Financially Wise
Financially Strong

Kerri Maharaj

Financially Wise Financially Strong

A Beginner's Guide to Master the Fundamentals of Personal Finance and Take Control of Your Money

© Kerri Maharaj 2024
kerrijmaharaj@gmail.com

ISBN 978-976-97291-0-0 (paperback)
ISBN 978-976-97291-1-7 (Kindle)
ISBN 978-976-97291-2-4 (e-book)

The views, opinions and comments expressed in this book are those of the author.

Design and Layout by Paria Publishing Company Limited
Typeset in Bembo and Cast
Cover design: Alice Besson
Icons: Freepik
Author photograph: Sarita Rampersad

Contents

To my mother, Gloria Maharaj, who introduced me to the importance of money. She knew nothing formally, but everything practically, and could have written her own book.

To my wife, Alisha, and son, Liam, who were incredibly patient while I wrote this book. It took 10 years to accomplish, and they supported me every day. Love you both forever.

Introduction

Everyone is probably familiar with the saying "money doesn't buy happiness." While aspects might be true, the importance of money is plain to anyone who doesn't have enough. Without it, what you have instead is a world of worries, problems, and unhappiness! This I know from personal experience.

Like many others, I started with almost nothing. Sadly, I had no natural talents to use nor were my parents able to help me financially. I therefore accepted I must earn success by working crazy hard and continuously trying to improve myself. When I was young, my simple wish was to have enough money to live comfortably. I didn't need to be wealthy, only worry-free.

I remember when I started my first job. It automatically made me the breadwinner for my mother and me. My income was ridiculously small, given that I had only a high-school education and zero work experience. After working for a few months, I noticed a pattern. I would run out of money by the third week of each month and my mother, an extremely proud lady, would have to seek a small loan to tide us over to my next payday. This situation continued, much to my mother's embarrassment, until a bank gave me my first credit card. The limit was small, but that was okay. I only needed a limit large enough to stop borrowing from friends and family.

But after I received the card, my situation didn't improve. And why would it have? All I did was trade one form of borrowing for another. My month-ends followed a similar pattern. I was paid around the 28th of the month. The first thing I did was pay off my credit card because I hated the thought of owing anyone, even a bank. Then, after paying the monthly bills due,

I was out of money. Until my next salary payment, I could only make purchases using my credit card.

It's funny when you are in the moment and life is happening rapidly around you, the obvious may not be so obvious. One month-end the reality hit me: I was just paid, yet I already had no money! Ideally, you should use your salary to cover your costs for the *next* month. But there I was paying off *old* expenses and had no money for expenses for the upcoming thirty days. I describe the expenses as "old" because my credit card bill was for purchases I made weeks ago, and the other bills I paid were for services I had already used.

I kept asking myself, why was I in this situation? I concluded that I just did not know any better. When I entered the workforce, I had gone to school for several years but still knew nothing about one of life's most important skills: managing my own finances. It was a frustrating moment for me. I faced options about money every day, but I did not know what to do. Eventually, I accepted that I had no reason to be guilty about my lack of knowledge because I had never learned how to make a wise financial decision. If you are near a hot stove, would you touch it? Never. Why? Because you learned it would burn you. You have the knowledge to make a wise choice.

Inexplicably, we often do not approach personal finance as something to be taught and learned. Across a lifetime, we will face endless financial situations that require us to act. The problem is that the wrong choice can cause pain. You often, however, cannot tell, unlike when you touch a hot stove. Put another way, **a wrong decision will make you poorer**, but owing to a lack of knowledge, you will not have realized it. If you had the knowledge, instinctively you would have made a different choice, like not touching the stove.

Who should read this book?

I wrote this book for people who want to learn how to make wise decisions about their money. And while writing it, I assumed you are as I was: with no money and no clue what to do next.

I do not focus on complex areas of finance, which many of us are unlikely to meet. I am interested in situations and transactions we face regularly. For example, the credit card I obtained was my first loan and serious financial transaction. I remember the lending officer had to explain how it worked. I could not follow anything that was said because realistically they don't have the time to ensure you understand what you are committing to. At that time, it didn't matter to me anyway. All I cared about was that the card allowed me to borrow easily. Nothing more. Only much later did I learn about the many pitfalls to avoid when using a credit card.

Financial decisions usually involve understanding detailed rules about a product[1] or transaction. It often requires you to think about legal and taxation aspects as well. But good news: I did not include any of these complications in this book. I believe **learning rules before you understand concepts is frankly a waste of time**. You may become frustrated or even give up because you believe the transaction is too complex.

Instead, I focus on the fundamentals of personal finance. I will show you how to keep it simple and how to do the simple things well. Of course, at some point, you will need to understand rules. But once you understand the basics properly, it's much easier to follow the detailed rules.

---

1   I'll refer to the term "financial product" often. All businesses sell a product or a service to their customers to earn revenue. Financial institutions are the same, but their products are intangible, not physical. For example, each type of bank account is a financial product you can obtain. Opening an account is the equivalent of a sale for a bank because they earn revenue when you use it.

Let's say you want to take a mortgage. You should first understand what a mortgage is, how to decide what option is best for you, and how to estimate how much you can afford. Otherwise, it makes no sense for a lending officer to tell you about the details of the loan agreement, the potential tax deductibility of the interest, the incentives available for first-time homeowners, or the rights of the lender if you cannot repay.

Whenever I wish to use a financial product or perform a transaction, I check the detailed rules because they change often. I don't memorize them. But how the transactions work and their concepts hardly ever change. Because I know these basics, I understand the current rules easily.

You can apply the principles and techniques from this book when you are earning income for the first time or if you are already in a bad financial situation. If you have experience, you may know some of the early material in the book. If so, focus on the areas you think are most relevant to your pain points. For example, if you have dependents, you may want to make Action 2: *Protect Yourself and Your Dependents* a priority. If your area of stress is too much debt, then Action 3: *Manage Your Debt* could give you immediate help. When you have greater peace of mind, then try to focus on the other areas. I still encourage you to read from the beginning because I've organized the content to build your knowledge in a logical way.

Why is this book different?

At the core, my focus is financial education. When you hear "education" you may think about school. Except you usually apply subjects you learn in school in specific circumstances, such as in your job. Whereas you'll apply the financial lessons in this book every time you reach into your wallet/handbag or whenever you make a financial decision. I want to empower you to make wise choices. Or, if you choose a "bad" option, you *know* that you did because it was deliberate and empowered. And yes, you can do so, guilt free.

The principle I tried to apply to each topic and chapter was "Show How; Don't Tell." Have you ever read something and thought you had a lot of information but still had no idea what to do? That's the problem I tried to tackle. I believe personal finance is about applying our knowledge to make everyday decisions about our money. I do share a lot of information, but I try to focus on what is practical and show you how to apply it. Be aware though, it is easier to show how with some topics, while others require a greater awareness of facts.

There is an endless supply of personal finance books. I read many when I was trying to get my own finances under control. After completing them, I often asked myself these questions:

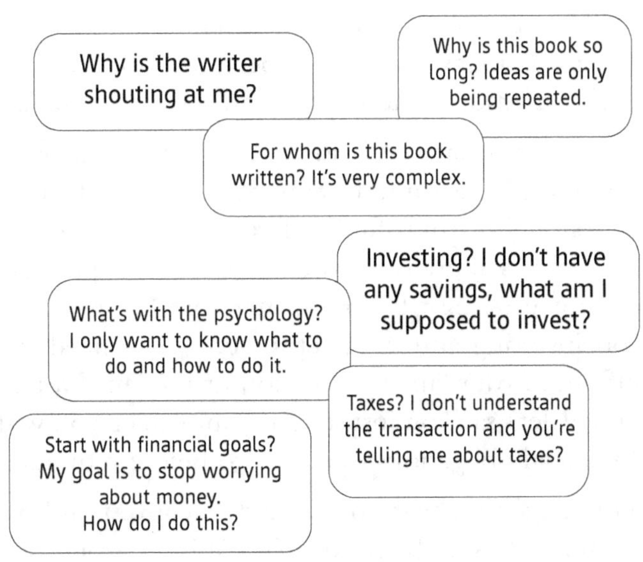

To avoid these problems, my approach is to teach each topic. When I complete each one, you should have enough knowledge to act confidently. Think about a subject you learned at school, for example, math. You began by learning to count, then performed basic calculations, and progressed to complex equations. I try to use the same approach. I'll build your knowledge slowly and gradually introduce the less straightforward areas.

You'll notice my approach loosely follows our life stages. Once we begin to work, we immediately begin to face choices about our money. At this stage, many decisions will affect us for a long time if we get them wrong. Eventually, different life changes arise, creating further complexities such as marriage, children, and mid-life responsibilities. Then, suddenly the priority becomes planning for life when our best earning years are behind us.

Investing and retirement planning

I do not cover investing and retirement planning, which is different from many books on personal finance. In those books, large portions tend to focus on these two areas.

In my view, these are two advanced topics, and practically speaking, most of us cannot begin to think about them until we have enough surplus funds. If you struggle to make ends meet or debt is burdening you, your present problems are much more pressing. It would, therefore, be impossible to focus on investing and your retirement. You need to work yourself out of your current situation first. Even if you are less constrained, let's say you just started your career, you will have many financial obligations to attend to before retirement.

I am not suggesting that you should not invest and plan for your retirement as early as possible. Quite the opposite: you absolutely should make it a priority. I am only being practical and recognizing that we often must balance this goal with other realities. Often, those other realities take greater priority.

My main objective, therefore, is to help build your knowledge, and show you how to apply it, to the point where you generate surplus funds. When you do so consistently, you can then focus on investing and detailed retirement planning. And frankly, most books cover these two topics in such a high-level way that they do not empower anyone to make a decision. It's a lot of telling but not showing how.

When I help you to take control of your money successfully, I bet you'll become *much* more interested in understanding how to invest and plan for your retirement.

Are you ready to begin? Let's start at the end.

Start at the End

When you arrive at the end of this book, I hope you have achieved these goals:

1. You are empowered to make wise financial decisions and you understand the financial effect of your choices.

2. You understand the fundamentals of personal finance and know how to use this knowledge to take control of your money.

3. You produce a steady (or better still, increasing) surplus each year, resulting in your net worth increasing over time.

In summary, I want you securely on the path to removing stress, building wealth, and becoming financially better off because there is truly no better feeling than financial freedom.

It's okay if some of the terms I used above or in the rest of this chapter are unfamiliar. I'll explain many of them in the chapter *Key Terms* and the others as we delve deeper.

There are telltale signs for those who are not in control of their finances. And I mean in addition to the dark cloud that accompanies them and their continuous stressed look.

If you recognize any of these signs in yourself, don't despair. It is possible to eliminate these problems and you'll learn how to do this by yourself. How will you know when you've succeeded? Of course, your dark clouds and stress will have vanished! But in addition to peace of mind, you'll find that:

☞ You are in control of your outflows.

☞ You have a pool of emergency funds.

☞ Your debt is manageable, or you are debt-free.

☞ You are ready for life's major events.

☞ You easily navigate common financial situations and make decisions confidently.

☞ You produce annual surpluses, which you use to invest and plan for retirement.

☞ You invest in yourself.

Are you wealthy?

Does financial independence sound as fantastic to you as it does to me? I hope you shouted an enthusiastic "Yes!" It does, however, introduce a question: is financial independence the same as being wealthy? I would say no. Being in control of your finances does not necessarily mean that you are wealthy. I believe wealthy individuals have three main characteristics:

1. Their income easily exceeds their expenses, meaning they are in a continuous surplus cash position, which they use to invest.

2. They own assets that earn income and have the potential to increase in value.

3. They enjoy a higher-cost lifestyle: their spending on Wants easily exceeds their Needs.

Don't let the thought that financial freedom is different from being wealthy discourage you. The majority in any country's population are not wealthy. Instead, the majority earn a normal income, have a small savings pool or none at all, and struggle to grow their net worth. Your personal challenge is to move beyond this situation and become financially secure.

> By applying the concepts in this book, you will no longer worry about money and will definitely be on the path to building wealth. Importantly, you will have enough knowledge to make wise financial decisions, so the chance of losing what you worked hard to earn is remote.

How to succeed?

Taking control of your money and putting yourself on a path to build wealth is possible. You succeed by:

- **Working hard to keep your money.** There is no magic formula. It's sad that many people work twenty-two days (or more) a month to earn an income, yet they spare little time making a real attempt to keep it.

- **Learning how to manage your money.** Could you return to the earlier list that describes someone who succeeded? Look at the last bullet, "You invest in yourself." We will explore this idea in greater detail later, but as far as the list is concerned, I left the best for last. Investing in yourself means, primarily, educating yourself. Educating yourself about personal finance is critical if you wish to take control of your money.

Six Actions

Whenever I assess if someone has strong personal finances, I use a checklist of six Actions and ask myself if the person has successfully completed them. I believe these six connect, and each strengthens the previous and lays the foundation for the next. When all are present, what appears is a picture of financial strength that withstands severe shocks and creates future wealth. The six Actions are:

1. **Control your inflows and outflows**

2. **Protect yourself and your dependents**

3. **Manage your debt**

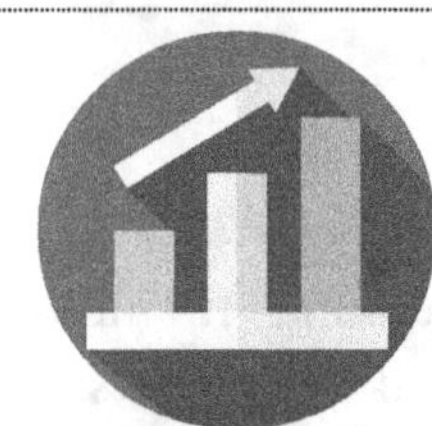

4. **Grow your income and net worth**

5. **Prepare for major life events**

6. **Invest and plan for retirement**

I'll guide you, step-by-step, to master each of these Actions. In each topic, I've assumed you have little prior knowledge. Some areas may therefore appear basic to anyone with experience. Experienced readers may also have alternative approaches or shortcuts to what I suggest. This is fine because there is no one right approach. If your different approach achieves the outcome that I described, keep doing it. Just remember, my focus in each chapter is to build a reader's knowledge from the ground up.

Where to begin?

We begin by understanding certain core principles. They form the foundation for everything I explain in later chapters.

If you are determined to take control of your money, you should not debate the core principles. I ask that you understand and accept them. We accept many things without asking why. For example, as a child you learned the alphabet, or that $1 + 1 = 2$. We never really question why the English alphabet has twenty-six letters or who decided that $1 + 1 = 2$. But we cannot read, write, or use math unless we accept these facts.

Similarly, if you are unwilling to accept the principles, you will struggle to understand and apply the six Actions that follow. Without them, your path to a better financial future may be left to chance, for example, winnings from a lottery or gambling. The irony is, even if you are lucky and receive a windfall, you may lose it because you never learned how to manage your own money.

By the way, as attractive as receiving a windfall without working sounds, gambling, or playing the lottery is a terrible financial decision for persons who are not wealthy. Using your hard-earned money on a minuscule chance that you could be lucky is not a sensible approach. Only individuals who have surplus cash should play the lottery or gamble. Unfortunately, the opposite usually occurs and many persons who gamble lack surplus funds.

Core Principles

The journey to financial security requires you to understand, accept, and master certain principles.

You build on those principles by learning and applying the skills to perform the six Actions that create strong personal finances. When persons struggle with money, it is a sure bet they either do not understand these core ideas or choose to ignore them. Of course, life occasionally deals some people a difficult hand. Having a disabled dependent or one who has a long-term illness could derail the best of plans. Excluding these challenging situations, I firmly believe anyone can manage their money properly.

Let's look at the principles that underpin the six Actions.

Understand the difference between Wants and Needs

A fundamental concept is the difference between Wants and Needs. Needs are the items you cannot live without, such as food, clothing, or housing. Wants are everything else and are usually what help us relax and enjoy life.

You may think Wants only include items such as vacations or the latest electronic device. But it is important to understand that the cost of food, clothing, and housing varies widely. If you overspend on these Needs, they essentially become Wants. Ultimately, your lifestyle choices determine what these items cost, and I'll cover this in more detail in Action 1, specifically *Step 3: Decisions About Your Deficit.*

The reality is that Wants often dominate our spending because finding ways to use one's hard-earned money is easy. Let me be clear: **I'm not suggesting that you should do without the things you enjoy. You should merely live on what you can afford.** My goal is to help you figure out what you can comfortably afford in a disciplined way. Only you can separate your Needs from your Wants.

Know your expenses

A more precisely worded principle would be "know your income *and* expenses." Knowing our income is not usually the challenge though. We tend to know precisely how much we earn. *The real problem is knowing what we spend.* The greater our financial difficulties, the more acute the problem.

You *cannot* achieve financial freedom without knowing what you spend. Unfortunately, most people *think* they know, but they cannot be precise. Try it yourself: think of a typical month and try to name your top five expenses and how much they cost. If you could put a specific description and cost to the five items, you are one of the few and on your way to being in control of your money! If you cannot, unfortunately, you are part of the majority. However, do not fear! You can fix this situation.

> You *cannot* achieve financial freedom without knowing what you spend.

I emphasize you *cannot* take control of your finances without knowing how much you spend. Remember, this is *your* money, and you *must* know where it goes.

Aim to live well below your means

Living below your means requires that your expenses be less than your income.

You cannot achieve financial freedom by earning $100 and spending $105. This is obvious. But you also will not be stress-free if you spend $97, even though it is less than $100. You'll be better off compared to spending $105, but you will not achieve financial independence.

You might be asking yourself, what then is a suitable gap between your income and expenses? Don't worry, I'll address this question as we go through the upcoming chapters. Right now, the principle to accept is you must spend less than you earn, ideally *much less.*

> It's fine if you cannot live well below your means at once, but you must set this goal and take specific actions to meet it.

It's not what you earn; it's what you keep that matters

The reality for most of us is our income does not change easily. If you earn a monthly salary, well, that's all you have. Unless you are promoted, obtain a salary increase, or find a better-paying job, your income is fixed. You don't earn more by working more, although it may lead to performance bonuses. If you are hourly-paid or are eligible for overtime, practically speaking, your potential extra income is still capped because you cannot work indefinitely. For most of us, therefore, our income is either fixed or fluctuates within a narrow range. The income of some people can vary, for example, if they earn sales commissions. In this case, while their income will still not exceed a certain amount, they have the added risk of their income moving up *and* down.

If your income is either fixed, or fluctuates within a known range, then you truly only have control over your expenses. The core principle is, therefore, it's not what you earn that matters, but what you keep. You keep what remains after you pay your expenses. Consequently, someone could earn the same as you, or even less, and be in a stronger financial situation because they keep more.

Another challenge arises when persons begin to earn more income: the less disciplined start to spend more. They believe having more income is a reason to improve their standard of living and increase their spending on Wants. So, despite having *more* income, they keep the same as before, or worse, they keep less.

Instead, they should remain disciplined and not be tempted to spend more when their income grows. The time will arrive when they are financially secure and can spend more. Of course, the irony may be that when this time arrives, their financial IQ could be so high, they make different choices.

Millionaires do not become or stay millionaires by wasting their money.

Cash is king: be debt-free

One of the major sources of financial stress is debt. Even if you are currently up to date with payments, loans dominate your decisions because overdue payments carry severe penalties. If you are not current with your obligations, I bet you cannot sleep.

Loans, and what they allow us to buy, create an illusion of joy. **But in most cases, a loan is consumption brought forward.** By this I mean, instead of being patient and saving to use cash later, you borrow to make the purchase now. The "buy now, pay later" approach has two problems:

1. You may over-borrow if you cannot assess how much is enough debt for you.

2. The cost of a loan (its interest rate) tends to be expensive. The interest paid is a significant hit when trying to build wealth.

If loans were unavailable, you would have no choice but to save before you spend. When you are trying to achieve financial freedom, this should be your starting point. Forget loans exist and pay only with cash. That way, you owe no one. You are in control.

> Forget loans exist and pay only with cash. That way, you owe no one. You are in control.

Once you accept that financial freedom and being debt-free go together, only then should you allow the thought that not all debt is bad to enter your mind. If, however, you are unable to decide if a loan is a wise financial decision, I suggest you approach debt as if it were radioactive: avoid, avoid, avoid!

When you read Action 3: *Manage Your Debt*, return to this principle to understand the previous paragraph better.

Look ahead

All of us must progress through certain life stages. We are initially dependents; then young adults; we become middle-aged; and lastly, are seniors. Each stage brings certain financial challenges.

Most of us do not have enough money to prepare for all challenges at once. If you wish to be in control, you must gaze a little into the future to anticipate the major life events ahead. You then prepare by setting funds aside for future Needs, then Wants.

The actual events will vary based on personal ambitions. For most, life events include entering long-term relationships, having children, buying a car, and buying a home. While these events are emotionally rewarding, they could have large, multi-year financial impacts. When they occur unplanned, they can easily become a source of stress.

With a little forward thinking, you can manage these life events easily. Even if they temporarily result in lower savings, you are not affected.

What destroys our confidence and creates stress is trying to figure out how to afford the event after it has already begun. With your gaze slightly ahead, you prepare for what's to come and remain in control.

Choose your friends wisely

You may be wondering how or why this is a principle about money. The company we keep has an outsized influence on our actions and whether we succeed or fail. Friends who live in the moment and binge on debt may not support us if we try a different approach.

Instead, we should surround ourselves with people who have a similar life plan. Each person builds off the positivity and energy from others, which in turn reinforces their own resolve. Think about successful people you know and who they associate with. I'll bet their circle includes persons with similar goals. I am not suggesting we cannot be friends with everyone, regardless of beliefs. We absolutely should have friends from various backgrounds to benefit from the richness of different experiences. But never underestimate the power and influence of the people around you.

Wrap up

As I said earlier, we'll apply these principles throughout the Actions to come. I'll understand if you are skeptical at this moment, but I'm confident that when you see the principles applied and understand how they contribute to strong personal finances, you will become an advocate.

Key Terms

Let's ensure you understand some of the words and phrases that we'll meet regularly. Nothing here is complex and you might already be familiar with these terms. Think of it as doing a quick knowledge check but paying attention to the finer points.

Cash

I use "cash" to mean both physical cash (that you keep with you) and funds you have in a bank account. If I am referring specifically either to physical bills or to an electronic transaction, the context will make it clear.

Inflows

Inflows refer to cash you receive. Your personal inflows could arise from three sources.

Income from work

Firstly, you receive inflows as payment for either working for others or from being self-employed. For most of us, this type of inflow will be our major source of cash. Over time you would want it to be:

- Regular, which means from an established career, profession, or business.

- Increasing, because you want your net worth to grow over time. Increasing your inflows is the best long-term approach to achieve this goal. I'll cover this in more detail later, including the concept of net worth.

- Ideally, from more than one source.

One-off events

You could receive cash from events or actions that happen only once. For example, selling something you own or receiving a gift or an inheritance. If you sell your sofa, the cash you receive is a one-off event because you can't sell the same sofa again. (Well, I hope not!) You can sell another item you own, but that also will be a one-off.

Investment returns

You could receive inflows from having cash on deposit with a bank or other financial institution. The inflow you receive is called "interest." Or you can have other investments that pay you. As you read, you'll notice that I do not focus on inflows from investments. Realistically, if you are a young adult or in a financially strapped situation, you are unlikely to have investments.

Outflows

Outflows refer to cash that you use, and like inflows, outflows arise from a few sources.

Expenses

The main source of outflows would be expenses, which are payments for Wants and Needs, including charity and other forms of gift-giving. The main feature of a Want or a Need (and therefore an expense) is that whatever you pay for is not permanent. You use what you purchase at once, or the benefit disappears within a brief period. If you buy food, it is gone after you eat it, and the benefit lasts a few hours until you get hungry again. The benefit from paying rent, which is getting a place to live, lasts for one month or a specific period. You must eventually replace clothes and shoes due to wear and tear.

I'm keeping loan payments separate because they require specific attention, which we'll get to later.

Outflows can be money used to purchase assets (I explain assets below). In most cases, these are likely physical assets, for example, real estate or a vehicle, or financial investments bought with our retirement funds.

Surplus and savings

As you read, you'll notice that I refer regularly to "surplus," often when you may have expected to hear "savings." I use these terms in a specific way. I'll explain in more detail in the upcoming chapters. For now, broadly, I refer to surplus as what remains after you deduct outflows from your inflows:

$$\textbf{Inflows - Outflows = Surplus}$$

Assets

Anything you own is technically an asset. But we need to be more precise because while you certainly own, for example clothing, financially savvy folks would not refer to them as an asset. Instead, I suggest you think of an asset as something you could sell for a reasonable amount of cash. Using this approach, clothing is not an asset because it is unlikely someone will buy it.

For you to sell an asset for cash, it must retain value for a period. When an asset's value falls over time, we say it "depreciates." Importantly, an asset could also become more valuable over time (it "appreciates").

Income

An asset could either earn income on its own or you use it to earn income. You need to be careful with those used to earn income. It may be valuable to you because you depend on it to earn income, but it may be worth much less to someone else. For this reason, I emphasize only treating an item as an asset if you can sell it for a reasonable value.

Collectibles

Some assets do not earn cash on their own, but their value might increase; therefore, if you sell them in the future, you receive more cash than you initially used to buy them. Examples include art, jewelry, and wine.

Examples

Let's look at a few examples to determine what qualifies as an asset.

Is a phone an asset? I would say, doubtful. Even if expensive, its value to someone else disappears quickly because new models arrive regularly. When an item is no longer in demand, it has become "obsolete."

Is a computer an asset? Moreso than a phone, it is saleable for a short time. Is it a great asset? Not really. Although you could use it to earn income, it does not earn cash directly and it depreciates over time.

Is a vehicle an asset? Yes, because you can usually sell it for something. Does it pay you anything while you use it? No, but you could use it to earn income. Could it appreciate as you own it? No, unless it is a collectible.

Is property an asset? Yes, because you can sell it for cash. Does it pay you anything while you own it? Yes, you could receive cash if you rent it. Could it appreciate? Yes. Real estate therefore checks all the boxes for a great asset.

Which to own?

While it is possible to own several types of assets, which should you place greater priority on having? Those that both pay you cash as you own them and appreciate the longer you keep them.

Liabilities

Also known as loans, debt, obligations, and borrowings. A liability means you owe cash to someone else. The "someone" could be an individual or a corporation. The idea here is you acquire an item (or receive a service) but pay for it over time.

How you bought the item may vary. You could have borrowed money from a friend or family member (not usually a clever idea) and used it for the purchase. You could buy a vehicle or property by borrowing from a bank or other lender. Or you could go to a store and make a purchase with a credit card.

In each case, the way the loan arose and what we call it could vary. The important question is whether it requires you to pay cash over time. Once yes, then that's a liability.

Wrap up

I'm sure you agree there was nothing complicated here. You may have already been familiar with the terms, but if they were previously unclear, I hope you now fully understand them. These are the ones you'll meet initially. I'll explain the others as I use them (for example, the concept of "net worth" that arose earlier).

Basic Banking Products

How comfortable are you dealing with banks? I would understand if you don't like to because they seem to speak a different language (a financial one). In addition, they must follow complex laws and rules, which make them seem inflexible at times. Having said this, banks do try to explain what they mean as plainly as possible, and competition forces them to simplify how they interact with you.

Although you may wish to avoid them, learning about these institutions will help build your confidence. They have many useful tools to help us get control of our finances and even accumulate wealth. To simplify the discussion, I'll focus on banks, but other institutions also offer bank-like services and are great alternatives to traditional banks.

Having a relationship with a bank is important because their basic services simplify several aspects of managing your money. This will become clearer as we progress through the book. Of course, you can achieve the same result by keeping your money at home and using manual methods. But your money is safer in a bank and doing some of the activities to come are hassle-free when performed electronically.

Certain banking products are complex. At this stage though, we will only look at straightforward ones you'll use in the next few chapters. Later, we'll meet those that are slightly more complicated, which usually are lending products. As a reminder, a bank's products are intangible, not physical, for example, each type of deposit account.

I'll return to this point later, but introduce it here. You should always bear in mind that the bank is *selling* you something. It earns revenue when you use the account/product. Like any other purchase you make, you must ensure you get the best price for the features you buy.

Checking account

A checking (or demand) account is a basic banking product used for day-to-day activities, such as deposits, withdrawals, or payments. The key features of the account are in its name. It allows you to write checks and your funds are available on demand, which means you can access your money without restriction.

A check is a convenient method for payments. With a few short scribbles you promise to pay someone (the payee) when you buy a good or service. Although the names of checking accounts vary by institution, all that matters is the main feature of the account is the ability to write a check.

Because of other developments, checks are used less often than in the past.

Savings account

A savings account is another basic banking product. Its purpose is again in its name: to encourage you to save. It is meant to be where you keep your funds for longer periods. In comparison, a checking account is for your day-to-day banking needs, which means your balance changes based on use.

Banks also call savings accounts by different names. They generally operate in the same way, but the amount of interest paid may vary. Additionally, each bank may have conditions, such as keeping a minimum balance every day for a certain period.

To reward and encourage you to keep funds in your savings account, it pays interest on your balance. In contrast, checking accounts do not normally pay interest. If you have excess funds in your checking account, you should transfer the excess to your savings account to earn at least a small return. If your checking account does offer interest, it is usually lower than what you could earn from a savings account.

There is an excellent reason why savings and checking accounts are important, which also explains why the interest earned is so low. I'll cover this when we meet deposit insurance later in this chapter.

Debit card

Debit cards are also known as ATM (automated teller machine) cards or bank cards. They are essential. You must have one and keep both the card and the security PIN (personal identification number) you choose secure and private. I think of debit cards as the "key" to bank accounts (like a key to your home) because they unlock several services.

- **ATMs are like mini banks.** To access your accounts at an ATM, you insert your debit card and enter your security PIN. From there, you deposit funds, withdraw cash, pay bills, and the list goes on.

- **Point-of-sale transactions.** At an almost infinite number of retailers, you can use your debit card to pay for goods and services instead of using cash. When you authorize the transaction with your PIN, the bank deducts the funds from your linked account. This cashless method of payment is incredibly convenient.

- **Online banking.** You access your bank's website using your debit card number.

I suggest you have the products described above as we move forward. They aren't mandatory, but they certainly make your life easier. Also, think positively! As you practice what I teach in this book, you'll begin to have surplus funds. You'll need somewhere to keep them safe, so you might as well open the accounts now! For most banks, it is an easy process, usually done online.

Let me explain a few other points that you should bear in mind.

Deposit insurance

Deposit insurance is the reason everyone who is now starting to build their finances should do so with a bank: **your money is protected up to a certain amount.**

Like any other business, it is possible for banks to fail, meaning they go out of business. They appear like fortresses with massive physical structures, but they have failed in the past and will in the future. They may fail fewer times than other businesses because of financial regulation and oversight, but they are not invulnerable.

Even though the bank goes out of business, you still recover your money.

Banks are a special type of financial institution because they are eligible for deposit insurance. Deposit insurance protects depositors against loss, and it applies to certain products, like checking and savings accounts. If your bank fails, you will not lose your money in these products, up to certain limits. For most of us, this will mean full recovery. Let me repeat. Even if the bank goes out of business, you could still recover your money. Importantly, because saving and checking account holders have no risk of loss below certain limits, the interest paid on the accounts is low. This reasoning will become clearer as you read the chapters.

If you are beginning to build your finances, it would be a disaster to lose all your money because your bank failed. Before giving a financial institution your precious funds, be sure to ask if they offer deposit insurance. If they do not, leave at once. If they do, ensure your accounts are eligible (not all types of accounts are). Also, find out the limit of coverage for each account and keep your account balance below the limit.

This investigation is critical. Do not overlook it!

Overdrafts

For most bank accounts, you use your funds until the balance on the account is zero. You obviously cannot use what is not there! To continue using the account, you deposit more money and then resume your transactions.

If, however, the account has an overdraft facility, the account balance can fall below zero. The amount below zero is known as an overdraft, and it is subject to a limit the bank sets. Once your account is below zero, you now owe the bank this amount. Put another way, you borrowed that money. When your balance is positive, this is your money—the bank owes you. When you are in overdraft, you owe the bank.

Let's say you have $200 in your checking account, and you write a check for $500. If you have an overdraft, the bank will honor your check, but you then owe the bank $300.

We'll cover loans in Action 3: *Manage Your Debt*, so at this point, just be aware that:

- An overdraft facility is often an optional feature on your checking account.

- Once you agree to it, you can become overdrawn at any time, so you must monitor the funds in your account carefully.

☞ Overdrafts are expensive. *Very* expensive.

Fees

Banks charge fees on almost everything. No-fee accounts and transactions do exist but are becoming rarer. No-fee products also tend to have fewer features. Always inquire or research what is the fee for any account you wish to open or transaction you plan to do. If you are now starting to build your finances, the basic no-fee options should be perfect for your needs. Do not pay for advanced features that you will not use; upgrading later is always an option.

> Fees quietly add up and you may be surprised at the accumulated cost. Pay attention!

Electronic transactions, records, and easy access

When you are now beginning, some of the advantages of using a bank as the center of your finances are:

☞ **Paperless transactions.** Most transactions are online or through banking apps on your phone.

☞ **Electronic record-keeping.** If you make all or most of your transactions through your bank accounts, keeping paper records is not necessary. This simplifies the activities you will perform in the coming chapters.

☞ **Convenient access.** You can access your records from anywhere.

Let's be thankful that the days of bank passbooks are well behind us. If you aren't familiar with what passbooks are, do a quick online search and learn about the pain that you are now lucky to avoid!

Fraudulent transactions

In essence, fraud is someone accessing your accounts without your permission and stealing your money. This is a realistic scenario, and it could definitely happen to you. For this reason, some people prefer to stay away from the banking system and only use cash. While this approach is understandable because your money is in your sight, it is not safe. You can still become a target for theft, and even if the culprit is caught, you are unlikely to recover your funds.

The advantage of using a bank is it offers strong protection against fraud. In addition, they will usually return any funds lost while they investigate the incident. The process could be painless. It happened to me more than once, and each time, the bank resolved the matter, hassle-free.

Direct debit

I previously mentioned that checks used to be the main way to make payments. Now, electronic methods have become more popular as they are quicker, safer, and more convenient.

Instead of writing a check to pay someone, you authorize the payee to withdraw the amount directly from your account electronically—this is a direct debit. Of course, you can also receive funds electronically—this is a direct credit/deposit.

For the upcoming *Steps*, try to avoid using checks to make payments or to receive funds. Checks are slow, they are sometimes lost, and you need to monitor your account to ensure they are cashed or deposited. Instead, I strongly recommend you use direct debits and credits for your transactions.

Useful but not essential: credit cards

A credit card is a complicated product, but it is one of the first a bank will offer you.

A credit card allows you to make an immediate electronic purchase. You do not need funds in your bank account to use it. Let's pause for a moment to ensure you understand the crucial difference between a debit and a credit card.

To use your debit card, you must have either funds available in your account or an overdraft facility. A credit card is not tied to either a checking or savings account. You can use it even if you have no funds available. Take a moment to read that again if you're still a bit confused.

Although your purchase is immediate when you use a credit card, you pay for what you bought sometime in the future. If you are unable to pay in full when the balance is due, you have automatically taken a loan from the bank. It sounds, and is, incredibly convenient but using it properly requires knowledge and careful management. We'll cover this in the dedicated chapters on credit cards.

You *do not* need a credit card to perform the *Steps* to come in Action 1. If you already have one (or more), and you use them actively, I'll explain what to do in the appropriate *Step*. If you already owe an amount on your credit card, you should aim to stop using it as soon as possible—you'll understand why later.

Wrap up

Excellent! We've covered quite a lot in this chapter, from everyday banking products to a few other points to note when dealing with a bank.

You are now ready to begin Action 1: *Control Your Inflows and Outflows*.

Action 1

Control Your Inflows and Outflows

Lay the Foundation

As a reminder, I've structured this book in six sections, which correspond to the six Actions that I believe are necessary to achieve strong personal finances:

1. **Control your inflows and outflows**

2. **Protect yourself and your dependents**

3. **Manage your debt**

4. **Grow your income and net worth**

5. **Prepare for major life events**

6. **Invest and plan for retirement**

The first Action lays the foundation for everything that follows: you must know your inflows and outflows. Why? Because **it is impossible to manage what you do not know**. Whenever I speak to individuals about their personal finances, I am always surprised how many have no idea how they spend their money each month. Most know how much they earn and can identify their major expenses, such as rent or loan payments. But for smaller outflows, and especially if it varies, for example, groceries or eating out, I often receive a pained and confused look.

How important this Action is to you, and therefore the amount of effort you put in, will depend on how much you are struggling. **If you battle to make ends meet, then you should know your income and expenses in detail**. If money is not as tight, estimates should work. Regardless, I will show you a complete approach and I hope you try it, because you'll learn something surprising about yourself.

Money has a way of disappearing, and you end up wondering, what exactly did you do with it? Figuring this out is normally an enlightening process.

Because my own financial situation was difficult, I had to know my outflows in detail. When I started paying attention, it led to *many* eye-opening moments. Sometimes I was surprised at what I spent on because I was only throwing away my scarce money. Often, I couldn't believe how individual expenses added up over a period. Of course, in the moment, I easily justified each silly purchase. When viewed over a longer period though, I kept asking myself, "You spent money on *that*?"

Once you truly know your financial self in dollars, you are in control to decide what to change. Notice I said *you* decide what to alter. **Taking control of your money is about what you are willing to do and the changes you are willing to make.** Along the path to financial freedom, there are areas where you seek help from others. For example, a lender can change your loan terms to help make your payments manageable. But there are several areas *only you* can change.

The problem with actions only you can perform is that you need to commit. To commit, you must genuinely want to improve your finances. The easy path is always to do nothing. But once you decide that you want to stop worrying about money, implementing the actions only you can do becomes much easier.

So, what's next? I've outlined the approach to our first Action in a series of steps. Remember, if you are struggling, these steps are important because they lay the foundation for the other five Actions. You'll start by gathering data to understand your financial self. You will never be in control without this information, and I repeat, you cannot manage or improve what you do not know. It only takes a little willpower and discipline. I have read several books that try to convince their readers that this effort is not necessary. Honestly, how that advice could help anyone become financially independent confuses me.

I therefore hope you complete the *Steps* and not skip any. If you have an approach to simplify them, feel free to use your approach once it leads to the result I describe. (Also, drop me a line and let me know what you did!)

It's time to learn a lot about your financial self!

Step 1:
Track Your Inflows and Outflows

Let's try the challenge from the last chapter: think of a typical month and try to name your top five expenses and how much they cost. Chances are, you can't identify the top five, and if you could, you aren't sure about the cost. You don't need to be correct to the dollar, but you should be in the ballpark. If you have an estimate, my follow-up question would then be, how do you know if you are correct? If you can't verify your answer, we still arrive at the same problem: you can't manage what you do not know.

Our first aim therefore is to determine, in enough detail, what are your inflows and outflows. We'll then use this information to learn if you have an overall surplus or a deficit.

Let's start with what you earn and spend for one month. You can do this in two ways:

1. If you already have the information, gather the details of your inflows and outflows for the month just prior to reading this book. For example, if you're reading this in May, focus on gathering information for April. In this case, proceed to *Step 2: Your 30-Day Financial Self.*

2. If your records are not easily available, use the approach I describe below.

To continue, you'll need a checking account and an ATM card linked to that account. You'll use this account to keep a record of your inflows and outflows, starting at the beginning of a month. I recommend using a checking account because you'll use a savings account in a specific way in the later chapters.

As much as possible, have all your inflows and outflows pass through this account for the next 30 (or 31) days. Even if you receive inflows elsewhere, transfer them to this account. If you receive physical cash, deposit *all,* and if you need cash, withdraw it from the account. (Don't keep some and deposit the difference.) Also, try to make all your payments using your bank card or direct debit, instead of using cash.

Having all your inflows and outflows passing through one account may sound strange. It may seem especially odd when I suggest, for example, deposit all cash first and then withdraw what you need. **The reason for this specific approach is to create a record, so you do not need to rely on your memory later.**

To use your debit card for outflows you must have funds in your account or an overdraft facility. Some persons may not have funds at the start of the month because their inflows arrive later in the month, but their outflows occur every day. To fill the gap, they will likely use a credit card for purchases until they receive money. In this case, also use those records for the Actions described below, but you'll need to remember you have two sources for transactions. To avoid complications, I recommend using only your bank account.

I emphasize that none of these activities is difficult. Once you do all or most of your transactions from your bank account, you can easily access the information later. During the month you choose, do not do anything different with your life's activities. It is important that you live normally: pay bills, buy groceries, go to the movies, and so on. The only change is, try to make your bank account your financial center. The month will pass quickly, and you may be surprised what you eventually learn about yourself.

As you go through the month, here are some points to pay attention to.

Inflows

Inflows are easy because most of us do not have many sources. I hope you recall the three main types. You should review the chapter *Key Terms* if anything here sounds unfamiliar.

Employment income

How much do you earn? Whether you're paid monthly or weekly, by check or in cash, deposit all amounts received into your bank account. If your employer pays you by crediting a different account, transfer the funds into the account you are using for tracking.

Importantly, ensure you receive the supporting wage or salary slip to understand the various deductions from your gross pay. For example:

- We need to know what you receive *after* mandatory deductions. Mandatory deductions are usually taxes and any other amounts required by law.

- Some persons make direct payments from their wage/salary, for example, loan payments or insurance premiums. This approach is by choice (not required by law) because it is a convenient way to ensure the payments are not forgotten. If you have a similar arrangement, you'll need to separate your net salary into two parts. First, you need the amount for your gross pay less mandatory deductions. Next, you'll need the details for the other payments. We'll treat the other payments as normal outflows covered in 2 and 4 below.

☞ Some persons also have direct deductions from their wage/salary for retirement products or other forms of savings. Pay attention to these amounts because I'll ask you to treat them in a specific way in the next chapter.

Non-employment income

You may be fortunate to have inflows from interest, investment income, or other sources such as rental income. Again, gather the details so you know how much you received and from what source. To the extent possible, have them all deposited into the account you are using for tracking.

Other inflows

You could have other inflows that usually do not repeat, for example, selling something you own. For this *Step*, *ignore* inflows of this nature. Do not deposit them into the account you are using for tracking.

Outflows

Tracking outflows is usually more difficult for a few reasons:

☞ **Many sources and transactions.** While most of us tend to have one or two sources of inflows, we have many types of outflows (food, clothes, entertainment, travel, etc.). In addition, our inflows occur on specific days, while our outflows occur often.

☞ **We forget.** Because we make purchases regularly, it is not possible to rely on memory for the details. For this reason, we often underestimate what we spend.

☞ **Many ways to pay.** In addition to having many types of outflows, we pay for them in many ways. For example,

credit cards, point of sale (using your ATM card), direct debits, checks, and of course, cash.

- **Cash is troublesome.** Unless you keep receipts, it is easy to lose track of what you spent.

Once you follow my recommended approach to make your purchases with your bank card, you should remove most of the problems with tracking your outflows. The record is in your account so there's no need to rely on your memory. Even if you had to use a credit card, you would also have an electronic record of your purchases.

Cash purchases

By asking you to use your bank card for all purchases, I am implying you should not use cash. Of course, this may not be possible for everyone. If you must use cash, withdraw what you need from the bank account you are using for your tracking. In this way, at least you'll know exactly how much cash you had.

The challenge after withdrawing cash is to keep track every time you make a purchase. The reality is cash disappears, and you often cannot remember what you used it for. You must therefore make a deliberate effort to track where your cash goes. Hopefully, you understand why using a bank card and having everything in one place makes tracking easier. Thankfully, there are many free phone apps that allow you to record cash payments. It only takes a few seconds to enter the information, and after a couple of entries, it quickly becomes second nature. I did this myself and it was quick and painless.

Cash count

With cash, despite your best efforts, you might forget to record a purchase, especially when rushed, so doing an occasional cash count will help. Let's say at the start of the month you withdrew $300. At the end of the first week, let's say your notes (or app) show that you used $120, which means you should have $180 left. Count your cash to check if you have $180. If you do not, you'll have to record the missing cash as "Unidentified" or a similar description. Once these amounts are small, they will have no impact. The more often you count your cash (for example, weekly), the more accurate your tracking will be.

A typical cash-count movement could look like **Table 1**.

Table 1	
Cash at the start of the month	$300
Funds withdrawn from bank during the month	$100
Payments	($250)
Cash at the end of the month	**$150**

Your effort here really depends on how much cash you use. If you use a lot, then you need to track the payments more carefully. Otherwise, you'll end up with a large amount of cash used without knowing how you spent it. If you do not use cash regularly, then using a mix of actual purchases plus estimates should work just fine.

Loan repayments

While loan repayments are an outflow, they require special attention. Loan installments could be a set monthly amount, for example, a mortgage or auto loan, or they could vary, such as with credit cards. They can also be informal, for example, loans from family or friends—not usually a wise idea, but if they exist, you must repay them.

Your loan payment may be deducted directly from your wage/salary, or you may even pay it from another account. In these cases, it is not possible to record the payments through the account you are using for tracking. That's fine once you know the amounts paid for the month.

Wrap Up

I hope you agree there was nothing difficult here. You live normally for one month, with the only change being recording all your transactions, ideally electronically. You can do this in several ways, but it is easy if you have your transactions in one place. I recommend using a bank account. While cash is a potential problem, an easy solution is to track your cash transactions using a phone app.

In the next *Step*, we will use your transaction data to understand 30 days of your financial self.

Step 2:
Your 30-Day Financial Self

At the end of the month, you should have a record of all inflows and outflows from your bank account (ideally this has most of your transactions), credit card statement, or cash tracking (for example, from an app).

Now, let's use the data. Much of this activity could be done using computer programs. But instead of directing you to an application, I am going to show you how to use a spreadsheet. Why? Although the programs are fairly easy to use, I realized I followed the invisible program logic better when I knew how to do it myself. Also, by not relying on an application, I had a more complete understanding of my finances. Realistically, you might only understand what I mean after you try it yourself. After you've worked through the *Steps*, you can certainly try using an application, as they will simplify some actions. But I am confident if you do the activities yourself the first time, you will not regret it.

Again, nothing here is complicated. **This is your information. No one should be more interested in what it says than you.**

Let's do it together.

Make the data meaningful

To make the data useful, you need to put each payment into a category that is relevant to your situation, such as food, entertainment, car costs, and so on. Using food as an example, having a list of 50 payments for food is not helpful. Instead, it would be better to have, let's say, three food-related categories, such as groceries, dining out, and other meals. You then assign the 50 transactions to the three categories, which allows you to see how much you spent on groceries and so on. Name the categories whatever you want, just ensure they accurately describe the payments you assigned.

Needs and Wants

In addition to creating categories, let's bring in the two broad reasons why you have outflows: Needs and Wants. When you name each category of outflow, place each category into one of these broad types. Deciding what is a Need versus a Want could vary by person or require a little judgment. Think about it like this: if you cannot live or work without it, then it is a Need; everything else is a Want.

I pointed out in *Core Principles* that some Needs may include a discretionary aspect (making it a part-Want). By "discretionary," I mean you can adjust the amount you spend, for example, food. While food is a Need, an expensive restaurant meal makes it closer to a Want because cheaper meals are possible by making lifestyle choices. But we aren't at that decision point yet. Right now, place this as a Need because you can't live without food.

If you used a bank account for most of your inflows and outflows, first download the transactions to a spreadsheet (for example, *Microsoft Excel* or *Google Sheets*). Once the details are in a spreadsheet, assigning transactions to categories is easy. Don't forget to include in the spreadsheet the cash payments that you were tracking.

Categories: an example

Here's an example to show how to place the amounts into categories, using ten transactions. Trust me, this does not take much time after you download the transactions into a spreadsheet. It is also an interesting exercise to identify the categories that work best in your situation. There isn't a right number of categories. Too few would not make much sense. Too many will prevent you from seeing the big picture. Play around with them and after a while you'll arrive at the right level of detail for you.

When you download transactions from your bank account, you usually get the transaction date, a description (the payee), and the amount. This information is shown in the first three columns in **Table 2**. Next, name the categories and put each amount under the category that best describes it. Then, add each category to create totals.

Once you have one month of transactions in categories, we need to summarize them. On a second sheet, create a layout where the categories are now on the left in one column, and the total for each category is shown in another column.

Table 2								
Date	Description	Amount	Eating Out	Groceries	Rent	Utilities	Fun	Transport
1-May	Payee 1	**$50**	$50					
2-May	Payee 2	**$300**		$300				
3-May	Payee 3	**$26**	$26					
4-May	Payee 4	**$85**					$85	
5-May	Payee 5	**$500**			$500			
6-May	Payee 6	**$70**				$70		
7-May	Payee 7	**$21**	$21					
8-May	Payee 8	**$90**				$90		
9-May	Payee 9	**$41**						$ 41
10-May	Payee 10	**$18**	$18					
		$1,201	**$115**	**$300**	**$500**	**$160**	**$ 85**	**$ 41**

Again, this is easy to do if you use a spreadsheet; it takes a few clicks to achieve.

An example of a list of categorized inflows and outflows is provided in **Table 3**. Notice I have the totals for the month in each category under the broad headings of Needs and Wants. Also notice I showed loan payments separately.

Remember, the categories I use may not apply to everyone. To understand your outflows properly, you should use categories relevant to you.

Calculate your Surplus or Deficit for the month

Next, let's calculate your surplus or deficit. Notice at the bottom of **Table 3**, I already included a line called "Surplus/(Deficit)," which is your total inflows minus total outflows.

This is your 30-day financial self.

Table 3	
Inflows	**30 days**
Gross salary	$8,500
Taxes	($2,000)
Other mandatory deductions	($650)
Net salary	$5,850
Other inflows	$50
TOTAL INFLOWS	**$5,900**
Outflows	
Loan payments	
Loan 1	$1,500
Loan 2	$600
Total Loan payments	**$2,100**
Needs	
Rent	$600
Internet/Mobile	$285
Utilities	$250
Groceries	$350
Clothing	$160
Transportation	$80
Insurance	$185
Total Needs	**$1,910**
Wants	
Entertainment	$600
Gifts	$20
Eating out	$400
Cable/Streaming	$125
Total Wants	**$1,145**
TOTAL OUTFLOWS	**$5,155**
Surplus / (Deficit)	**$745**

Check for completeness

This action is optional, but undeniably useful. For those who like to be complete, they may even think it is essential. The question you are trying to answer here is, have you picked up *all* your inflows and outflows for the 30 days?

If you used a bank account to capture your inflows and outflows, then answering the question is easy. Let's assume you used your bank account for all your transactions and used no cash during the month. Then, your surplus is in your bank account balance at the end of the month. If in a month you received $100 and used $90, your surplus is $10. That should be the amount in your account at month end. If you had $5 in your account at the start of the month, you should have $15 at the end: the beginning amount of $5 plus the surplus of $10.

You can show this in your spreadsheet by adding your bank balance at the start of the month to your surplus from **Table 3**. The result should equal your bank balance at month end. It would look like **Table 4**.

Table 4	
Surplus / (Deficit)	$745
Opening bank balance	$5,000
Closing bank balance	$5,745

It is fine if you're missing a few dollars; minor differences will not matter. What you're trying to ensure is that you aren't missing anything large.

Cash

Cash presents a small, but manageable, complication. If you withdrew cash from your bank account during the month and spent it all, you will include these outflows in their respective categories.

Let's say your starting bank account is $5,000 and you withdrew $500. If you had no other inflows or outflows for the month,

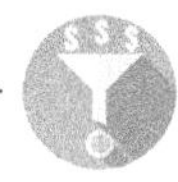

Assess your 30-day picture

Let's now take a moment and review your outflows over the last month. Why outflows? Usually, we do not have much ability to increase our inflows, so we must ensure our outflows fit within our inflows (we must aim to live well below our means).

After looking at your month's outflows, what you spent could shock you. It is often an "Oh no!" moment. If you were not overly surprised, just wait. Your "Oh no!" moment could come in the next chapter.

The reason I said you could be surprised is because if you have not tracked your outflows in the past, I'm certain you don't know what they truly are. Even if you were familiar with the types of your expenses, their size could be larger than what you expected.

Don't be concerned if you have a deficit for the month. The main goal right now is to ensure you know where your hard-earned income has gone. If you incur a deficit more often, we'll deal with that situation in an upcoming chapter.

Wrap up

Was this exercise that difficult? It required you to make a little effort, but I am certain seeing your 30-day financial self was worth it. For the next *Steps* you no longer need to perform any tracking. If what you learnt about yourself was eye-opening, think about continuing to track for a few more months.

I remember when I tracked my expenses for the first time. I was so astonished about my spending that I continued to track my inflows and outflows for six months to understand exactly where my money was going.

Feel free to continue tracking because it doesn't hurt to keep learning about yourself. For our purposes though, we can use this 30-day data to continue with the rest of the *Steps*.

Step 3:
Estimate for 12 Months

If you worked through the last two *Steps* and gathered one month's worth of inflows and outflows, this third *Step* is easier and more important. While one month's inflows and outflows is useful, it is critical to have a 12-month estimate. This doesn't mean you must track your money movements for one year! Instead, we'll estimate your 12-month amounts using the 30 days of data that you gathered.

Let's understand why a longer time frame is important.

First, one of the sources of financial stress is large outflows that do not occur often. For example, if you pay car insurance once a year instead of monthly. You know the outflow must occur because if you own a car, you must buy insurance. But in your busy day-to-day activities, the upcoming expense is not usually top-of-mind. Suddenly, when the time to pay arrives, you're not ready and you scramble to find the funds.

Second, another "Oh no!" moment arises when you realize how much you spent on certain items over the course of a longer period. Each outflow by itself is easy to ignore. But over time, it is shocking how they can add up to a large amount.

As with the previous chapter, we'll take a do-it-yourself approach using a spreadsheet. Let's walk through the process.

Table 7

	Jan	Feb	Mar	Apr	May	Jun	Jul	Aug	Sep	Oct	Nov	Dec	Total
INFLOWS													
Gross salary	5,000	5,000	5,000	5,000	5,000	5,000	5,000	5,000	5,000	5,000	5,000	5,000	60,000
Taxes	(1,200)	(1,200)	(1,200)	(1,200)	(1,200)	(1,200)	(1,200)	(1,200)	(1,200)	(1,200)	(1,200)	(1,200)	(14,400)
Other mandatory deductions	(650)	(650)	(650)	(650)	(650)	(650)	(650)	(650)	(650)	(650)	(650)	(650)	(7,800)
Net Salary	3,150	3,150	3,150	3,150	3,150	3,150	3,150	3,150	3,150	3,150	3,150	3,150	37,800
Other Inflows	50	50	50	50	50	50	50	50	50	50	50	50	600
TOTAL INFLOWS	3,200	3,200	3,200	3,200	3,200	3,200	3,200	3,200	3,200	3,200	3,200	3,200	38,400
OUTFLOWS													
Loan payments													
Loan 1	1,000	1,000	1,000	1,000	1,000	1,000	1,000	1,000	1,000	1,000	1,000	1,000	12,000
Total Loan payments	1,000	1,000	1,000	1,000	1,000	1,000	1,000	1,000	1,000	1,000	1,000	1,000	12,000
Needs													
Expense 1	500	500	500	500	500	500	500	500	500	500	500	500	6,000
Expense 2	500	500	500	500	500	500	500	500	500	500	500	500	6,000
Total Needs	1,000	1,000	1,000	1,000	1,000	1,000	1,000	1,000	1,000	1,000	1,000	1,000	12,000
Wants													
Expense 1	300	300	300	300	300	300	300	300	300	300	300	300	3,600
Expense 2	300	300	300	300	300	300	300	300	300	300	300	300	3,600
Total Wants	600	600	600	600	600	600	600	600	600	600	600	600	7,200
TOTAL OUTFLOWS	2,600	2,600	2,600	2,600	2,600	2,600	2,600	2,600	2,600	2,600	2,600	2,600	31,200
Surplus / (Deficit)	600	600	600	600	600	600	600	600	600	600	600	600	7,200
ALLOCATIONS													
Emergency fund	100	100	100	100	100	100	100	100	100	100	100	100	1,200
House deposit	250	250	250	250	250	250	250	250	250	250	250	250	3,000
College fund	150	150	150	150	150	150	150	150	150	150	150	150	1,800
TOTAL ALLOCATIONS	500	500	500	500	500	500	500	500	500	500	500	500	6,000
Unallocated Surplus	100	100	100	100	100	100	100	100	100	100	100	100	1,200
Opening bank balance	4,000	4,100	4,200	4,300	4,400	4,500	4,600	4,700	4,800	4,900	5,000	5,100	
Closing bank balance	4,100	4,200	4,300	4,400	4,500	4,600	4,700	4,800	4,900	5,000	5,100	5,200	

Time period

I recommend using a calendar year for your 12-month period (January to December). If another 12-month period (for example, May to April) suits your situation better, feel free to use that. Just ensure you cover 12 months.

Aim for a layout like **Table 7**.

Don't panic if it looks like a lot of information. It's exactly what you prepared for one month. You're only adding more columns for the next 11 months. The total column is the sum of the 12 months.

Repeat 30-day data

Repeat your 30-day information for each of the other 11 months. Starting this way assumes your inflows and outflows are **the same** each month. Your annual unallocated surplus (or deficit) should therefore be 12 times your one-month number. Notice the 12-month surplus is $1,200, which is 12 times the January amount of $100.

We'll make this closer to reality next.

Adjust monthly inflows

You want your projected 12-month inflows to be as accurate as possible. One approach is to start with your exact inflows from the *previous* year. Locate your records for last year and update your spreadsheet using these amounts. You then adjust these monthly amounts if your inflows changed from last year, for example if you switched jobs and now earn a different salary. Of course, there is no need to use this "look back" approach if you already know your inflows for the next 12 months.

Adjust monthly outflows

Let's now review each category of outflow. Initially, I asked you to repeat the 30-day amount for the other 11 months. While this approach may work for some categories (for example, loan payments or subscriptions), it will not work for all. You must therefore review each outflow to decide whether to adjust any specific month. Importantly, think carefully about payments that are not regular and include them in the month you expect to pay them. Create new categories as needed.

Here are a few guidelines:

PARTYING Consider events that you celebrate, for example, religious occasions, birthdays, anniversaries, or even a long-weekend get-away. Include the outflows for these events in the months you expect them to occur.

HOLIDAYS Outflows like vacations can be tricky depending on the cost. If you take annual vacations, include the cost in the month you expect to pay for it. Remember, you may have to pay hotel, airfare, and other costs in an earlier month.

Some persons take vacations every two years because trips are expensive. The easiest approach for this type of outflow is to divide the total estimated cost by two and include half in your current estimate. When the month arrives, you'll need to remember to put away the funds that you estimated (and don't spend it!). Next year, you'll add the second half to pay for your vacation.

You can use this approach for any large expense. Use your savings account to keep the funds that you set aside.

MAINTENANCE Think about maintenance for vehicles, air conditioners, and other equipment. Search for records from the past year to help estimate the costs and when they might occur.

KIDS If you have children, some costs for their upkeep could be shared, for example, groceries because you'll buy for the whole family. Other costs will be specific to them, such as clothes, shoes, school supplies, activities (for example, camps), and toys.

UNDERESTIMATES You are more likely to underestimate your outflows than overstate them. Your estimate could be low because you either missed an item or the actual cost is higher than you thought. You can cover both these situations by including an outflow category called "Contingency" and using a reasonable monthly estimate.

MEDICAL You will incur certain costs every year, but it may be difficult to know when or the amount in advance, for example, doctor or dentist visits. You can include these if routine, let's say if you do checkups every six or nine months. Unfortunately, you cannot predict what month you may have a toothache or the cost of a more serious medical issue. It's easier to treat events where timing and cost are uncertain by using an emergency fund. We'll discuss this in *Step 6: Build an Emergency Fund.*

You may notice that you have a large outflow in a month, which caused that month to be in deficit. You might be tempted to spread the cost over several months, but don't. The monthly balances, even if in deficit, aren't important yet. This will become clearer as you continue.

If you tracked more than one month's outflows, naturally your 12-month estimate would be more precise. **Tracking your outflows over a longer period could be necessary if your monthly outflows are often close to your inflows.** By this I mean you are effectively spending what you earn.

If you plan to track additional months, you'll notice it quickly becomes second nature, like blinking. Also, the need for precise tracking ends quickly because you begin to estimate your outflows more accurately. Remember, if your estimates are slightly off when compared to your actual outflows, the small difference will not affect your overall financial picture.

Your 12-month estimate

After completing the previous changes, you will arrive at your estimated 12-month inflows and outflows. Before continuing, I'd like to point out that this is NOT a budget. It is only your projected inflows and outflows as they currently exist. **Put another way, it is a portrait of one year of your life in dollars and cents, assuming you continue to live exactly as you normally do.**

Now it is time to step back mentally and do the following:

- ☛ **Review each total outflow.** Look at the 12-month totals for each outflow category. This will be the last column to the right if you followed my layout. You might be surprised about how much you spend on items, such as entertainment or buying food. Each monthly amount might not raise your eyebrows, but when viewed for 12 months, you may begin to think that some outflows are not a smart use of scarce funds.

- ☛ **Review your total surplus or deficit.** Staying with your 12-month total, focus on the surplus or deficit balance. If the surplus is small, you effectively will spend the next year working to pay your bills. Yes, you are making ends meet, but continuing with that approach will not result in financial independence. If the amount is a deficit, meaning your outflows are greater than your inflows, you must act to reverse the deficit, otherwise you may need to borrow soon.

- ☛ **Review each month's surplus/deficit.** I mentioned earlier that some months could be in deficit because of a large outflow. If you have an overall surplus for the 12 months, it means you will use cash from the months in surplus to cover the months you are in deficit. If you did not take a 12-month view, you may have fooled yourself into thinking the excess cash in a particular month was

available to spend. In fact, **the 12-month view shows that you must keep the surplus cash to cover the upcoming months in deficit.**

Wrap up

I'd like you to pause for a moment and understand the importance of the exercise you just completed. You have taken a major step towards taking control of your money by figuring out if you have an overall 12-month surplus or deficit. You are no longer living day-to-day. You are no longer stressed by large upcoming outflows or expenses arising unexpectedly. A slightly longer view allows you to plan for the year ahead and decide how to avoid upcoming problems.

You should celebrate because this is an excellent achievement!

At this point, two questions may start to form in your mind:

1. If I am in deficit, what should I do?

2. If I am in surplus, what should I do with it and what size of surplus should I aim for?

Let's tackle these.

Step 4:
Decisions About Your Deficit

We ended *Step 3* by completing a 12-month estimate of your inflows and outflows. What you should do next depends on whether you have a deficit or a surplus. Let's look at the situation where your estimate shows you could be in a 12-month deficit. In summary, once you're projecting a deficit, you must find ways to "fund" the deficit, either by:

- Reducing your estimated outflows.
- Finding new sources of inflows.
- Using any money that you have saved.
- Borrowing.

While a 12-month deficit is a serious situation, there is a small silver lining. You now know in advance it could happen, and you can eliminate the deficit proactively. This is exactly what being in control means.

As you evaluate your options, the one you must avoid, if possible, is borrowing. And if you are not aware that you could be in a 12-month deficit, you will likely fund the deficit by using a credit card. You will learn later that credit card debt is one of the worst forms of borrowing, and because using it is so easy, we may ignore the effect on our finances.

Until we review borrowing fully in Action 3: *Manage Your Debt*, I'll say you should take loans in a financially responsible way. If you don't make a deliberate, well-thought-out decision, it could damage your finances.

I do not believe borrowing to fund a 12-month deficit is a smart move.

Your immediate objective

Let's focus on the main point to understand at this stage. Unless you convert your 12-month deficit to a surplus, you cannot achieve financial security. Achieving a 12-month surplus is your first key milestone. All other actions to develop financial independence start from this point.

> I'm sure it is obvious you cannot spend more than you earn for an extended period.

Let's think about what could happen if you keep making annual deficits because you either were not aware or chose to ignore the situation. I'm sure it is obvious you cannot spend more than you earn for an extended period. Yes, you could fund the outflows for a "longish" period by borrowing or selling assets you own. Eventually, however, you'll run out of assets to sell, and your lenders will start to demand you repay your loans. When this downward spiral reaches a certain critical point, it is difficult to recover. It could lead to your personal bankruptcy, and the stress could shatter your emotional health.

I know you agree that you must avoid this result no matter what. It is, therefore, important to pause here and decide how to correct it. Even if these decisions are difficult, they will turn your finances towards a sustainable path. Right now, this means ensuring your 12-month inflows less outflows are in surplus.

Reduce your outflows

Start by reviewing all outflows to select which ones to reduce. Within outflows, focus initially on your Wants. Remember, Wants are outflows you do not need to survive. Often you can convert your deficit to a surplus by just reducing these expenses. If, however, you reduced Wants as much as possible, but you are still in deficit, then it's time to tackle your Needs.

Lifestyle choices

The advantage of choosing a different lifestyle is that the benefits are long-lasting.

I previously explained that while Needs represent the basics to survive, the cost of those basics could vary a lot. But reducing Needs is more difficult than cutting Wants. You can always choose to do without a vacation or drinks with your friends. In comparison, to these short-term sacrifices, reducing Needs requires you to make lifestyle choices. Lifestyle decisions are more difficult because they are longer-term changes. But the advantage of choosing a different lifestyle is that the benefits are long-lasting.

Examples of lifestyle adjustments could include living in a cheaper location, using public transportation, or cooking instead of buying food. Each of these changes will result in lower outflows every month. Once you make the first difficult step to a lower-cost lifestyle, it is remarkable how quickly it becomes normal.

Loan repayments

The combination of reducing Wants and making lifestyle choices should be sufficient to convert your 12-month deficit into a surplus. But if not, try to reduce a third set of outflows: your loan payments. Of course, you'll need your lender to work with you to lower the payments. To be clear, I am recommending that you *reduce* your loan installments, not to

stop making payments. Never stop making payments unless your lender agrees.

In Action 3: *Manage Your Debt* you'll understand why the approach to lower your loan installments is not in your best long-term interest. Right now, though, the focus is getting to a 12-month surplus, which makes achieving smaller loan payments a valid approach. Once you arrive at a surplus, you will then be able to make other decisions.

New sources of inflows

Assuming you cannot reduce your outflows further, next you must search for a new source of inflows. The first approach to get cash could be to sell any assets you do not use. The second approach is to find a part-time job (a second or even a third job). As tiring as this sounds, remember, your immediate goal is to reverse the potential deficit. Getting another job, until you have a longer-term plan, is often the only way to avoid the option I describe next.

Draw down your savings or borrow

If you cannot reduce your outflows further and you are not able to improve your inflows, you've arrived at what you really should do your best to avoid. The first option is to use any savings you have and the second is to take a short-term loan to fund the deficit. There are a few points to consider here.

These are only valid options if a one-off event caused your 12-month deficit. By this I mean, your inflows are lower, or outflows higher, due to something specific that is unlikely to recur in the *following* year. Once the reason is not repeated, next year you will return to a 12-month surplus.

If this is your situation, then using your savings to offset the deficit, or borrowing if you have no savings, are reasonable actions. To repeat, they are only acceptable if you expect your deficit to be temporary and you have truly exhausted the other options.

If your only choice is to borrow, do not use your credit card. Instead, I suggest you approach your bank to ask for a short-term personal loan. This approach will make more sense after you learn how to manage debt.

Wrap up

Before moving on to consider how to use your 12-month surplus, I must underscore a point. If you genuinely wish to stop worrying about money, you MUST arrive at a point where your 12-month inflows exceed your 12-month outflows—you must be in surplus.

You will not obtain the greatest benefit from the next chapters until you achieve a 12-month surplus. If you are in a 12-month deficit, I urge you to make the difficult choices now. **Your future financial self depends on the decisions you make at this moment.**

Step 5:

Decisions About Your Surplus

I hope you took a moment to celebrate if this was the first time you performed *Steps 1 to 4*. Celebrate a little more if you decided what actions you intend to take to correct a deficit. Remember, these are deliberate actions to take control of your finances. You are no longer "winging it" or living month-by-month. It's an incredibly liberating feeling to know you are in control of your financial destiny!

Let's continue with our second question from *Step 3*. There were two parts: (a) If I am in surplus, what should I do with it? And (b) What size of surplus should I aim for?

To answer part (a), I recommend using it in four ways:

1. Build an emergency fund.
2. Repay debt faster than scheduled.
3. Save for medium and long-term goals.
4. Invest and plan for retirement.

I expect for most of us our surplus is only large enough to focus on one goal at a time. This is fine and the list is in the order that I suggest you follow to put your surplus to work. For example, if you are currently completing 1 (building an emergency fund), do not start 2 (repaying debt more quickly) until you finish 1. If your surplus is large enough to allow you to tackle more than one goal at the same time, then definitely proceed. I am therefore answering the second question as well: what size of surplus should you aim for? You should aim for an amount that allows you, at a minimum, to achieve 1. When you complete 1, you should aim for an amount that allows you to achieve 2. And so on.

Let's look at the four uses briefly, as we'll meet them in more detail in the later chapters.

Build an emergency fund

This is essentially "rainy day" money. This means you set aside some funds in case the unforeseen happens. I cover this activity in the next chapter.

Repay debt faster than scheduled

Most loans have a fixed repayment schedule, and those that do not, have at least a minimum payment. The goal here is to pay *more* than the set payments until your loans are repaid.

Save for medium and long-term goals / Invest and plan for retirement

Did you notice that I put 3 and 4 together? I did this because we normally consider retirement planning as a long-term goal. But I like to treat retirement as a separate use of your surplus because it is important. I'll cover this in more detail in our closing chapter *The End of Our Journey*, but for now, let me make two points:

- Although retirement planning is fourth on the list, *whenever* you have money that you are unlikely to need, you should use it for your retirement funds. I stress these must be funds you realistically do not intend to use.

☞ Retirement funds are what most individuals should use for investing.

Let me expand on the last point briefly until we return to this topic in the closing chapter. In my view, only the truly wealthy have enough money to have both a retirement pool and an investment pool. They generate large surpluses that easily meet their retirement needs, and the excess is available for other investments to build wealth. Of course, this wealth is also available during retirement.

Most of us, however, are not that fortunate. Our surplus funds are smaller, and we usually must work through the list I provided one-by-one. We only focus on retirement when 1 to 3 are under control and at this point, we allocate every available dollar to retirement savings. In our case, we have one pool of money: a retirement pool, which we invest.

Savings

Let's spend a few moments discussing the concept of "Savings." Did you notice that the action of "saving" only arises in the third use of your surplus? This is deliberate because it helps ensure the different uses of your surplus are clear.

The word "Savings" can be used in a general way, which does not necessarily mean the person doing the saving is becoming wealthy. So, to avoid any misunderstanding as we move forward with the *Steps*, let's agree on what savings is definitely *not*.

What is *not* Savings?

Have you ever heard people say they are saving for a vacation, for Christmas presents, to buy a phone or a gaming system? We should find a unique way to describe this intent because the funds gathered for these uses are not part of our savings. Yes, you are setting aside money over a period to buy something. **But these funds are for a *current* expense. As such, they are not part of your savings.** To emphasize, these funds are to pay for a present Need or Want.

Deciding to gather funds before spending is exactly the discipline you need to achieve financial freedom.

Recognizing that you are setting aside funds to meet a short-term Need or Want is important. It is easy to mislead yourself by thinking you are actively saving but feel disappointed when you aren't more financially secure. But let's acknowledge something important. Deciding to gather funds before spending is exactly the discipline you need to achieve financial freedom. The easy approach would be to buy the item using a credit card. You'll learn in a later chapter that this is a bad financial decision. So yes, "saving" before you buy something is an excellent habit. My point is, do not consider these amounts as real savings.

What is Savings, and why are they important?

Real savings are for your medium to long-term benefit. They are what is left after you pay all outflows and allocate money for specific goals such as an emergency fund. You do not use real savings to meet day-to-day living expenses (Needs or Wants).

While the act of saving might seem like a short-term action, you should view it as part of a larger plan. Each month of savings adds up to a year, and each year builds over time. You use these accumulated amounts to meet your medium-term goals or invest for your long-term goals. Medium-term goals could include saving for a deposit on a home, higher education, or some other significant aspiration. Long-term goals could include children's education or your retirement.

It is easy to believe an impulse purchase or loose spending only has a short-term impact. A different picture appears if you think it was money you could have saved to meet your long-term, and more important, goals.

For context, $1 saved today, continuously invested at 4% will become $2 (it will double) in around seventeen-and-a-half years. Think about that for a moment, with larger amounts instead.

Imagine how secure your future financial self could be if you save instead of spending in a way that has no lasting value beyond the present. **The bottom line is your current spending decisions have a major impact on your ability to meet your future goals.**

What is Savings used for?

To summarize, when you actually "save," you gather funds to achieve medium and long-term goals. In your 12-month estimate, these are included in the allocation lines at the bottom of **Table 7** in *Step 3*, repeated here:

Table 7

	Jan	Feb	Mar	Apr	May	Jun	Jul	Aug	Sep	Oct	Nov	Dec	Total
Surplus / (Deficit)	**600**	**600**	**600**	**600**	**600**	**600**	**600**	**600**	**600**	**600**	**600**	**600**	**7,200**
ALLOCATIONS													
Emergency fund	100	100	100	100	100	100	100	100	100	100	100	100	1,200
House deposit	250	250	250	250	250	250	250	250	250	250	250	250	3,000
College fund	150	150	150	150	150	150	150	150	150	150	150	150	1,800
TOTAL ALLOCATIONS	500	500	500	500	500	500	500	500	500	500	500	500	6,000
Unallocated Surplus	**100**	**100**	**100**	**100**	**100**	**100**	**100**	**100**	**100**	**100**	**100**	**100**	**1,200**

The "Surplus/(Deficit)" line at the top is the difference between your total inflows and outflows. From your surplus, you now allocate funds to meet specific goals. In the example, you'll notice there were no specific allocations for retirement because there isn't enough surplus. That's unfortunate, but often a reality. In the example, this person would first have to gather funds for any current goals. After reaching that goal target, the person then begins to set aside funds toward a new goal, which could be retirement.

Maintain order

I previously recommended using a checking account as your financial center for day-to-day transactions. When you start to have regular surpluses, you'll notice your bank account grows. Once this begins, to help keep things in order, you should separate true savings (your allocations) from day-to-day funds.

I suggest using a savings account to hold the funds you saved/allocated. You can also use a savings account to hold funds you are setting aside for an upcoming purchase. Eventually, you'll want to move your allocated funds to a long-term savings option. I'll cover this approach in Action 6: *Invest and Plan for Retirement*. For now, use your savings account to hold the allocations. I'll explain emergency funds specifically in the next chapter.

Wrap up

This was an important chapter. Having arrived at the key milestone of an estimated 12-month surplus, next, I'll show you how to put that surplus to work. I suggested four uses and the upcoming chapters will explain each in detail.

Step 6:
Build an Emergency Fund

In *Step 5*, I identified four ways and the order in which to use your surplus:

1. Build an emergency fund.

2. Repay debt faster than scheduled.

3. Save for medium and long-term goals.

4. Invest and plan for retirement.

In this chapter, I'll focus on the first use: build an emergency fund, a concept I first introduced in *Step 3*. Let's understand what an emergency fund is, why it is important, and why it should be the *first* use of your surplus.

What is an emergency fund?

It is a pool of money set aside to use when the unforeseen happens (the "emergency"). You do not use your emergency fund for outflows already included in your 12-month estimate. It is for outflows you have *not* identified. What makes it an emergency is the need to deal with the issue quickly.

Why do you need it?

Despite how carefully you plan, unexpected events occur. While you cannot say in advance what they will be, you are sure *something* will happen. For example, you lose your job

or are temporarily unable to earn income; medical issues arise; you must replace a major appliance; you have a minor car accident; or you sat on your glasses and broke them. The list is endless.

Unforeseen costs occur more often than we would like, but as no one lives protected in a bubble, we know a costly problem *will* arise sometime. We just can't predict when or the size of the outflow. **If we can estimate what, when, and how much, the outflow is not an emergency.** You should then include the estimated cost in your 12-month outflows.

One of the causes of personal stress is trying to find funds to deal with the unexpected. On the other hand, when you know you can afford unexpected costs, it is liberating and a sign of being in control.

Without an emergency fund, if an unexpected expense arises, often the only option to pay for it is to borrow. If we are forced to borrow, using a credit card or bank overdraft tends to be the easiest way. As I've said before, borrowing in an unmanaged way will damage your finances. Do your best to avoid this situation.

Is it part of your savings?

An emergency fund is not part of your savings. Yes, it is money you set aside, but you intend to use these funds for short-term outflows. You just can't identify now, with certainty, when, or how much. As discussed in *Step 5*, you should think about genuine savings as funds that you set aside for your medium and long-term goals.

You'll notice in the previous chapter that I treated an emergency fund as an allocation of your surplus, although it is not part of your savings. This is because you should focus on it as a *specific* goal.

How much do you need?

The amount will vary by person because it could depend on a few factors, for example:

- The more uncertain your income, the higher the fund.
- The more stable your job, the lower the fund.
- If you want greater peace of mind, then the higher the fund.

It's often easier to set an amount based on your monthly outflows. For example, one approach is to consider a situation where you had no income. If you lost your job, how long would it realistically take you to get a suitable alternative? If the search will take, let's say 5 months, then build your emergency fund to cover 5 months of outflows.

The exact amount is not important because you cannot predict how you will use it. You are only trying to ensure you have something set aside.

Try to be realistic and don't aim for an amount that is too large. Otherwise, you'll end up having a large pool of cash that you could use in a better way. Returning to the example above, consider setting aside an amount only for Needs, as opposed to total outflows. Or assume you'll take a part-time job until you find the right opportunity, in which case, your fund need not be as large.

Once you've reached your target fund size, stop allocating funds and focus instead on the next use of your surplus. Remember, this could be either accelerating payments on your debt or saving for a particular medium or long-term goal.

Replenish

Importantly, whenever you use your fund, your first action is to allocate new money immediately until you return the total fund balance to your targeted level.

Keep it safe and separate

Earning interest on the money is not the primary aim—your key objectives are ensuring not to lose it and accessing it when needed. While you're building the fund to your target, the most convenient place to keep the money could be in your savings account. Remember, savings accounts are eligible for deposit insurance, so your funds are safe (up to a limit) if the bank fails.

Once you reach your target, if you'd like to earn a little interest, you should discuss the options with your bank. They may be able to offer a money market account, a fixed deposit, or another option. If you must put the funds on deposit for a fixed period, choose a short time, for example, six months, or twelve at most. You may face a penalty if you are forced to withdraw the funds early. In my view, a penalty is fine, once you receive at least what you put in; it should *not* be less.

Because the fund is for emergencies, you should not dip into it without good reason. It may, therefore, help to introduce a little hassle to access it. For this reason, I don't recommend leaving it in your savings account once you reach your targeted level. **Know yourself.** If you could be tempted to use the funds for something that is not an emergency, then make it a little difficult to access. If you stay disciplined and use the funds only for emergencies, then you can ignore this extra precaution.

Make automatic transfers

Building your fund is a priority. As a result, a useful approach is to create an automatic transfer from your checking to your savings account for the amount you allocate each month. If you think about it, once you make the transfer, your checking account would only hold funds that you expect to spend each month (your estimated outflows). If you make the transfer early and automatically, you are not tempted to spend it and you would not forget to do it later.

You should not touch your savings account because these funds are for a specific purpose.

Making automatic transfers to a savings account for *all* allocations (the four uses of your surplus) is a good practice to adopt. You know you should not touch your savings account because these funds are for a specific purpose. Instead, you focus solely on your checking account for your daily transactions.

Wrap up

Having an emergency fund is another key milestone along the path to financial independence. This is your personal insurance policy for when things go wrong. Don't forget to celebrate a little when you reach your fund goal. It is another significant achievement!

Before leaving this topic, let me describe an alternative to having an emergency fund: standby credit, for example with a credit card. When you begin to generate continuous surpluses, you could choose to stop having a separate fund and use your credit card if an emergency arises. This approach is valid because you will pay off the card fully from your surpluses. Using a credit card in this way takes discipline. I don't recommend using this approach until *after* you become financially secure.

To continue with the remaining ways to use your surplus, we must first discuss a few other important topics, starting with net worth.

Step 7:
Calculate Your Net Worth

Step 3 Estimate for 12 Months led to a few important takeaways:

1. You cannot begin to build wealth unless you have a 12-month surplus.

2. You should use your surplus in four ways.

3. The first use is to build an emergency fund. These funds are your personal insurance plan to deal with unexpected outflows. We know the expense will happen, but we can't identify for what, when, or how much.

4. With your emergency fund in place, you then use your surplus to repay debt faster than scheduled, save for medium and long-term goals, and invest and plan for retirement.

Because these are critical goals, the question that must arise is: what size of surplus should you aim for? When this question came up earlier, I answered you should aim for a surplus large enough to cover all four uses. If this is not possible, you should approach them one at a time.

Admittedly, this was vague advice because you still may not know how to estimate an amount for each use. Have no fear; I'll address this later. At this point though, I want to focus on a situation where you need $X for one of the goals, but your 12-month estimated surplus is too low. For example, let's say you need $20,000 for a particular goal, but your 12-month estimated surplus is $8,000. What do you do now?

The answer is to create a budget.

Key financial metric

For budgeting to make sense, we must first understand the most important financial metric for individuals: net worth. Your net worth is like seeing a picture of yourself in dollars instead of pixels. It is an easy calculation. It is the difference between your assets and your liabilities:

Assets less Liabilities = Net Worth

We covered what are assets and liabilities in *Key Terms*, so you may find it useful to revisit that chapter for a refresher. As a quick reminder, consider an asset as anything you own that you could sell for a reasonable amount of cash. A liability is money that you owe.

When calculating your net worth, you should apply the following guidelines:

- For assets, use values that reflect their selling price. Technically, I should say less taxes owed from the sale, but you can ignore taxes if they are expected to be small. The reason for using selling values is it forces you to recognize real assets, not just any item you own.

- For loans, use the balance currently owed, not the original loan amount. Put another way, use the amount your lender would require if you had to repay the loan today.

Net worth indicates wealth

I am sure you have heard people described as "wealthy." What this means is they have a high net worth. You want your net worth to increase over time. The more it grows, the stronger your personal finances and the closer you will be to achieving financial peace of mind.

You want your net worth to increase over time.

If your net worth falls or becomes negative (yes, negative is possible), your finances are worsening. You are moving away from financial freedom and towards financial distress.

How does your net worth change?

Your net worth increases or decreases when the value of either your assets or your liabilities change. **Ultimately, making wise financial decisions is about whether the decision increases or decreases your net worth**. Let's look at each aspect.

Assets

If you increase your assets faster than you increase your liabilities, your net worth will grow. For most individuals, the major way we increase our assets is to increase our savings. It should now be clearer how *Steps 1* to *6* were building you to this point. Those steps showed you how to take control and produce a surplus. You need to have surpluses to grow your net worth. The other way to increase your assets is to own an asset whose value appreciates over time. Let's look at an example in **Table 8**.

Table 8			
	Now	**Change**	**Later**
Assets			
Bank	$5,000	$3,500	$8,500
Vehicle	$12,000		$12,000
House	$250,000	$5,000	$255,000
	$267,000		**$275,500**
Liabilities			
Credit card	$10,000		$10,000
Home loan	$200,000		$200,000
	$210,000		**$210,000**
Net Worth	**$57,000**		**$65,500**

This person's starting net worth was $57,000. It increased by $8,500 to $65,500 because they saved more, resulting in a larger bank balance, and their home also appreciated by $5,000.

The opposite can happen, meaning your net worth falls if your assets decline. This also happens when we use our savings for consumption, which means having outflows that do not lead to an increase in your assets.

Liabilities

When you take loans in an undisciplined way, your net worth falls.

When your liabilities increase, your net worth declines. Even if your assets increase, your net worth declines if your liabilities grow faster than your assets. You might recall, in the earlier chapters I warned that increasing your debt could have a negative effect on your finances. Let me now state this more precisely. When you take loans in an undisciplined way, your net worth falls. To be clear, not all debt is bad, but to make a wise financial decision you must understand how it affects your finances.

Table 9

	Now	Change	Later
Assets			
Bank	$5,000		$5,000
Vehicle	$12,000		$12,000
House	$250,000		$250,000
	$267,000		$267,000
Liabilities			
Credit card	$10,000	$7,000	$17,000
Home loan	$200,000		$200,000
	$210,000		$217,000
Net Worth	**$57,000**		**$50,000**

In **Table 9**, let's say instead the person used their credit card for consumption (outflows with no lasting value), resulting in their net worth falling from $57,000 to $50,000.

Table 10

	Now	Change	Later
Assets			
Bank	$5,000	($5,000)	–
Vehicle	$12,000		$12,000
House	$250,000		$250,000
	$267,000		$262,000
Liabilities			
Credit card	$17,000	($5,000)	$12,000
Home loan	$200,000		$200,000
	$217,000		$212,000
Net Worth	**$50,000**		**$50,000**

Table 10 shows the person's net worth is unchanged while the debt from **Table 9** is being repaid. An increase will happen when surpluses are made in the future, which should increase the bank balance and provide funds to continue repayment.

Relationship between net worth and surplus

Let's connect a few dots. You should remember the four ways to use your surplus:

1. Build an emergency fund.

2. Repay debt faster than scheduled.

3. Save for medium and long-term goals.

4. Invest and plan for retirement.

Do you realize the impact of actions 2 to 4 on your net worth? When you repay debt faster than scheduled, you increase your net worth because your liabilities decline. Additionally, when you begin to save actively for medium and long-term goals (including retirement), your net worth improves because your assets increase.

The key, therefore, to increasing your net worth and building personal wealth is to have a steady, or ideally, increasing surplus over time.

I suggest you read the previous sentence again. It is important. We'll return to this critical point in the Action 4: *Grow Your Income and Net Worth.*

Measure periodically

I believe net worth should be your only metric to evaluate if your finances are improving. You should calculate it periodically, let's say every 6 months but at least once a year, and compare it to your past calculations. You want to see an increasing trend over time.

Your calculation

At this point, you should try to calculate your own net worth, which is not difficult. You know what assets you own, so you only need to estimate their selling value. Be realistic because

it doesn't make sense to fool yourself with inflated values. For most of us, our liabilities will be loans from a financial institution. Check your balances for what you currently owe, *not* the original loan amount.

Once you have a list of your assets and liabilities, calculate your net worth as shown in the examples. If your net worth is positive (even if the balance is small), you are in a good place to apply the *Steps* to come. If your net worth is negative, your priority should be to reduce your debt to convert your negative net worth to a positive balance.

Do you remember when you estimated your 12-month inflows and outflows? If the outcome was a 12-month deficit, you had to adjust to convert it into a surplus. I emphasized that you could only achieve financial independence when you achieve a 12-month surplus consistently. That point is worth repeating here. If you wish to grow your positive net worth or convert a negative net worth to positive, you *must* be in a surplus 12-month position.

Wrap up

At the beginning of this chapter, I said you need to create a budget when you are trying to achieve a targeted surplus. But I temporarily diverted to introduce net worth, a key metric in personal finance. This is a measure of your financial strength, and you become wealthier when your net worth increases. For most of us, that means generating a steady or growing surplus over time.

Once you understand the importance of your net worth, you will better appreciate how a budget helps you achieve a higher net worth over time.

Step 8:
Create a Budget

I introduced budgeting in the previous chapter. We arrived at that action because building wealth and planning for your financial future depend on your achieving an annual targeted surplus. The problem you will most likely encounter is your 12-month estimated surplus is lower than your target to achieve a particular goal. To close the gap, you need a budget.

What is a budget?

If you followed the logic in the previous paragraph, it should be clear that having a budget is essential to achieve financial freedom. You might be asking: didn't I already do a budget when I estimated my 12-month inflows and outflows? The answer is no; that was not a budget. That exercise only identified what you *currently* earn and spend over 12 months.

A budget is not a list of current inflows and outflows. It is a plan. A plan designed to deliver a targeted surplus each year. A budget is, therefore, not about what you earn and spend right now, but what you *should* earn or spend to meet your medium and long-term financial goals. When you create a budget, you consciously decide how to produce a particular outcome: your target surplus.

You should recall from *Step 4: Decisions About Your Deficit* that I asked you to take immediate action to convert the deficit to a surplus. In that situation, you took short-term tactical decisions to achieve the immediate goal of arriving

at a 12-month surplus. Those actions (and the outcome) are similar to what is needed to create a budget.

Can you succeed without a budget?

Only a few people earn enough income to cover their desired lifestyle and have enough surplus to achieve long-term financial security. Most of us do not make enough income to cover our Needs, Wants, and goals in total. To fulfill our financial needs, we must adjust our outflows over time to fit our current income. Or we must earn more income. The objective of each decision about your inflows and outflows is to achieve a specific financial goal.

Without a budget as a roadmap to guide you, I don't know how you can balance the competing variables in your head. When you create a budget, you target a particular financial outcome, and importantly, you assess your progress along the way. If you are not achieving your financial target, you take suitable corrective actions.

> I can also tell you, with certainty, what a budget is *not*. It is not counting pennies or a stranglehold on your ability to live freely. I know this may be the impression that some have. If you believe this, I understand why you would avoid budgeting. Instead of being an enabler of financial freedom, you believe it destroys your freedom.

I think of a budget as a picture of a healthy body. If we are trying to become physically fit, we imagine what our healthy body looks like and then strive to achieve it. If you try to arrive at that mental picture with restrictive short-term actions, your success will not last. It takes time, patience, and sustainable actions to arrive at a healthy body, and similarly, a healthy financial state.

A budget is the equivalent of your healthy body, but in numbers.

Unless you have a large enough surplus, I do not believe it is possible to achieve financial peace of mind and stability without having a plan. This plan, when described in numbers, is your budget. Creating a budget is not difficult. The good news is, if you worked through the earlier *Steps*, creating your budget is straightforward. Your first task is deciding what level of surplus to target over the next year.

Select a target surplus

To begin, let's return to your 12-month estimated inflows and outflows. As a reminder, you should already have your emergency fund and you are working to save funds to:

* Repay debt faster than scheduled.
* Save for medium and long-term goals.
* Invest and plan for retirement.

The later chapters will help you understand the financial and net worth impact of both debt and future goals. You'll use this information to estimate what surplus to target. You do not need, however, to wait until you read those chapters. You can make certain decisions right now. After you review the later chapters, return to this *Step,* and adjust your target surplus.

Let's, therefore, focus on the exercise where you estimated your 12-month surplus. You might recall when you completed that exercise, the size of the surplus was not the priority. My only ask then was to ensure you were in surplus. If you projected a deficit, I urged you to act to convert the deficit to a surplus. This was your first concrete action to take control of your finances. (Yay!)

Your aim now is to work backwards. Instead of your surplus being the *outcome* of your estimated inflows less outflows, I am asking you to *choose* a surplus amount and alter your

inflows or outflows to arrive at that balance. For example, let's say the result of your 12-month estimation was a surplus of $5,000, but instead you decide you need $12,000. To repeat, how you arrived at $12,000 isn't the immediate focus; we'll refine the number later.

You now must decide what to change to arrive at the target surplus of $12,000. Thankfully, you only have two variables to adjust: your inflows or outflows. It's usually easier to start with your outflows.

Before continuing, let's take a moment to understand how important this is. By making these decisions, you are continuing to take control of your money. You are charting your own financial path, and this mindset and discipline leads to financial security. Be proud of yourself!

Reduce your outflows

The first step is to review your outflows to find which ones to reduce, focusing initially on your Wants. This should be familiar if you converted your 12-month deficit into a surplus. Remember, Wants are outflows you do not need to survive, which means you can forego them. If you reduced these as much as you could, then you'll have to tackle your Needs.

As discussed in *Step 4: Decisions About Your Deficit*, while Needs are for survival, the cost to obtain those basics could vary widely. If you realize that you must reduce Needs, it requires you to make lifestyle choices. The examples I listed in *Step 4* included living in a cheaper location, using public transportation, and cooking instead of buying food. There are many others. While initially these may appear to be difficult choices, think long term. Your financial picture is telling you that you will not achieve financial security without adjustments. The advantage of making lifestyle choices is that each adjustment could result in lower outflows every month. The choice leads to continuous long-term expense reductions.

Obviously, reducing Wants also saves money. But practically, you cannot strangle your discretionary outflows over a long period. Cutting Wants is like an adrenaline shot, a short-term boost, but eventually you must live a little.

Recall at the beginning of this *Step* that I told you a budget should not be about counting pennies or a stranglehold on your ability to live. When you try reducing Wants alone, you must watch each dollar you spend like a hawk. No one realistically has the time, or frankly, the willpower to apply this level of constraint for a long time. Don't rely solely on reducing Wants. Make sensible lifestyle choices and give yourself a greater chance to succeed over the long term.

Adjust your inflows

If you reviewed your outflows and adjusted them as much as possible, then you need more income to reach your target surplus. More income could mean a part-time job or trying to earn more at a current job (for example, from a promotion or working overtime) or developing a side business.

I believe arriving at this conclusion can itself be liberating. Knowing this is the direction you must take, you then dedicate your energy completely to this goal, especially if it requires you to invest in yourself. I'll cover this point in *Step 11*.

Uncertain income

While reviewing your inflows, I suggest you pay attention to which of them are doubtful or those where the amount received could vary. I recommend being conservative with items of this nature. Either remove them from your budget completely or include the smallest amount you expect to receive.

This approach "forces" you to assess your whole financial picture more realistically. It may lead you to make lifestyle choices to fit this lower level of income. Or the realistic view could make it even clearer that you need to increase your income. Because you budgeted conservatively, if the inflows happen, they boost your surplus. Examples include:

- **Performance bonuses.** Excluding these from your budget is smart because you have no control over a bonus payment. Avoid creating a lifestyle that depends on uncertain inflows.

- **Variable income.** If your income fluctuates weekly or monthly, such as from sales-based commissions, don't overstate your earnings. Use the lowest amount or an average.

Interest and investment income

In *Step 1: Track Your Inflows and Outflows*, I said some individuals may be fortunate to receive inflows such as interest or dividends from funds on deposit or investments. When completing that *Step*, we included these amounts to show your complete financial picture.

As we are now creating your new financial self, I recommend that you *exclude* these inflows from your budget. I believe it is a mistake to base your lifestyle on income of this nature. When you begin to receive interest and other forms of investment returns, your money is now working for you (instead of you working to get money). You should begin to develop the habit of reinvesting these returns so that your money makes more money for you. This action is called "compounding" your returns. We'll return to this concept in later chapters; I'll explain it fully at that point.

Living the budget

If you followed the above guidelines, congrats! You just produced your first budget, and it is yet another milestone along the path to controlling your money! Remember, a budget is your north star guiding you towards a financial goal. To achieve each goal, you must produce a target surplus for the next 12 months by altering your inflows and outflows.

> A budget is your north star guiding you towards a financial goal.

After creating your budget, maintain it by doing the following:

1. **Perform periodic check-ins.** To make sure you are on track, for the first few months you should confirm that you are achieving your monthly targets. Importantly, it will also ensure you did not omit anything major from your budget.

   If you followed the layout I used in *Step 3: Estimate for 12 Months* **(Table 7)**, and transferred allocations to your savings account, the checking process is painless. You only need to compare the month-end balance on your checking account to your target surplus after allocations. If you did not transfer any allocations to your savings account, all your funds should be in your checking account. In this case, you'll need to deduct the allocations from your checking account balance and then compare that amount to the bank balance in your spreadsheet.

   Once the funds in your bank accounts are close to your budgeted surplus, then you are fine. Ignore any minor differences: your budget is a guide, not a straitjacket. If, however, you discover large differences, you will have to review your actual inflows and outflows and compare them to your budget to see what caused the difference. Once you know what caused it, include the omitted item in your budget, so your budgeted monthly surpluses will be close to your actuals.

I suggest you perform these checks every month initially. As soon as you are comfortable, then aim for every 3-4 months instead. Trust me, once you get the hang of it, the check is as quick as: I budgeted a surplus of $3,000 by X month; my bank account balance was $2,900; close enough, I'm done until my next check-in.

2. **Update your target surplus.** Each time you achieve a financial goal (we'll discuss what this means in later chapters), estimate your new target surplus based on your next goal. Then adjust your budgeted inflows and outflows to achieve your new target surplus.

3. **Reassess your financial goals.** At least once a year, reassess your financial goals for the next year and adjust your inflows and outflows if your target surplus has changed.

4. **Rejoice.** You are now in greater control of your money!

Once you build this habit, the amount of time you spend actively budgeting quickly declines. Many of these actions will happen unconsciously, and I assure you it will take far less time than you may think.

Potential increases in inflows

At some point in the future, your inflows may increase. For example, you get promoted or you start to earn income from a second job or side business. **Unless your outflows were too tightly constrained and you absolutely must spend more, try to "pretend" this extra income does not exist.** Yes, include it in your budget, but do not increase your outflows just because you have new inflows. This takes discipline.

You should aim to keep your outflows stable until you are confident you will meet your financial goals. For example, if you are trying to be debt-free, use any extra inflows to accelerate your loan payments until you achieve this goal.

> Always remember that finding reasons to spend is easy. Stay disciplined and focus on improving your future financial self.

Wrap up

In summary, this chapter laid the groundwork for you to achieve various financial goals by using a budget as a key tool. For the discussion to proceed, I asked you to pick an amount that you could target as your surplus. Something challenging but achievable. You then created a budget to produce the desired surplus.

We can, however, improve the estimate of your target surplus and make the number more precise. Let's see how this works.

Step 9:
Improve the Estimate of Your Target Surplus

To recap, in *Step 8*, we used your estimated 12-month inflows and outflows as the starting point; we selected a target surplus; and then adjusted your estimate until you achieved the targeted figure. Together these actions created your budget. The key focus at that point—the chosen target surplus—was a random number. There isn't anything wrong with this approach because we often select an amount to save based on instinct. But if we could improve the estimate of your target, you would have a more direct relationship between the target, your financial goals, and wealth creation.

Two approaches are possible to refine your target:

1. Use a percentage of your inflows.

2. Estimate an additional amount to repay your debt faster or an amount you need to achieve a specific medium or long-term goal.

Percentage of inflows

Using a percentage of inflows as your target is easy. If you aren't sure what percentage to use, I have two suggested budget "profiles," one if you are presently debt-free and one if you have loans. I emphasize these are only guides and you should not expect to achieve them perfectly or immediately. If you use my suggested targets, or if you create a profile more suited to you, *gradually* adjust your budget until you reach the target profile. Be patient and realistic with the amount of time you need. It doesn't make sense to aim for drastic changes and frustrate yourself when you can't achieve them.

The way the approach works is, use your inflows as the base and multiply the base by a percentage. In other words, you are saying to yourself, "I'd like to save X% of my inflows." As the target surplus is really the goal, distribute your Wants and Needs according to your circumstances. In my profiles, I also suggest percentages that you should *not exceed* for Needs, Wants, and Loan repayments. Remember, the target surplus is your ultimate goal: distribute your outflows between Wants and Needs based on what works best for you. This will be clearer using an example.

Let's assume a 12-month estimate as shown in **Table 11**. I hid the inflow and outflow categories to make it easier to follow.

Table 11														
	Jan	Feb	Mar	Apr	May	Jun	Jul	Aug	Sep	Oct	Nov	Dec	Total	Current
INFLOWS														
TOTAL INFLOWS	3,000	3,000	3,000	3,000	3,000	3,000	3,000	3,000	3,000	3,000	3,000	3,000	36,000	
Needs														
Total Needs	1,500	1,500	1,500	1,500	1,500	1,500	1,500	1,500	1,500	1,500	1,500	1,500	18,000	**50%**
Wants														
Total Wants	1,300	1,300	1,300	1,300	1,300	1,300	1,300	1,300	1,300	1,300	1,300	1,300	15,600	**43%**
TOTAL OUTFLOWS	2,800	2,800	2,800	2,800	2,800	2,800	2,800	2,800	2,800	2,800	2,800	2,800	33,600	
Surplus/ (Deficit)	200	200	200	200	200	200	200	200	200	200	200	200	2,400	7%

The example assumes you currently have an estimated surplus of 7% of inflows ($2,400 ÷ $36,000). You calculate the other percentages in the same way, using total inflows as the base. For example, Needs are $18,000 ÷ $36,000 = 50%, and so on.

First, let's look at the debt-free profile.

Debt-free budget profile

If you currently have no debt, I recommend you target one-third (33%) of your inflows as your surplus. Even though the target surplus is the objective, if you wish, you can similarly target 33% of your inflows for Needs and 33% for Wants. (Put the missing 1% wherever you like!)

You do not have to apply the same 33% to Needs and Wants because it may not be possible in your circumstances. For example, if the cost of living in your location is high, your outflows for Needs could be greater than 33% of inflows. You must, therefore, adjust the percentage targets for Needs and Wants, once the total does not exceed 66%. I like a balanced approach, so I aimed for 33% in each area when I did this exercise personally.

Continuing with the example, with inflows of $36,000, your target surplus will then be one-third or $12,000. I have shown this in the "Target" column in **Table 12**. Also shown, Needs and Wants are 33% each, but as I explained, feel free to vary these. Once you choose a target, your aim is now to reduce outflows to reach the target surplus. In the example, you will need to reduce outflows for Needs from $18,000 to $12,000 and Wants from $15,600 to $12,000.

Table 12				
	Total Jan-Dec (as Table 11)	**Current**	**Target**	**Target**
INFLOWS				
TOTAL INFLOWS	$36,000		$36,000	
Needs				
Total Needs	$18,000	**50%**	$12,000	**33%**
Wants				
Total Wants	$15,600	**43%**	$12,000	**33%**
TOTAL OUTFLOWS	$33,600		$24,000	
Surplus/(Deficit)	**$2,400**	**7%**	**$12,000**	**33%**

Importantly, it is fine if your current 12-month surplus is far away from 33% of your inflows. My debt-free budget profile is an ideal to aim for. In the example, your surplus is currently 7% and trying to jump to 33% immediately may be too great a challenge. Instead, it may be more realistic to make gradual changes to your budget and get closer to 33% over time.

> If 33% is not possible, that's fine, but realistically you should aim for at least 20% of your inflows as a target. This is the only way to make a meaningful attempt at achieving all your financial goals.

Let's pay more attention to these percentages. In the example, did you notice the "Current" percentage for Needs is large at 50% of inflows? It indicates the cost of living may be too high. You might need to make lifestyle changes to save more.

Obviously, assessing if the level is adequate or too high will require judgment. Think of it this way. In an extreme situation, such as loss of employment, you could have large costs that are difficult to change in the short term. **You will, therefore, deplete your emergency fund quickly when Needs are high**.

If instead the percentage for Wants was large, again let's say 50%, then an opportunity exists to reduce them and set aside more for your financial goals.

With-debt budget profile

The with-debt profile works in the same way as I described above, except in this case, it assumes you have debt. Consequently, a target is set for loan repayments. My recommended profile is: 20% Surplus; 30% Loan repayments; and 50% Needs and Wants.

To illustrate with numbers, let's again assume you have inflows of $36,000:

- The target surplus will be 20% of inflows or $7,200. Of course, it could be higher, in which case you'll lower the other percentages.

- Loan repayments will be 30% or $10,800 (this is the *maximum*).

- Wants and Needs in total are 50% or $18,000. Or separate them as Needs at 30% and Wants at 20% of inflows. As with the target for loan repayments, you should *not exceed* the combined 50%.

Although the target surplus (20%) is lower than the debt-free profile (33%), it is still at a meaningful level.

Even if you have debt, you must still have a surplus to meet other goals and to keep growing your net worth.

How to estimate an accelerated loan repayment target?

The second approach is to choose a target surplus based on the additional payments you wish to make on your loans each year. By paying more than scheduled, you repay your loans faster. You'll understand the benefit of doing this when you read Action 3: *Manage Your Debt*.

This second approach is also straightforward. It begins with your net worth calculation from *Step 7*. To arrive at your net worth, you would have deducted your loans (and other liabilities) from your total assets. Using your loan information, create a table that lists each loan type, the current balance owed, and the scheduled monthly and annual repayments. An example could look like **Table 13**.

Table 13

Loans Outstanding	Balance	Monthly Repayment	Annual Repayment
Credit card A	$8,000	$250	$3,000
Credit card B	$5,000	$150	$1,800
Personal loan	$6,000	$300	$3,600
Auto loan	$15,000	$400	$4,800
Home loan	$250,000	$1,200	$14,400
Total loans	**$284,000**	**$2,300**	**$27,600**

The total annual loan repayments in your table should equal the 12-month total in your budget.

Once you have this information, the idea is to target a surplus to pay off all loans, even if you do one at a time. You then approach the accelerated repayments in the following order.

1. **Repay credit card debt.** If you have more than one card, start with the one with the lowest balance. From **Table 13**, you will first target a surplus of $5,000, pay off card B, then target $8,000 and pay off card A.

2. **Repay unsecured personal loans.** If you have more than one, again start with the one with the lowest balance.

3. **Repay vehicle loans.**

4. **Repay housing loans.**

The reason for this order of repayments, and the other approaches you could use, will become clearer in Action 3: *Manage Your Debt.*

Your aim is to arrive at the position where the only loan remaining is housing related. I assume it will show a large outstanding balance and a long period for full repayment. Once you are at this point, it makes sense to begin focusing on other medium and long-term goals as well. By this I mean you should target a surplus that allows you to set aside funds for *both* your future goals and accelerated loan repayments.

If you prefer to tackle one goal at a time, then pay your housing loan as scheduled (not on an accelerated basis) and target a surplus for your other goals. Whenever you believe you are financially ready, return to the specific goal of repaying your housing debt faster.

What about medium and long-term goals?

I previously identified the final use of your surplus as saving for medium and long-term goals, including retirement planning. It is difficult to guide how much you should target for these goals. They will vary widely by person, ambitions, and intended future lifestyle. I can, however, help you understand some of the financial aspects you should think about when setting these goals. I like to describe these as life events, and I'll cover the more common ones in Action 5: *Prepare for Major Life Events*.

Once you begin to plan for medium and long-term goals, protect your financial security by:

1. **Saving as much as possible.** Your income from employment will eventually stop and your future outflows could be higher than you estimate today. For example, your health could be worse than you expect, leading to unplanned medical expenses. Consequently, you should protect your future financial self by saving as much as you can *today*.

   Use the debt-free budget profile as a future savings target: 33% of your inflows. Once you keep your expenses in check and keep your medium and long-term goals affordable, this level of surplus should be sufficient to sustain "the future you" comfortably.

2. **Managing your outflows responsibly.** I am not suggesting you live frugally. You should, however, acknowledge that it is easy to find reasons to spend or ways to increase your outflows permanently. As a result,

even if your income increases, try not to increase the cost of your current lifestyle to the detriment of your future self.

Wrap up

Using a budget to target a specific financial goal is an incredibly useful tool to shape your future financial self. As you have learnt, there are several ways to decide what surplus to target. What's great is you see a direct relationship between achieving your medium and long-term goals and growing your net worth.

To complete our discussion on budgets, let's look at some of the challenges you could face.

Step 10:
Avoid Budget Pitfalls

If you step back and take a high-level view of the previous *Steps*, I'm sure you realize the process to create a budget is not difficult. In summary:

1. Track your transactions for a month (or more) to understand your inflows and outflows. If you're confident you know them already, you can bypass this activity. But if you haven't tracked your inflows and outflows in the past, I'll always bet that you'll learn something surprising about yourself.

2. Create an estimate for 12 months, using the information for one month.

3. Target a surplus amount that allows you to achieve a particular financial goal.

4. Finally, alter your inflows and outflows to arrive at the desired target.

From this point, periodically confirm your actual surplus is close to what you budgeted. The comparison is easy to make if you use bank accounts as I suggested. If your actuals are far away from your budget, adjust the budget to correct, and keep reviewing occasionally. Once you develop the habit, this entire process is quick, and you will reap tremendous benefits.

Let me help by identifying some challenges you could meet when creating or living by your budget. Hopefully, you avoid them.

Unable to commit

It is useful to think of spending as an addiction: we all want to buy things because they bring us joy.

For some, committing to a plan is difficult even if *they* created the plan. In the case of their own finances, they often prefer to spend at will. It is useful to think of spending as an addiction: we all want to buy things because they bring us joy. It is often easy to surrender to the impulse to spend, but another impulse soon follows when the mini euphoria from what you bought ends.

You must be prepared to close your eyes to the unending distractions you meet every day that tempt you to use your scarce funds. For example, it is easy to make an online "therapeutic" purchase after a tough or annoying day. (Feel free to replace online shopping with your own form of temptation.) **You need to build your resolve that your future financial self is more important than a snap purchase**. Learning to ignore, however, takes practice, and it may be easier initially simply to avoid these temptations. For example, leave your bank and credit cards at home and only carry a small amount of cash. You can't buy anything if you have limited funds.

Being unnecessarily influenced

Consciously or unconsciously, we tend to look to our neighbor to influence or validate our own lifestyle. Of course, it may not be your literal neighbor. It may be someone who appears richer than we are, or something we wish to own that represents wealth, such as a luxury vehicle. To an extent, this is understandable, and even useful if it helps us create our goals.

The potential problem is when you try to mirror a lifestyle you cannot afford.

The potential problem is when you try to mirror a lifestyle you cannot afford. Disturbingly, the person you are comparing

yourself to also may not be able to afford it! Being able to afford a lifestyle is not only about expensive items. It matters in smaller ways as well, for example, eating out regularly, owning the latest tech, a fantastic wardrobe, or entertainment. For these individually smaller, but collectively expensive items, a less costly option *always* exists.

To embrace the options, you must ignore peer and social pressure and accept that your future financial self cannot afford these items. You also must be comfortable knowing that despite the appeal of brands, the cheaper option is often perfectly fine. Pay attention to, and rise above, the power of marketing that tries to convince us that we need to replace or upgrade an item every year or two.

Learn to ignore!

Unrealistic expense cuts

Avoid expense reductions that are unrealistic. You will only demotivate yourself when you can't achieve them. Or you achieve them but feel financially strangled. Yes, sometimes you must act aggressively to deal with a problem. For example, if you estimate a 12-month deficit, you must convert it to a surplus by slashing your Wants. But the point is you cannot maintain prolonged austerity. Instead, be realistic and make sensible lifestyle changes to reduce your total outflows. **These choices will allow you to enjoy the specific Wants that bring you the *most* satisfaction.**

Magic money

I covered this already although I didn't call it "magic money." I'm referring to inflows that may not occur. Examples include: a salary increase you're hoping to get, alimony or child support that you do not receive regularly, or a bonus. I recommended you exclude these items from your budget. **Reset your**

lifestyle to live without them. If you eventually receive these uncertain amounts, use the windfall to help achieve your various goals.

Omissions and unexpected events

We also covered this point, but it is important enough to repeat. It is obvious that your budget should include all your outflows. But when you created your 12-month estimate for the first time, it is possible you did not remember all outflows. It is easy to forget those that arise once a year or irregularly. This is normal and don't be disappointed if you forgot something. Adjust your budget and keep moving forward. You will quickly understand your outflows better and the chance of further omissions will become smaller.

Wrap up

The previous *Steps* showed you how to take control by firstly understanding, and then shaping, your future financial self. It's easy for the detailed descriptions to make the activities appear more difficult than they are. Once the *Steps* become routine, however, you don't spend much time doing them. Yes, if they are unfamiliar, you must invest time initially to learn. But if you follow my approach, learning takes less time than you might think.

If you are comfortable using personal finance applications, you can simplify the *Steps* even further. But as I mentioned before, I do not recommend using apps when you are doing the *Steps* for the first time. They perform the work invisibly and you will not understand what happened. Instead, use a spreadsheet first. I guarantee you will learn so much. Afterwards, use personal finance software if you wish. This is the approach I took. I remember trying several programs before choosing one. I had to review several because I discovered each one

only did certain things well and not everything I wanted. I was able to make this conclusion because I understood the mechanics from doing it myself.

Please remember, the only purpose of a budget is to target a particular surplus. The only reason for the target surplus is because you are trying to achieve a particular goal. And when you hit that target surplus, I cannot describe the feeling of accomplishment. **You are now in control of your future financial self.**

Step 11:
Invest in Yourself

Before moving to our next Action, I'd like to pull together some principles I discussed along the way and explain how they represent an investment in yourself.

The best overall investment: educate yourself

Usually when we hear the term "Investing," we think of placing money in a financial product to earn a return such as interest or dividends. Examples of products are a bank deposit, a bond or stock or mutual fund. Often, however, your best investment, which provides the greatest return, is to educate yourself. This could be from using your spare time to learn something new from free online courses, or by reading (for example, this book to learn to make wise financial decisions), or by pursuing formal education.

The return you receive from investing in yourself would be earning more income from new skills. The more income you earn, the greater your chance to create wealth because as your surplus increases, your net worth will grow over time. Of course, I assume you stay disciplined and control your outflows.

The "problem" with investing in yourself is that you do not normally enjoy the return at once. It is therefore easy to believe the action of investing either time or money in

yourself is not valuable. Instead, I urge you to think long-term and embrace a guilt-free attitude whenever you invest time or money to learn something new. Knowledge lasts forever and it is one of the surer paths to higher income in the future.

The best financial investment: reduce a dollar of expenses

The general belief is the best financial investment is a product that produces an amazing return. I disagree. I believe the best financial investment for most people is to try to reduce a dollar of outflows. It leads to an immediate positive impact on surplus and net worth for two reasons:

1. Boosting your surplus by reducing one dollar of your outflows is far easier to achieve than earning one more dollar of income.

2. Even if you earn an extra dollar of income, it is different from reducing your outflows by one dollar because you need to factor in income taxes. As taxes must be deducted from income, you receive less than one dollar. Whereas if you reduce a dollar of outflows, you save the entire dollar.

To be clear, growing your income is critical, which I explain below. My point is, if this is not possible in the short term, an opportunity for an *excellent* financial return still exists.

The second-best financial investment: accelerate payments on loans

For most of us, one of our best financial investments is to repay our loans faster than scheduled and save the interest cost. This will make more sense after you complete Action 3: *Manage Your Debt*. But you should understand from our earlier discussion that reducing your loans boosts your net worth and improves your financial strength. In many cases, accelerating your loan repayments alone could bring about your greatest wealth creation.

The third-best financial investment: invest today a dollar saved

The faster you take control of your money and begin to produce surpluses to use for medium and long-term goals, the sooner you can invest and plan for retirement.

Having enough savings to invest as soon as possible is important for two reasons:

- During your retirement, you could regret not saving more in your early years.

- The sooner you start investing, the more time you give your money to work for you and grow. For example, $100 invested now, earning 4% on average, with interest continuously reinvested, will be worth $219 in 20 years or $324 in 30 years. These returns could lead to invaluable retirement savings and illustrate the power of compounding. We'll return to this topic in more detail later.

The best way to increase your savings: earn more

After a while, you'll realize it is difficult to reduce your outflows below a certain level. When you arrive at this point, the only way to increase your savings is to earn more. I've already explained the first approach to earning more: invest in educating yourself to learn new skills.

The second way to earn more is to obtain another source of income. The second source could be either a part-time

job or a side-business, ideally related to a passion you have. Regardless of the source, having different income streams will help boost your surplus.

The third way to earn more income is to become self-employed. Unless you aim, while employed, for a reasonable level of seniority, your earnings may be low in less senior roles. The potential for major wealth creation, however, lies with businesses and their profit growth potential. Let's recognize that owning a business is risky. But it is definitely the ultimate demonstration of investing in yourself and your success. As you continue to build your knowledge about controlling your money, keep this thought floating in your mind. Also, if you decide to become self-employed, some of the skills you learn in personal finance are transferable to business finances.

I'll return to this topic in Action 4: *Grow Your Income and Net Worth*.

For most of us, our best working years are between our thirties to fifties. These are the years when we earn the most income and when, importantly, we have the most energy to work. It is critical, therefore, to maximize those years by trying to earn as much as possible.

Wrap up

I urge you to pay close attention to the way these various forms of investing in yourself could lead to prosperity.

Excellent! We have now completed our first action about taking control. It establishes a proper foundation from which you build and strengthen your finances. While you do this, danger lurks from events that could destroy what you took so much effort to build. Let's now consider some of the ways to protect yourself and those who depend on you.

Action 2

Protect Yourself and Your Dependents

Conceptual Challenges

Congratulations on completing the first Action! If you tried the *Steps*, I hope you understand why I said it lays the foundation for the remaining Actions. Let's start with a reminder of the six Actions that I believe you must complete to have a strong, full financial picture:

1. **Control your inflows and outflows**

2. **Protect yourself and your dependents**

3. **Manage your debt**

4. **Grow your income and net worth**

5. **Prepare for major life events**

6. **Invest and plan for retirement**

While the first Action focused specifically on taking control of your inflows and outflows, building a stable foundation has a second aspect. You also take control by protecting yourself, and those who rely on you (your "dependents"), from future financial hardship.

As you'll soon learn, insurance is the cornerstone of protection. I must confess, however, I found this Action difficult to write for a few reasons:

- **Complexity.** By its nature, insurance is complicated. As it has evolved, this complexity seems to have increased. I tend to have a mental block whenever complexity exists or arises. I become skeptical and it forces me to pause and ask myself, "Is this difficult to understand on purpose?"

Consequently, I risk introducing personal bias into these explanations even though my aim is to teach objectively how to make a wise financial decision.

- **Knowledge-sharing.** The complexity I referred to leads to another problem. In the first chapter, *Introduction*, I explained that my approach to each topic is "Show How; Don't Tell." I want to share practical knowledge that you apply, not just theory. Unfortunately, understanding insurance requires quite a bit of telling, which again might defeat one of my goals.

- **Judgment.** Deciding whether to use insurance is a personal risk management decision (I'll explain this concept soon). The implication is that most forms of insurance are *discretionary* purchases—you choose to buy it. Legally, you must have some types, which obviously makes that decision straightforward. Many other decisions, though, are not clear-cut, and you need to use a lot of judgment. The final decision may depend on how much you are willing, or can afford, to spend.

With these confessions off my chest, I'll do my best to explain, but I ask you to be patient and read this Action carefully. To help you with your insurance decision, I will explain the various aspects, so you have the relevant information. You can then either continue with research specific to your situation or have an informed conversation with an adviser.

Let's understand the main issue. If certain events occur, they could leave us or our dependents with a lower standard of living or an uncertain financial future. Let's consider a few examples:

1. **Premature loss of life.** We will all eventually pass away, but the problem is if we pass away before our dependents are financially secure.

2. **Ill health and major medical complications.** There are two aspects:

    a) Medical care is expensive and the cost to treat certain ailments could be significant.

    b) A medical issue could prevent you from working fully or at all (referred to as "disability"), so you face the prospect of less or no income.

3. **Loss of personal property.** It may be difficult or impossible to replace expensive assets if stolen or destroyed.

Insurance helps us manage these risks. But before we dive into the details of insurance, I'll emphasize an earlier point. I believe insurance should be primarily about risk management. This statement is important because you will learn in the upcoming chapters that insurance has crossed over into investment. Consequently, the line between buying insurance and investing could easily become blurred.

I am not implying anything sneaky. I only mean it has become easy to confuse using insurance as a tool to manage risk, with making a financial investment. When we think of an investment, we naturally want to know what return we could receive. When insurance, as a risk management tool, is confused with making an investment, it forces us to look for a return on the premiums paid. **We lose the perspective that paying the premium protects us from a risk—the coverage, the peace of mind that we will survive the event financially, is the return.**

As we go through this Action, let's keep the two goals separate: risk management versus investing. Once you understand the difference between the two concepts, you are free to decide if you want to approach them in a blended way.

We'll begin by focusing on what is risk management.

How to Manage Personal Financial Risks

Life is full of risk, and we all adopt active or passive ways to manage those risks. A financial risk exists if an event or a situation could reduce our net worth, or it prevents our net worth from growing once it takes place.

Understanding these risks and knowing the approaches to manage them and protect our finances is critical. I think of my finances like rooms in a house. We construct a roof and walls for shelter and security, or in other words, for protection. It is possible to live in the same space without exterior walls or a roof, but you'll face threats such as from the weather or burglary. Our personal finances also face various risks, and we need the equivalent of walls and a roof to protect us.

Broad approaches

You use two broad approaches to manage risks:

1. **Transfer.** The first way is to transfer the risk to third parties and pay them to accept it. The third party who accepts the risk is usually an insurance company. "Transferring" means if the event happens and you face a loss, the insurer reimburses you for part of or the whole loss. Consequently, the insurer bears the loss, and you (the "insured") use the funds received to restore your net worth. You cannot transfer every risk, and while it is possible to transfer several, it eventually becomes too expensive.

   We'll cover using insurance to manage personal financial risks in more detail in the next two chapters.

2. **Assume.** The second broad approach is to assume the risk personally, which means you accept the impact of any loss. You are forced to accept the risk when there is no third party to transfer it to. In some cases, although you can transfer the risk, you could deliberately decide to "self-insure" (you accept the risk yourself). We'll return to this concept in the chapter *Insure or Self-insure?*

   When you have no other choice, or willingly decide to assume risk, you instinctively manage it in three ways:

   a) **Avoid.** For example, you avoid risks associated with ill health by not smoking or you avoid a vehicle hitting you by not jaywalking.

   b) **Reduce.** For instance, you reduce the risk of theft of your household property by installing an alarm system or reduce the risk of fire damage by installing smoke detectors.

   c) **Prepare.** As it is impossible to avoid all risks or reduce them to zero likelihood, you manage any remaining risk by preparing for the potential financial loss.

We'll return to these approaches in the chapter *Insure or Self-insure*, where I'll modify them slightly after we learn about insurance.

Specific risks

Let's consider a few specific personal financial risks and examine the approaches you can use to manage them. Some should sound familiar. Where the solution involves insurance, I'll leave the detailed explanations for the next chapters.

Net worth

The size of your net worth and the financial cushion it provides is a crucial factor when deciding to insure. We need insurance when we cannot afford the loss from certain risks. You do not necessarily need insurance, however, if your net worth is large enough to comfortably absorb a financial loss. Put another way, after the loss, your financial security remains intact. **This is an important paragraph, so please read it again.**

In the approaches described below, I am assuming that your net worth is not yet large enough to absorb potential losses from these risks.

Overspending

I expect the problem with overspending (spending more than you earn or spending in an uncontrolled way) should be obvious. First, you are not in control; therefore, any surplus you make is accidental. Second, if you spend more than you earn, you must fund the shortfall by either selling something you own to raise cash, or more likely, by borrowing. In Action 3: *Manage Your Debt*, you'll learn adding debt in an uncontrolled way is a recipe for future financial hardship.

Approach

You avoid overspending by being in control of your money. It is impossible to be in control unless you know how much you earn, how much you spend, and what is your target surplus. We explored this extensively in Action 1.

Too much debt

Having too much debt reduces your financial flexibility. If your monthly payments are too high, you are vulnerable because small adverse changes in your inflows or outflows could make it difficult to pay your loans and living expenses. Additionally, you must often pledge your assets as collateral. When you do so, you give up certain ownership rights.

You should also not underestimate the emotional aspect: a mountain of debt creates a mountain of stress.

Approach

You avoid this risk by knowing how much debt you can afford. It's fine if you didn't understand some of the terms I used in the previous paragraph. I'll explain everything when we explore Action 3: *Manage Your Debt*.

Variability of income or unexpected expenses

A common risk is earning income that could change each month. For example, if someone is paid daily or works for sales commissions. In addition, while we often think of our outflows as regular, such as monthly rent and cable/streaming bills, the unexpected happens. Unpredictable outflows could include broken spectacles, minor car accidents, appliance repairs, or plumbing/electrical issues.

Approach

You manage these situations in four ways. The first is to prepare by having an emergency fund, which we already discussed.

The next two approaches are possible although less easy to do. You reduce the risk by having a low level of outflows for Needs and by developing another income stream. A low level of Needs allows you to use a smaller amount of your income for outflows that you do not control easily. This provides a lot of flexibility. The benefit of having a second income is obvious.

The fourth approach is to prepare by having credit available, which means having the ability to borrow at will. Options that allow you to borrow quickly include having a pre-approved personal line of credit or a credit card. Of course, as soon as you restore your finances, you should quickly focus on paying off the debt you incurred. Again, I'll cover these details in *Manage Your Debt.*

Vulnerable dependents

When we have dependents, a disruptive financial event is more significant. For example, a family where both partners must work to support young children and one partner dies suddenly. If the surviving partner struggles to make ends meet on one income, the family's financial security would suddenly be in jeopardy.

Approach

This situation is best handled by using insurance.

Loss of income

You could lose your ability to earn income from ill health or disability. Disability means you are unable to work owing to injury or illness. While the risk of income loss is important because you must support yourself, it is more significant when you have dependents.

Approach

You can protect yourself from loss of earnings by buying insurance. Additionally, I am sure you agree that we could reduce the chance of becoming sick by following healthy habits and lifestyles.

Loss of assets

Losses could arise from two types of assets:

(a) Certain assets could be expensive or impossible to replace if damaged or stolen, for example, homes or vehicles; and

(b) Losses from financial investments.

Approach

We could use insurance to protect against loss from damage to or theft of physical assets.

Losses from financial investments might occur for many reasons, especially as you must accept a higher level of risk to obtain a higher return. In summary, two actions could minimize this risk:

a) The first is to follow the adage "Do not put all your eggs in one basket," which means you should diversify where you put your money. Do not buy only one type of investment or only one stock. Also, do not rely only on one issuer. By spreading your investments across different issuers and products, you reduce the risk of a loss from which you can't recover.

b) Secondly, do not put your money into an investment you do not understand.

I must emphasize that these two points on investing are a tiny part of a wide-ranging topic. I only mention these approaches for you to know it is possible to manage the risks in an investment portfolio.

Inadequate retirement income

As we grow older, our capability or enthusiasm for work tends to decline, and when we enter this phase of life, we retire from active work. Naturally, our earnings decrease as a result. Many persons also wish to retire early enough to enjoy, in good health, aspects of life that were not possible during their full-time employment.

To have a financially secure and stress-free retirement, you must have a reasonable pool of funds to meet expenses. You accumulate this pool while you work. The obvious personal financial risk is not setting aside sufficient funds to meet your retirement goals. The added risk is that inflation could erode the purchasing power of your savings over time. When your purchasing power declines, it means the same amount of money buys less than in the past. Inflation refers to the general increase in prices over time.

Approach

The best approach is to prepare by saving as much as possible, as early as you can, by following the techniques outlined in Action 1. In addition, you must focus on growing your net worth, which I cover in Action 4: *Grow Your Income and Net Worth*.

Certain insurance products also address your need for income in retirement.

Wrap up

Although we face several personal financial risks, we have many approaches to minimize or prepare for them. Several of these actions are within our control. Often, we take them instinctively without realizing we are risk-managing our personal financial affairs.

With this background and awareness that you might already be an excellent risk manager, let's review how insurance helps us manage certain risks.

Understand the Basics of Insurance

In *How to Manage Personal Financial Risks* I described various risks we face and explained the different approaches we can take to manage or reduce them. One of the important tools available to us, but not covered in the last chapter, is transferring the risk to an insurance company.

Let's begin by understanding a few insurance basics, including certain products that insurers offer.

What is the purpose of insurance?

If certain events occur, the financial loss could ruin us, or at least cause major damage to our current or future net worth.

Although we answered this question in the last chapter, it's worth repeating. If certain events occur, the financial loss could ruin us, or at least cause major damage to our current or future net worth. One way we protect ourselves from the impact of these events is to buy insurance.

When we buy insurance, we enter a contract (called a "policy") with an insurer to assume a risk from us. The payment we make to transfer the risk is called a "premium." It is paid either monthly or annually.

If an unfortunate event occurs and you incur a loss, you then make a "claim" with the insurer. Once the claim conforms to the policy conditions, the insurance company will pay you an amount based on the value of coverage you bought. The amount of coverage you buy depends on how much risk you

wish to transfer. The greater the coverage, the higher the premium. The insurer may also impose a limit to the coverage.

"Transferring the risk" to an insurance company therefore means:

- If an unfortunate event occurs, the insurer bears all or part of the financial loss, not you. The insurer accepts the loss when they pay your claim.

- The payment allows you to recover either partially or fully from the event.

- Let's say you insured an asset and it is destroyed. Yes, you no longer have the asset, but when the insurer pays your claim, you have the funds to replace it if you wish. After receiving the payment, your net worth is effectively the same.

I emphasize that you could bear some part of the loss. Depending on the policy, you may incur the full cost upfront and receive reimbursement later. Additionally, insurers often investigate claims, which could delay settling your claim. It is easy to overlook these points.

How does insurance work?

The way insurance works is smart. Many people could face the same risk, but it is unlikely they will all incur a loss at the same time. For example, all drivers face the risk of a car accident. The outcome of an accident could be costly repairs, damage to someone's property, or even injuring another person. If this happens, the loss could be too great for each driver to afford individually.

While all drivers continuously face this risk, the chance is remote that all or even the majority would get into an accident at the *same* time.

The insurer pools funds from a large group and uses it to pay the losses of a small group.

Instead, each driver pays a premium to an insurer for protection. The many small premiums will form a large pool of money. When someone suffers a loss, the insurer will use money from the pool to compensate the few who incurred the loss. In other words, the insurer pools funds from a large group and uses it to pay the losses of a small group. This way, while a loss for an individual could be catastrophic, the insurer absorbs it easily.

The "spreading" or "sharing" of risks among everyone who contributed to the pool is why insurance is sometimes described as the "pooling of risks." When a pool is large enough, insurers can predict with reasonable accuracy the amounts they are likely to pay in claims. They use their experience from past claims and mathematical techniques to estimate future claims.

Types of insurance

Insurance can protect many risks. For personal risk management, I think of insurance products in three buckets:

1. Long-term insurance, which I consider to be two types: life and retirement

2. Health and disability

3. Property and casualty

Before an insurer enters a contract with you, they will assess your risk to estimate how much your coverage will cost. Remember, this is the premium you will pay.

Long-term insurance

Long-term insurance means the insurer issues a policy that covers you for many years, or in certain cases your whole life. The insurer usually requires a medical examination to estimate your premium. It is normally a fixed monthly amount. Under

certain circumstances the insurer may revise it later, but you should not need another medical.

In comparison, a short-term policy could be for a few months or a year. When your policy expires, the coverage ends. You'll need a new policy if you wish to continue protection.

I'll cover long-term insurance in the next chapter and focus here on health and disability, together with property and casualty. Health and disability could be considered as long-term insurance because they both could protect you for a long time. For example, critical illness or long-term disability policies cover you for several years. I am, however, including health and disability in this chapter because they also have short-term elements. I can then reserve the next chapter specifically to discuss life insurance and annuities.

Health and disability

Health insurance is wide-ranging and includes medical, vision, dental, or critical illness. For many of us, our employer usually offers health insurance, but it is possible to have a separate individual plan.

I am discussing disability with health, but while related, they are two distinct forms of coverage. If you become sick or injured, health insurance covers your medical costs. There may be a period, however, when you are too ill or injured to work and unable to earn an income. Disability insurance provides you with an amount that replaces part of your income during this period. The amount and length of time the insurer pays varies by policy.

Property and casualty insurance

Property and casualty insurance is also known as "general" insurance. Property insurance covers your assets, such as your home or car. Casualty insurance protects you if you are responsible for injuring someone or damaging their belongings. It might be helpful to think of casualty insurance as "liability" coverage. It covers you if you are "liable" to compensate the other person. Insurers usually combine both types in one policy and common examples are homeowner's insurance and auto insurance.

Insurance terminology

I am sure you realized insurance has its own jargon, some of which I have already introduced. Let me explain a few other terms you'll meet regularly. Having a working knowledge of an insurer's language is important to have an informed discussion with an adviser or to read and understand your policy.

Underwriting

During a conversation with your insurer, you may come across this term when they refer to their "underwriters." When you ask an insurer to accept a risk, their underwriters assess the risk and set the price at which they will accept it. Put another way, when a risk is "underwritten," it means the insurer accepts the risk for a price. The price is the premium that you pay.

Peril

You'll come across this term often in property and casualty insurance. It is a way to refer to the risk or unfavorable event that you are trying to manage, for example, fire, theft, earthquake, or flood.

Deductible

You'll also come across this term in property and casualty as well as health insurance. Insurance companies almost never pay 100% of a claim. A deductible is the portion of the claim

you pay before the insurer begins to reimburse you. For example, let's say you make a claim of $300, and your plan has a $75 deductible. You bear the cost of the $75 deductible, and the insurer will cover the remaining $225. You should be aware that depending on the policy rules, the insurer may only cover *a part* of the $225.

While a lower deductible seems ideal to have more of your claim covered, lower deductibles make the policy more expensive because the premium is higher.

Lapse

Lapse means your policy is no longer active or "in force." A policy lapses when you have not paid the premium set in your contract. The insurer usually gives a grace period before the policy lapses, but once lapsed, the insurer will not honor claims afterwards.

A policy lapsing is different from a policy expiring. Some policies have a set expiry date, at which point, you stop paying premiums and your coverage ends. If you wish to continue coverage, you need a new policy. A lapse occurs *before* the policy's expiry date. The policy lapses because you did not pay your premiums.

Policy rider

A "rider" is a change to the basic policy to include more coverage. Policy riders allow you to tailor a policy to one more suited to your situation. You have several riders to choose from and each costs extra.

Group insurance

You can obtain life and health insurance either personally or as part of a group plan. A personal or individual plan means you have bought a policy in your name. A group plan is arranged by employers for their staff members, using a master policy. The terms of the master policy cannot be tailored to your specific needs. Group plans are often cheaper than personal ones, with employers sometimes paying a part of the premium. If you leave your employer, your coverage ends.

Wrap up

Although we covered quite a bit in this chapter, I hope you agree the basics are not difficult to understand. In the next chapter, we'll look at long-term insurance. After, I'll bring everything together when we consider ways to use insurance to manage our personal financial risks.

Understand the Basics of Long-term Insurance

Many of the concepts and terms from the last chapter apply here, so you already have a great foundation. Having said that, I want to focus on long-term insurance specifically because it has unique aspects.

As mentioned earlier, I think of long-term insurance in two broad categories: life insurance and retirement. I refer to them as "long-term" because the policies could exist for many years. Consequently, to be covered, you must commit to paying premiums for a long period (possibly decades).

Let's start with life insurance.

Life insurance

In summary, when you die, these policies pay an amount to someone you appoint. You are the insured person—every policy must have an insured person. The individual you appoint to receive the payment is the policy's "beneficiary" (the industry refers to the payment as a "benefit"). The amount the insurer pays when you pass away is the policy's "sum assured" or coverage. You pay for the coverage with a monthly premium.

You may hear the terms "life assurance" versus "life insurance" used interchangeably but there is a difference. Life insurance covers you for a specific term, for example, ten years, and you are only covered if you die within this period. On the other hand, a life assurance policy covers you for your whole life.

Life insurers offer several types of products to meet diverse needs, but the basic premise is the same: a beneficiary is paid when an insured person dies. Let's consider some of the more popular types, but I stress these are brief explanations. Evaluating individual products is not my focus. My aim is to ensure you have a good working knowledge to have an informed discussion with an adviser. I will, however, point out some key areas.

Term

"Term" refers to a specific period, for example five, ten, or twenty years. Term life insurance pays the sum assured (or "death benefit") if the insured person dies during the specified period. The coverage ends when the term expires. If anything in these sentences is confusing, re-read the previous paragraphs.

To emphasize, although your premature death is the risk covered, the insurer will only pay a claim if you die within the stated period. If you are alive at the policy's expiry date, the coverage ends, and you stop paying premiums.

Term life insurance is pure insurance protection and all premiums paid cover the cost of protecting you. This is an important sentence. Remember it when we discuss the other types of policies below. Term insurance is the least expensive form of life insurance.

Term insurance works well when you need cover only for a specific period. For example, while you have a loan outstanding, until your children complete their education, or if you have family members who rely on your income. In each case, if you die during the period covered, your beneficiary receives a payment. **The amount helps them achieve the financial goals that you would have worked towards if you were alive.**

Whole life

This product protects you for your *whole* life, with your beneficiary receiving a payment whenever you pass away. Of course, your premiums must be up to date. Whole life is "permanent" insurance because you are always covered, whereas term insurance covers for only a specific period. In both cases, once the insurer sets the premium, it does not change during the life of the policy.

> Whole life is "permanent" insurance because you are always covered.

While term policies are pure insurance protection, whole life includes another aspect. They have a guaranteed savings component built into the policy. This means your premiums have two parts: insurance protection and savings.

Over time, the savings portion grows and is called "cash value." You have options to use a policy's cash value:

- As collateral for a loan from a lender or the insurer.
- To pay your premiums.
- You could withdraw the amount under certain conditions, but certain penalties and taxation obligations could result.

Whole life policies are more expensive than term life because of the cash-value element as well as you pay for protection over a longer time.

Universal life

Whole life insurance, with its set premiums and guaranteed cash values, is sometimes regarded as "old fashioned" and inflexible. Consequently, the industry introduced universal life insurance and *variable* universal life. While the features vary by insurer, here are the main points.

Firstly, universal life is a type of permanent life insurance—it covers you for your whole life. Like whole life policies, they have a cash value, which you use in the same way as whole life policies.

While whole life premiums do not change, universal life allows you to adjust premium payments. This flexibility is useful if the amount you can afford changes over your lifetime. The key point to know is that when you reduce your premiums, your coverage could decline. Additionally, if you want to keep your original coverage, you may have to pay higher premiums later. Also, insurers do not guarantee the cash values for universal life policies.

Its alternative, variable universal life, has the same basic features described in the previous paragraph. In addition, you have more investment options that may help your cash value grow faster (the returns could *vary*).

As you can imagine, the flexibility in universal life policies introduces a bit of complexity, which might be more than some people could manage easily. **These policies require regular monitoring to ensure you obtain the benefits you expected.**

Retirement

Individuals have many options for retirement planning and insurance companies offer a specific product to help us: annuities. There are several types of annuities but let us stick to the basics.

Annuities pay a steady, guaranteed amount for the rest of your life. As with life insurance, you pay a fixed monthly premium until you retire. During retirement, annuities pay a steady, guaranteed amount for the rest of your life. Of course, you assume your insurer will continue to operate over this longer term. Few people seem to think about this risk.

One common type of annuity is an "immediate" annuity. Instead of paying premiums monthly, you could instead make a lump-sum deposit and begin to receive annuity payments relatively quickly.

Taxation advantages

There could be taxation advantages to both life insurance and annuities. You should obtain suitable advice to learn more about their current tax benefits.

Wrap up

Congrats! You made it through the two chapters on the basics of insurance! Remember, insurance is a specialized industry, and it's fine if you do not grasp the concepts at once. Be patient and re-read both chapters if necessary.

It is possible that our understanding of insurance also suffers because transactions tend to be less frequent. As a result, we can't learn from regular exposure and experience. Let's use life insurance as an example. Once you buy the policy, all you do afterwards is pay the premiums. Eventually, the details evaporate from your memory, and you must check the policy if you have a question later. The policy types that you meet more regularly, such as homeowners, renter's insurance, and car insurance tend to be easier to understand because we renew these policies every year.

Now, let's connect the dots between the various insurance products I explained and the personal financial risks you are trying to reduce.

Use Insurance to Reduce Personal Financial Risks

In the chapter *How to Manage Personal Financial Risks* I identified several risks we face and the methods we use to manage them. There are certain risks, however, that we cannot manage on our own because they are significant. By significant, I mean if they occur, the impact could be too large for us to afford, and we will struggle to rebuild our net worth. Examples include loss of income, losses to personal property, and losses from personal liability.

For these risks, we need help, and insurance offers the support we need.

In this chapter I'll explain which insurance product you can use to manage each risk. As a reminder, I think of insurance products in three buckets:

1. Long-term insurance, which I consider to be Life and Retirement

2. Health and Disability

3. Property and Casualty

Two points before we continue. First, if it is possible to use more than one product for a particular risk, I am not focusing on which is the right product to choose. Second, I am also not focusing on what is the optimal amount of coverage. Both these decisions depend on personal circumstances. But I'll still give you some pointers in the following two chapters.

Let's look at the risks and relate them to each type of insurance.

Loss of income

Being unable to earn income is a major problem when you have dependents. But as I pointed out, even if you have no dependents, you must still support yourself. You can lose the ability to earn income in four main ways: premature death (obviously!), ill health, disability, and aging.

Let's examine the approach in each situation.

Premature death

Remember, premature death means you die before you provided for your dependents' future. Your early passing affects those you leave behind in several ways. They could face a lower standard of living because your income is no longer available to them. Your passing could leave them liable for any loans you had as well as prevent you from building an estate to afford future life events that relate to them (for example, higher education).

You can address the risk of premature death with life insurance. As a reminder, the product options I explained briefly were term, whole life, and universal life insurance.

Ill health

Medical issues could require basic physician services, such as dental and vision. Or they can lead to complications requiring hospitalization or surgery. Or you could be affected by more serious conditions, such as cancer, stroke, and heart disease. Depending on the severity, it may not result in your loss of income, but you may have to pay for unplanned expensive treatment.

You can protect yourself from the cost of becoming sick with various forms of medical/health insurance. These could be offered by public health care, by employers as a group health plan, or by buying insurance privately. You can protect yourself from more serious diseases by using critical illness coverage.

Disability

Most of us must work to earn income to support ourselves and our dependents. If we experience serious medical issues, it could lead to long recovery periods with no income and financial hardship.

You can mitigate this risk with disability insurance.

Aging

Sometime in the future we will stop working, either because we choose to, or because we are unable to work productively. At this point, we retire. The challenge when we are no longer employed is knowing if we have enough funds to afford retirement. Insufficient funds could lead to a fall in our standard of living, or worse, we could run out of money in retirement.

You can address this financial risk in retirement by using annuities, as they provide a guaranteed monthly income for life.

Losses to personal property and personal liability

Physical assets such as vehicles or real estate (for example, our home) are often expensive, and we must sacrifice to buy them. If the asset is stolen or damaged, the loss could seriously damage our net worth or the loss could be so large that we cannot recover.

Additionally, if we are responsible for causing harm to another person or damaging their property, we could be liable to compensate that person. The cost could be significant.

We protect ourselves from both situations by using property and casualty insurance. You might recall I explained that insurers normally combine the protection for both loss and liability in one policy. We must buy the minimum liability coverage required by law, but of course, we can purchase more. In the case of auto insurance, we will also have to decide what other protections to buy. These could include collision and other perils, such as fire, theft, and natural disasters. We face similar decisions when insuring our home.

Wrap up

I hope you now better understand that some risks are too great for us to bear on our own. For these situations, we need insurance to provide financial peace of mind. Consequently, insurance is regarded as an essential part of a good financial plan.

Let's continue by identifying a few points to consider when choosing a suitable level of insurance cover.

Insure or Self-insure?

Earlier in this Action, I described the main approaches we use to manage our financial risks. They were to transfer or assume the risk. If we accept the risk, we must then decide whether to avoid, reduce or prepare for it. Now with our understanding of insurance, we can adjust the approaches slightly to:

1. **Avoid.** For example, we would not choose to live in an area prone to major flooding. The large, frequent financial losses would be unbearable.

2. **Self-insure.** When you choose to self-insure, you decide to accept the financial loss if the risk occurs. We manage the potential loss by reducing the risk or preparing for it.

3. **Insure.** You pay an insurer to take the risk and bear a part or the whole loss.

In this chapter, we'll focus on deciding when to insure or self-insure. First, I'll identify a few important points to bear in mind and then provide you with a list of questions to ask yourself. The answers should help point you to a decision.

Key points

Let's start with the points you should always remember.

You are managing risk

In this Action's introduction, I emphasized that insurance should be primarily about risk management. I urged you to decide about insurance coverage in this context. You are paying to reduce or eliminate a risk that could destabilize your finances. For a moment, let's think about the return you receive from eating a meal. It is not a financial return; instead, eating satisfies you and you receive nutrition. Buying insurance is similar. **The return you receive is peace of mind and comfort that your finances are safe and secure.**

Purchasing insurance is not the same as making an investment. While many insurance products include (or "bundle") a savings or investment component, these are two separate financial decisions.

> Purchasing insurance is not the same as making an investment.

Make an informed decision

As a tool to manage risk, insurance is a discretionary purchase—you choose whether to buy it. But the power of choice should not lead you to adopt an outlook of "no harm shall come to me." **When you ignore significant risks, you leave yourself and your dependents exposed.** Obviously, the previous comments exclude the types of coverage we are legally required to buy.

You can, however, make an informed decision not to insure after a deliberate and careful assessment of your insurance needs. Or you walk away if you are uneasy with an adviser's recommendation.

Insurance is a cost

The cost of insurance is an outflow for you. Like any other outflow, it must be worthwhile and affordable. It is easy to lose sight that insurance is potentially expensive.

Focus on realistic risks

If you browse the websites of insurers, it seems they offer a product for nearly every type of risk an individual could face. As you review, you might even convince yourself that every risk is likely to happen to you soon! It is, however, expensive to insure yourself against all risks. And you do not need to. Selecting what to insure and a suitable coverage involves first knowing the risks you *realistically* face. You must accept that a lot of judgment is needed: a right answer does not exist. It often involves balancing the cost to insure with what loss you could bear.

Financial cushion

If you are sufficiently wealthy, you have no need for insurance. When your net worth is large enough, you can comfortably withstand losses and still support yourself and provide for your dependents. Put another way, as your net worth grows, your need for insurance as a financial cushion eventually disappears because you built your own cushion.

This point is important to understand and decide if you personally agree, because of course, you can choose to still buy insurance. There is only less need for it. You'll understand the relevance when we review the questions below.

The insurance self-questionnaire

In the past, like you, I had to decide about my own insurance coverage. I realized that I was easily distracted and confused by various scenarios about my future and trying to assess every possibility. I therefore tried to simplify the decision with a series of brief questions, which kept my focus on risk management. I asked myself:

1. Who am I trying to protect?

2. What realistic risks should I insure?

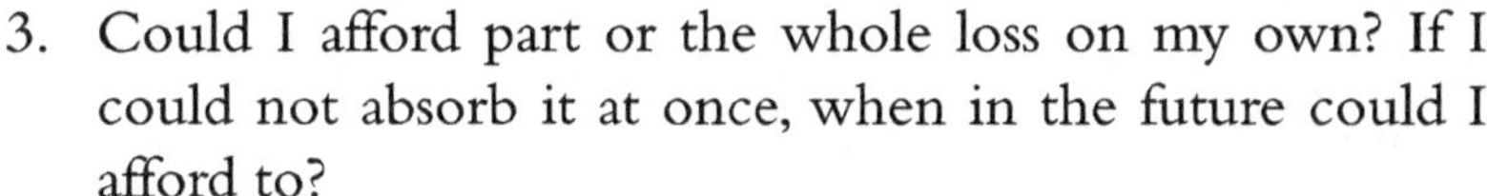

3. Could I afford part or the whole loss on my own? If I could not absorb it at once, when in the future could I afford to?

4. What is the minimum cover I need until my risks either diminish or I can afford them?

Let's use an example to illustrate how to approach the questions. The scenario is:

a) Married partners with two young children (under ten).

b) Partner A has a much higher income than Partner B.

c) The partners own a home, which has an outstanding loan.

d) They own a new vehicle, which they also bought using a loan.

e) The partners have a small but growing net worth. They expect to afford all remaining risks in fifteen years, especially as their children will have completed university.

f) Neither partner has employer-sponsored group life or health plans.

Let's assess what risks the partners should insure or self-insure. As you'll see, you often need to use judgment, together with balancing cost versus benefit. I exclude legally mandated insurance from the discussion below.

Who needs protecting?

We buy insurance to protect either ourselves or those who depend upon us. We could protect our dependents by having replacement income if we cannot work and ensuring they have enough funds available if we die. Persons without dependents should still try to ensure they have not only replacement income if they cannot work but also sufficient income in retirement.

From the situation, the standard of living and future financial security of Partner B and the children depend on Partner A's income. The dependents are therefore Partner B and the two children.

What realistic risks to insure?

We should insure what we are either unable or cannot afford to replace. Expensive physical assets may leap to mind, but we may be unable to replace our ability to earn income if we become injured (and obviously if we die).

From the situation, A's income is key to the family's future. B's income becomes more important if A has already passed away. In addition, the family has two significant assets, a home and vehicle that they cannot afford to replace. The family therefore faces these main risks:

- The loss of A's income from premature death. Without A's income, B will struggle to repay the loans and meet the children's current and future expenses (including education).

- Costly damage to both home and automobile and theft of the vehicle or household items.

- The likelihood of A or B needing expensive medical support or experiencing a critical illness.

- A becoming disabled. If A is unable to work and earn income for an extended period, the family could struggle to make ends meet.

When could the loss be absorbed?

At present, the family's net worth is not enough to absorb the financial impacts of the risks they face. They expect they can

do so in fifteen years due to a growing net worth, reduced outflows related to the children, and smaller outstanding loans.

Possible coverage

a) The family should protect their home and vehicle from the range of perils. They could decide to insure their home only for property damage and self-insure for damage or theft of personal belongings. For their vehicle, it would be sensible to obtain both comprehensive and collision insurance while it is new. They could reduce or eliminate both when its value has declined over the next five years or so.

b) Next, the family should buy life insurance for A (there is no group life option). They expect to take fifteen years to build their net worth to a level that can absorb losses without losing financial stability. Consequently, term insurance would be best in their circumstances. As it appears they can live on A's income alone, they could choose not to insure B's life currently. If A dies prematurely, then B's life can be insured to support the two surviving children. Of course, if A's coverage is enough, insuring B's life may not be necessary.

When deciding A's sum assured, they should include an estimate for:

☛ The cost to support the children's living expenses.

☛ The cost for university education.

☛ The value of the loans outstanding.

☛ The shortfall in the partners' future net worth due to A's death.

---

c) The last issue for the family to consider would be health and disability. Deciding on this coverage could require the most judgment. The issues to balance are a potentially large financial loss and how likely it is to occur, against the cost to insure.

If the family can't afford to insure medical, critical illness, and disability, the question to consider is the likelihood and impact of disability occurring. For example, dangerous jobs carry a higher risk of injury. Or if a job is specialized (for example, a surgeon's), finding alternative employment to earn comparable income could be difficult. If A's risk is low, it reduces the need to buy insurance.

The decision to insure or self-insure would depend on how much risk the family is prepared to bear. A family history of major disease would be a factor when deciding whether to buy critical illness insurance. Even if they decide to self-insure, basic medical coverage seems a minimum necessity.

If the Partners had access to employer-sponsored life and health insurance, they could reduce the amount of coverage they need to buy.

Wrap up

It is worth remembering that no "right" answer exists, and the thought process described previously is only one option. Other approaches are possible, and seeking professional advice is important when deciding what works best for you. Additionally, insurance products evolve, and cheap, flexible options could exist to cater for your needs.

It is worth observing that at no point in the analysis did I consider how any investment component of an insurance product would perform. I focused on risks faced and the ones to mitigate because the loss would be unaffordable. I then

balanced these aspects against the cost to insure the risk and prioritized which protection to buy.

The final area I'd like to address in this Action is pitfalls you could meet when trying to make an insurance decision. I've already touched on a few, but it will be useful to bring the threads together in one place. Despite the undeniable benefits of insurance, if we are uninformed, these pitfalls could be a minefield to navigate.

Potential Pitfalls with Insurance

It is difficult to imagine how we could manage certain risks without insurance—it plays a key role. Unfortunately, pitfalls exist that could cause the inexperienced to stumble or force them to be skeptical in general.

Challenges

At the core could be five challenges.

More difficult to understand

As I mentioned in the chapter *Conceptual Challenges*, insurance is complex. It is certainly more complicated compared to banking, the other financial services sector that we deal with often. The difficulty is evident in the products insurers sell. Even the basic ones have a dizzying array of riders and options that often only persons familiar with the industry can follow. The industry has tried to make the products easier to understand, but they are still not as straightforward as banking (and may never be).

Difficult to compare

There seems to be a product for every imaginable risk that we face. Instead of having the benefit of catering to any need, we could easily feel overwhelmed. In addition, as consumers, we should always be able to compare offerings from different providers to get the best deal. Unfortunately,

only basic insurance products seem similar enough to allow us to compare.

Focus on the negative

Insurance requires us to discuss potentially unpleasant events. No one wants to speak about tragic events like critical illnesses, disabilities, catastrophes, and death. We prefer to focus on the positive and hope the unfortunate events do not happen. The need to focus on the negative doesn't naturally lead to a warm enthusiastic feeling towards insurance.

Possible conflict

Because individuals are reluctant to face their most feared possibilities, insurance suffers from low demand. To counter this situation, companies engage salespersons (usually called "agents") to inform the public about the value insurance provides. That leads to another problem. Insurers must motivate these persons to sell a product when the words they will hear most often are "no thanks." Insurers therefore offer sales commissions to encourage the agents.

As you can imagine, basic products pay lower commissions. Insurance advisers, therefore, are naturally inclined to offer more sophisticated products, which pay higher commissions. I am not implying that the products might not be useful or suitable, but a conflict exists that you should be aware of.

What may not always be obvious is that you bear the cost of the commissions. You pay for them with your premiums, and for permanent policies and annuities, they can be substantial.

Honoring claims

Individuals may be skeptical whether their insurer will pay their claims. An insurance company's largest cost is likely settling claims, and like you, it must control its outflows.

Insurers therefore scrutinize claims carefully to ensure they are in line with policy rules. Fraudulent claims happen often, so we cannot blame the industry for being vigilant. For persons who diligently paid their premiums over a long period, it would, however, be a nightmare to learn that their insurer will not honor their claim.

Having identified a few general challenges, let's examine some of the pitfalls.

Protection from loss

The concept of buying protection from loss (of income or life) can be a difficult one to grasp fully. Normally, when we make an outflow, we receive something in return. It could be tangible such as clothes and books or a service such as appliance repair. But in the case of insurance, you receive protection for yourself, or someone else, from *loss*. And because the loss may not occur, it is unsettling to think you received nothing in return for your payment.

This is a mental hurdle we *must* get past. We only appreciate the importance of insurance when we need to use it or regret not having it.

Excess coverage

Excess coverage means you are over-insured. Why is this a problem? Because there is a cost involved, and in some cases, you commit to a cost over your life. Excess coverage can arise in a few ways:

- The sum assured on the policy is too high.
- The coverage period is too long.
- The bells and whistles (riders) attached to the policy are unnecessary.

☞ You paid to insure risks that you could self-insure.

Let's think about life insurance. It certainly does not have to be for your whole life. Your goal is to protect someone from hardship if you die *prematurely*. Your death prevents you from providing for your dependents over time, including leaving an inheritance if you were so inclined. Let's explore this from a few angles.

No dependents

It is difficult to justify why you need life insurance if you have no dependents. For example, if you are single or just started your career, who specifically is depending on you and your ability to earn an income? Most likely no one. The balance you are trying to strike is deciding whether to incur an expense now when the real need has not yet arisen.

Yes, your monthly outflows should be smaller when you buy insurance early. Is this necessarily cheaper than buying it later? It depends, but an early purchase also means outflows exist for a longer period.

Optimal coverage

In other situations, you can easily identify your dependents, for example, a life partner, children, or an ailing family member. If you have a dependent, you must assess what coverage level you should buy. The optimal coverage to balance cost and benefit should be large enough to provide financial security until a date in the future when they would no longer be dependent. For example, for children, a suitable level of cover could be one that supports their needs until they leave university. At that time, they should no longer be financially dependent.

Net worth

As discussed in the last chapter, you don't necessarily need insurance if you have sufficient financial resources to support your dependents if you die prematurely. Or alternatively, you only need coverage until you believe you will have a large enough net worth. Or you only cover the shortfall between what you need less your current resources.

Debt

We also discussed in the last chapter that you should include debt when you quantify your coverage amount. If you have a mortgage loan or other debt, you should not burden your dependents with repayment. You should therefore choose coverage that allows them to repay these obligations if you pass away. You should also be wary of buying insurance from the same provider as your loans. While it may be convenient to transact with one institution, it makes sense to shop around to double check that your premium is competitive. Remember, you could be committing for many years, so ensure you get the best deal.

To address the matters above, in most cases all you really need is term life insurance. It is cheap and covers you for a specific period, but long enough to cater to most situations. You pay a low premium and receive pure protection in return. Once you pass the mental hurdle described in *Protection from loss*, term insurance is usually the wise decision. But this leads to the fourth general challenge I described that affects insurance. Cheap term insurance is not a "sexy" product for agents to sell because sales commissions are low.

Protection vs investment

It could be that insurers developed hybrid policies in response to the mental barrier that persons have about paying and receiving no financial return. (Hey, I am guessing here!) By

hybrid (or "bundled") I mean the product serves more than one goal. In this case, it protects but also adds a savings or investment component.

While the dual aims sound appealing, I urge you to evaluate the pros and cons carefully.

Excess coverage?

These policies are usually permanent insurance. Unlike term policies that end after a set period, these policies cover you for your whole life, committing you to an outflow "forever." Permanent insurance, therefore, could be a form of excess coverage if not carefully evaluated.

The questions to answer will always be:

a) Who do you need to protect?

b) Can they live comfortably using the net worth you leave behind now?

c) If not, how long would it take you to accumulate a large enough net worth?

Remember, if your net worth reaches a level where you can absorb financial hits, you have less need for insurance. If you need additional time to build your net worth, you only need insurance coverage during this period. Even if it takes a long time, it is unlikely you need your *whole* life to do it. Extra coverage may be a nice boost for your dependents, but it comes at a potentially unnecessary cost to you.

Savings/Investment challenges

The premiums for permanent policies have two portions: one part pays for insurance protection and the other part is for the savings/investment component. Savings in a whole life policy comes from the cash value that you build over the life of the policy. While you have no control over how the cash value builds in a whole life policy, other types of permanent insurance offer flexible investment options.

These savings/investment components offer appealing features but there are several challenges.

a) They are expensive and it is possible that you could build a greater cash value on your own (outside the policy).

b) The insurer usually keeps the cash value you build when you die. Pay attention! The cash value may not be paid to your beneficiaries. In addition, if you used any of the policy's cash value, the insurer deducts the amount you used from the policy's death benefit.

c) The policies that add investment options usually transfer the investment risk to you. This means that while you benefit from any gains, you also bear any losses. These options add different challenges to your financial life and require you to monitor the policy. Most people do not have the time or knowledge to do this effectively.

Cash value

More generally, I am skeptical about policies that build cash value. Yes, you can use the cash value in a few ways, but my mental hurdle is the cash value only arises because you are *overpaying* upfront. If I pay more than needed for the insurance protection, why am I being touted the benefits of using my own money? Even worse, it does not work like a bank savings account, where I can easily access my funds. There are several restrictions. No matter how I look at it, cash value insurance seems to have many drawbacks, unless you genuinely have a need to protect your dependents for your whole life.

While it could be convenient to have multiple goals addressed in one policy, it is often better for individuals to manage insurance and investing separately. This way, you ensure you understand each part and are clear about the respective costs and benefits.

Fees and charges

Insurance products have *many* fees and charges, several of which could be incurred upfront. Their impact is not always easy to understand until you experience the charge. You may not realize their effect until you wonder why returns in early years are low. Or you may face penalties for trying to end or alter a policy before a certain period (think five years as a rule of thumb). You should ensure you are familiar with the details and limits stated in your policy contract.

> It is easy to zoom past this point and not appreciate its importance, so I am going to repeat it: insurance products have *many* fees and charges.

Before you commit to a policy, I suggest you meet your adviser to discuss all the fees and charges that could arise. Do not discuss any other aspects of the policy. Get into the details and look for costs that may not be called a fee or charge. How does the insurer determine the return you earn on the cash value? If it is lower than what you can earn elsewhere, that is a type of charge (even though many may not realize it). What would be the interest rate if you took a loan against the policy's cash value? I'll bet it is not straightforward, and if it is higher than other loan types, that's another type of charge.

You might have a headache at the end of the conversation with your adviser.

Wrap up

As part of this wrap up, I'd like to discuss a commonly stated reason for buying insurance: as a forced-savings strategy. The thinking here is you use life insurance to leave an inheritance for your loved ones. The idea of "forced" arises owing to the way the transaction works:

- You enter a formal contract.
- Your premiums are deducted automatically.
- You fear "losing" the premiums you already paid if you allow the policy to lapse.

These factors effectively force you to keep paying the premium to ensure your dependents receive funds when you pass. Another reason for this approach is your dependents can often receive the benefit payment free from taxation.

I understand the rationale, but I have my doubts about this strategy. The cost of permanent life insurance potentially makes it uncompetitive as an investment. You may achieve a better return using another form of professional investment management. If you wish to use insurance as a forced-savings strategy, I recommend you evaluate this approach carefully.

With that final thought, I can now bring this Action to an end. Just be aware that once you begin to think about insurance, it forces you to pay attention to events that you want to be prepared for. You will naturally want to address the risks urgently. But I hope you are in a better position to understand that buying insurance (especially long-term insurance) is not a transaction you should do hastily. They:

- Are expensive, multi-year commitments.

- Use terms that you do not meet every day.

- Are sold by persons with more knowledge than you, who are paid to sell as much as they can.

Remember, insurance is a key aspect of taking control of your money by helping to manage significant risks. Just be aware about the pitfalls you could meet. Keep them in mind when you are discussing options with an adviser/agent/broker.

Excellent! Let's continue to our third Action and learn all about debt.

Manage Your Debt

The Big Monster

We've completed the first two Actions and I hope you better understand why I said they interlock and strengthen each other. In Action 1 you took control by learning how to manage your inflows and outflows. In Action 2 you protected yourself and your dependents by taking control of events that threaten financial security. Now, let's turn our attention to slaying a big monster: uncontrolled borrowing. I don't mean that we borrow without a care in the world, although this happens sometimes. I am referring to borrowing in an unmanaged way, which eventually leads to problems.

One could loosely describe debt as the financial equivalent of other guilty pleasures (mine is coffee!). The comparison highlights that they share some broad traits: many sources to obtain them exist, qualifying to use them is "straightforward", and they are accepted in most societies. These factors could contribute to overuse, leading to our physical health being affected with one and our financial health being seriously damaged with the other. The eventual stressful outcome ultimately points to the need for moderation.

Think back to the exercise when we estimated your twelve-month inflows and outflows. If your estimated surplus was small, one way to improve it was to reduce your outflows. But one outflow that you cannot change easily is loan repayments because you entered into a contract with your lender. If you have too many loans you could feel like you are suffocating because it is not an easy situation to correct. Poor debt decisions can eventually become a constraint, especially if your expenses increase or your income declines unexpectedly.

To be truly in control of our money, we must learn about all aspects of debt and know how to make wise choices when deciding whether to incur new debt.

By the end of this Action, I hope you understand:

1. How debt can hurt or enhance your net worth.

2. How to estimate the most debt you should have and still be financially comfortable.

3. How to approach a conversation with a lender.

4. How the main types of loans work.

5. Credit cards and their hidden dangers.

6. The approaches you can use to reduce debt.

I mentioned debt a few times in the earlier chapters, but explaining debt was not my primary focus then. It might be useful, therefore, to recap the points already made, so you connect all the dots when you complete this Action.

Be debt-free

In *Core Principles*, I described one of the principles to achieve financial freedom as being debt-free. I explained in most instances a loan is consumption brought forward— you borrow to make a purchase now instead of saving to use cash. By borrowing, instead of sacrificing to save, you have surrendered part of your freedom to a third party. The promise to repay, and penalties if you don't, are signs that you have partially lost control of your money and your freedom to choose.

Even when you learn to take loans responsibly, always remember complete financial freedom is ultimately having no obligations. Always strive to be debt-free.

Debt

I first defined the term debt (and its different names: liabilities, loans, obligations, and borrowings) in *Key Terms*. Debt is money you owe to someone else, either a person or corporation. Loans could arise in several ways:

- Borrowing from friends or family (always a bad idea).

- Using a personal overdraft or line of credit. You can use up to the authorized limit without consulting the lender.

- Certain purchases could be financed directly, for example, a house, a vehicle, furniture, or appliances.

- Making a purchase with a credit card.

In each case, the way you took the loan, and what the loan was called, could vary. The important question is whether you must repay money over time. If yes, then you have a loan.

One last point on lending lingo: lenders often refer to loans as "credit" facilities. Receiving credit means you obtain an item now but pay for it later. I'll use this term at times to help you get familiar with it.

Loan repayments in your budget

When we performed *Step 1: Track Your Inflows and Out-flows* and *Step 3: Estimate for Twelve Months*, we treated loan repayments as a separate outflow because I said we must manage them directly.

After creating your budget in *Step 8*, we refined how to target your surplus in *Step 9: Improve the Estimate of Your Target Surplus*. In *Step 9*, I explained an approach to use your surplus and link it to your financial goals. One goal was to repay debt

faster than scheduled. I introduced the use of "profiles" based on a percentage of your inflows and my with-debt profile was:

- 20% Surplus
- 30% Loan repayments
- 50% Needs and Wants

If we assume an individual has inflows of $36,000, the profile suggests they should aim to have total loan repayments of 30% or *less* ($10,800). I also emphasized you could achieve this over time.

Net Worth

In *Step 7: Calculate Your Net Worth*, I explained the importance of net worth to measure your increase in wealth. You learned that debt reduces your net worth. Consequently, one way to increase your net worth is to repay debt faster than scheduled. I also suggested in *Step 11: Invest in Yourself*, that accelerating your debt repayments is one of your best financial investments.

Wrap up

Having pulled together the major threads about debt so far, let's begin by learning about types of debt. In *Core Principles*, I said treat debt as radioactive—avoid it until you understand how to manage it. You will soon learn that debt can be either good or bad. Your challenge is to avoid *bad* debt.

Understanding how to manage debt is not actually the challenge some of you will face. After you work through this Action, you'll see it's not difficult. The real challenge will be dropping the "buy now; pay later" habit. I'm confident you'll follow the logic and methods I show you, but the final hurdle will be a *mental* one. You must stop using credit as a substitute for cash, unless you incur good debt. You must force yourself to be patient and wait until you have cash to make a purchase. And who knows, while you wait, you may even decide that you don't need that item you wanted to buy!

Good Debt vs Bad Debt

Although I previously said one principle to achieve financial freedom is to be debt-free, I can now place that statement in the proper context. You will learn in this Action, it does not mean you should *never* borrow. Quite the opposite; debt is a powerful tool if used correctly. In fact, your finances could be stronger when you have credit options available, such as credit cards, lines of credit, assets to secure loans, and so on. But you must use the credit available in a disciplined way.

Problems with debt

Although we might have good reasons to borrow, being in debt has several problems:

- **It is restrictive.** You now have a *legal* obligation and are *accountable* to a third-party who sets rules you must follow. In the future, this obligation is your priority, and it dominates your decision-making.

- **It ties up assets.** Lenders often require "collateral" before you can borrow. When you supply collateral, you give them temporary rights over one or more of your assets. If you cannot repay the loan, they will seize the asset and sell it to recover the amount owed. Once you give an asset as collateral, you have effectively lost control over it.

- **Most persons cannot assess if they have too much debt.** If you are not in control of your money, it is easy to borrow more than you can comfortably afford.

☛ **You lose flexibility.** When your debt is high, small decreases in income or increases in expenses could create a lot of stress.

☛ **Debt is expensive.** When you borrow, you incur a cost, and we often ignore how it affects our net worth.

☛ **Debt can make us poorer.** If we borrow for the wrong reasons, our net worth falls, which means we are less financially secure.

Why our comfort with debt?

Despite its problems, bingeing on debt is common. Some reasons why we borrow in an uncontrolled way are:

☛ **Credit is easy to obtain.** Because it is easy to borrow, it encourages us to satisfy our Wants by an immediate purchase rather than saving over time.

☛ **Being in debt is more widely accepted.** In the past, being in debt was not viewed positively, but cultural norms have changed.

☛ **We allow entities that *sell* loans to decide for us.** If you cannot assess if borrowing is a smart decision, you have no choice but to rely on a lender's recommendation. As their job is to sell loans, the advice you receive could be skewed to their best interest, not yours. I am not saying this is definitely the case, but the reality is a conflict exists.

☛ **We lack enough knowledge to decide wisely.** Persons may not understand the credit products they use (for example, credit cards), how much they cost, or whether cheaper and better options exist.

Good debt and wealth creation

Once you understand how badly managed debt affects you, it becomes obvious you should borrow carefully, not casually. You should agonize over having to borrow.

When deciding if debt is right for you, a major consideration should be its impact on your net worth. Whether the debt improves or erodes your net worth depends on the purpose of the loan, which means you can have either good debt or bad debt.

> A major consideration should be the impact of new debt on your net worth.

Good debt *creates* wealth over the long term. Let's look at a few examples.

Residential loans

Although buying a home provides peace of mind and stability for your family, it could have financial benefits as well. It tends to be a good purchase because the value of your home could increase over time. Of course, no asset is perfectly safe, and housing market declines do occur. Regardless, taking a loan to buy a home is regarded as good debt because the potential increase in its value could exceed the cost of home ownership.

Home improvements

Home renovations, such as remodeling a kitchen or upgrading to modern styles, might increase your home's value.

Investments

Once you begin investing, you'll learn about using debt as a tool for buying investments. If an investment earns a return that exceeds the cost of the loan, you have good debt because it adds to your net worth.

Investment options range from financial investments (bonds or stocks) and real estate to starting or buying a business. Obviously, each of these options has risks as well as benefits. For instance, starting or buying a business has many challenges and uncertainties. But if successful, the business could grow over time and your wealth/net worth would increase.

Education

In *Step 11: Invest in Yourself,* I said one of the best forms of investment is educating yourself, as it could help you earn higher income. Borrowing to fund your education is therefore good debt.

Bad debt and wealth erosion

While good debt creates wealth over time, bad debt reduces your net worth. Let's look at a few examples.

Consumables

By consumables I refer to a wide range of everyday items such as groceries, clothes, or entertainment. It is anything that has no lasting value because you use it quickly. Often, we create these loans by using a credit card.

> It is not a sensible financial decision to use an expensive loan (that you repay over time) to buy an item that you use at once.

Think back to your net worth calculation. If you add no assets (by buying consumables) but increase your liabilities with loans, your net worth declines immediately. This is the definition of wealth erosion.

Depreciating assets

You should recall from *Key Terms* that "depreciate" means an item loses value over time. Some purchases are not consumed at once, but they eventually lose value, for example, furniture and appliances. These items usually last for years, and as they could be large outflows, we tend to buy them using credit. The problem with items of this nature is their low resale value. Even if the item was expensive, it tends to have more worth to the purchaser than to someone else.

Remember, our definition of an asset is that it must be saleable for cash, which requires it to have value. I doubt you would pay much for used furniture and appliances. If you skip back to *Step 7: Calculate Your Net Worth*, you'll notice I did not include these assets in the examples. Once bought, what you could sell them for declines rapidly, although you use them for a long time. From a net worth perspective, they are low-value assets, but you deduct the full value of any loans taken to buy them.

Cars are another type of depreciating asset. They lose significant value quickly. Bear in mind, cars could be the second most expensive item we buy; homes being first. Borrowing to buy a car is, therefore, the net worth problem I described with furniture and appliances, on steroids.

You buy an expensive asset that declines in value quickly, and worse, it could decline faster than you repay the loan. This situation is important to understand. It is possible that your loan balance could be *greater* than the vehicle's value during the loan. If you are forced to sell the vehicle to repay the loan, a shortfall might exist that you must fund.

Wrap up

I hope it is now clear that you should not use debt for all purchases. You should instead prioritize good debt, as it could improve your net worth over time. If you must incur bad debt, borrow as little as possible for the shortest time possible, otherwise you could seriously damage your net worth.

Let's now consider the second way debt can harm your net worth: the interest cost.

Interest:
The Not-So-Hidden Cost
(Part 1)

I described interest in this chapter's title as "Not-So-Hidden" because although it is a critical concept in finance and easy to find out, it may as well be hidden because it is mostly misunderstood or ignored. The irony is: what we ignore or consider unimportant is what lenders use to earn revenue. It is, therefore, *extremely* important to them.

You will not be truly in control of your money unless you have a proper working knowledge of interest and how it affects you. I'll cover this topic in two parts, and I stress that both are important because interest is a key factor when making a smart borrowing decision.

Let's approach it slowly and build to the slightly more advanced aspects.

What is interest?

Broadly, interest is like any other expense you incur. There is a cost to receive goods (such as buying clothes) or a service (for example, paying for a repair). With a loan, you receive money, and the cost for the money received is interest.

Interest is either received or paid. The cost of a loan is the interest you pay a lender. The interest they receive is their income. The lender treats the loan to you as an investment and requires a return, which is interest.

I'll focus the discussion in this Action on interest as an expense to you, the borrower.

Loans differ from goods and services in an important way. With goods and services, you normally make one payment to receive either, for example, a technician does not keep returning for more payments unless he supplies another service. In contrast, you keep paying interest until you fully repay your loans. If any part of the loan is unpaid, you will continue to have a cost.

Loan principal vs interest

When we borrow, we tend to base our decision on what size of loan payment we can afford. This makes sense because we treat the payment as another outflow that our inflows must cover. Although we think of the installment as one outflow, it has two parts:

- Repayment of the loan itself, referred to as the loan principal.
- Payment for interest, the cost of the loan.

Importantly, the interest portion could be more significant than we realize.

It is possible to have interest-only loan payments, but they are always temporary. Eventually the payment will revert to a loan installment with principal and interest, so let's stay focused on this.

Interest rates

The other way the cost of a loan differs from the cost of everything else you buy, is the way it is presented. If you buy

food, groceries, or a plane ticket, the retailer presents that cost to you in dollars and cents. A precise amount. You then quickly assess whether the purchase is expensive or if you can afford it.

The cost of loans, however, is not presented in dollars and cents. While lenders certainly can estimate the amount, they will not present that estimate. This is because the amount of interest you pay depends on the length of time you borrow (referred to as "loan term" or "tenor"). The amount paid also depends on whether the interest rate changes during the loan term. As either the loan term or interest rate could change, lenders quote the loan's cost as a percentage.

This difference between displaying the cost of loans (%) and the cost of all other items ($) is not meant to confuse you or hide the actual cost. Using a percentage is the best way to show the cost over time. If you want to know the dollar value of the interest cost, the easiest calculation is:

Loan principal x interest rate x loan term

Let's say you borrowed $10,000, for one year, and the interest rate was 5% per year. The interest paid for the year would be:

$10,000 x 5% x 1 = $500

If the loan tenor was instead two years, the amount for both years would be:

$10,000 x 5% x 2 = $1,000

If the tenor was six months, the amount would be:

$10,000 x 5% x 6/12 = $250

Let's set aside the calculations for a moment. My point is you should not expect a lender to state the interest cost in dollars. Yes, they can estimate it, or you can calculate it, but the amount will only be correct if the tenor and interest rate do not change over the life of the loan.

You must therefore become comfortable using percentages to describe the cost of loans. And importantly, like any other purchase you make, you must be able to evaluate if it is expensive.

Loan comparisons

Quoting the loan cost as a percentage helps to compare the cost quickly and easily from different lenders. Let's say you know how much you'd like to borrow and for how long. If you provide this information to a few lenders, the interest rates quoted will allow you to decide who has the cheapest offer. We'll consider the impact of other costs in the next chapter.

Impact on net worth

In *Step 7: Calculate Your Net Worth*, we learned that your net worth declines when your liabilities increase, assuming you do not add assets of equal value. Let's recap with an example to show how debt could affect your net worth. Remember net worth is your total assets less your total liabilities, both in current realistic values. In the case of assets, realistic means resale value, and for liabilities, what you currently owe.

Assume you have cash savings of $10,000 and no debt. Your net worth is $10,000 − $0 = $10,000. Let's assume you then used your credit card to buy everyday items for $2,000. As these are not assets, you have only added $2,000 in debt.

Your assets therefore stay at $10,000, but because of the debt, your net worth has fallen from $10,000 to $8,000 ($10,000 assets less $2,000 debt).

The example shows if you take loans for purchases that do not add assets (bad debt), your net worth declines. You are now less wealthy and less financially secure. The example only includes the loan principal, not the cost of the loan. Let's factor in interest, but also include a purchase that increases your assets.

Let's again assume you have cash savings of $10,000 and no debt; therefore, net worth of $10,000 − $0 = $10,000. You then buy furniture and appliances on credit costing $15,000. At the date of the loan, your net worth is unchanged because the new assets and new debt have the same value:

Assets: ($10,000 + $15,000) $25,000

Debt: ($0 + $15,000) $15,000

Net worth = $10,000

But over time, your net worth will decline by the interest cost paid. If you assume 10% for three years, your net worth will reduce by $15,000 x 10% x 3 years = $4,500. I'll show the $4,500 as a reduction in assets because your savings will fall as you pay it.

Assets: ($10,000 + $15,000 - $4,500) $20,500

Debt: ($0 + $15,000) $15,000

Net worth = $5,500

Notice, the value of the furniture and appliances as well as the loan remained unchanged. Of course, in reality this will not happen because:

1. As you repay the loan principal, your cash and the loan balance will decline.

2. In addition, I previously explained assets of this nature lose value, so your net worth declines as the asset values fall. Also remember, the assets in your net worth calculation should be based on their resale value. Used furniture and appliances do not have much resale value, so technically we should not have increased your assets by $15,000. We should use a lower amount.

Let's return to our interest discussion. The takeaway is **the interest cost of a loan causes your net worth to decline *further*.** This is one drawback of quoting interest as a percentage and not a dollar value; the financial impact is not quickly understood.

175

As you learned in the earlier *Steps*, building wealth is about growing your net worth, so you must proactively manage anything that could *decrease* your net worth.

Even if you borrow to buy an asset that might appreciate, which is good debt, your net worth will *always* decline by the interest cost. Your hope is the increase in the asset's value will be *greater* than the interest cost on the loan. When you review how much your asset appreciated, you may focus on the purchase cost only and compare that to the asset's current value. It is easy to forget about the total interest cost.

Let's say you bought an asset for $10,000 by taking a loan for the same value. Let's assume the asset's worth increased to $15,000. Was this a good purchase? It looks so because its value increased by $5,000. But if you paid interest of $8,000 over the same period, you are actually worse off by $3,000. You hope that the *future* increase in value will exceed the $3,000 gap. The point is, saying the asset cost you $10,000 and is now worth $15,000 is only part of the picture.

Accelerated debt repayments

If you look back to *Step 5: Decisions About Your Surplus*, I hope you now understand why I recommended using your surplus to repay debt faster than scheduled. **By repaying your loans as quickly as possible, you avoid the interest cost and prevent a future decline in your net worth.** In addition, reducing your debt quickly improves your finances by removing the constraints a loan imposes.

The amounts involved can be *substantial.* For example, let's assume you took a loan to buy a home for $550,000 at a rate of 4.5% for twenty-five years. Assuming neither the interest rate nor the loan tenor changes, you would have paid nearly $367,000 in interest, so the total cost of the house would have been about $917,000. Yikes!

Of course, few can purchase a home for cash, so we have no choice but to borrow. (If you could use cash, you would not need this book!) Do you follow the point I am emphasizing? **After taking the loan, if you focus on repaying it faster than scheduled, the potential saving in interest cost could be *staggering*.**

Every dollar of interest you avoid improves your net worth. This is why in *Step 11: Invest in Yourself,* I stated that one of your best financial investments is to repay debt early. Let's think about this from your lender's perspective. When they lend, they seek a return on their investment (as we should expect). They charge an interest rate that is competitive, but from which they earn enough profit to make the risk of lending worthwhile.

Realistically, you are unlikely to find an investment that makes a better return than what lenders earn from your loan. Given this is a cost to you, I therefore believe that one of your best financial investments is to avoid incurring this cost. Using the previous example, your challenge is to find an investment with a suitable risk level that earns 4.5% or better. If you cannot, your best financial investment is to *avoid* incurring that cost.

To summarize, good debt = buying a home (for example).
Best debt = early repaid debt!

Wrap up

In this chapter I covered the basics that you must understand to allow us to build from here. The importance of focusing on not only if you can afford a loan installment but also *the cost* of the loan should now be clearer. It could have a significant impact on your future net worth.

Whenever I had to decide whether to borrow, I always compared the rate I earned on my savings accounts (or alternatives like term deposits) against the interest rate I would pay on the loan. That comparison always made me walk away from the loan because the difference was usually *significant*, for example, 1% on the deposit compared to 7% on the loan.

To be clear, I am not suggesting the rates should be the same. A lender could have valid reasons for the difference. But in that moment, I was making a financial decision that was best for me. I could not understand why I should accept receiving so little as a return but give up so much as a cost.

It brings into focus good debt and bad debt. Sure, it is convenient to buy something now using debt instead of saving to buy the item. But instead, you should think of loan interest as a "tax" on the transaction. You should quickly estimate what would be the total cost of the purchase. By this I mean the cost of the item plus loan interest. And yes, you can *estimate* this in seconds by using rounded values. Then decide if the total cost is worth the convenience of buying the item at once, or whether it is more sensible to wait, save, and buy the item using cash.

Usually, there is only one right answer if you are focusing on your future financial self.

The discussion continues in Part 2!

Interest:
The Not-So-Hidden Cost
(Part 2)

To introduce *Part 2*, let's quickly recap the last chapter. We learned that interest is a cost like other outflows, and as a cost, it reduces your net worth. I explained that interest is different from other costs because lenders quote the cost as a percentage and not in dollars. Quoting a percentage is helpful because it allows us to compare the cost of similar loans from different lenders to ensure we get the best deal. Apart from the size of a monthly loan installment, we also learned to pay attention to the cost of the loan. Over time, the interest cost can be substantial.

In this chapter, let's delve a little deeper into the way interest rates could be quoted. You'll learn that it is possible for lenders to use a rate that makes their offer appear more appealing. To combat situations like these, knowledge is our power, so let's jump in and learn about some complications!

What time period?

If you focus only on the percentage quoted, low rates could tempt you. You must ask the question, for what period does the rate apply? For marketing reasons, it may be more attractive to advertise, for example, 1% per month instead of 12% per year. Although both quotes are the same, and the amount of interest paid does not change, 1% appears more attractive than 12%. If the per month quote instead was 1.5%, it is even *more* expensive than 12% per year.

You must ensure the rate quoted is for a *one-year* period. If it isn't, you must "annualize" it. Annualizing means making it equivalent to one year. For example, for a rate of 1% per month, you multiply by twelve to make it annual. If the rate was 1% a quarter (which means every three months), you multiply it by four to get the annual equivalent. The quote of 1.5% per month in the previous paragraph is 18% per year (1.5% x twelve months), which is more expensive when compared to 12% per year.

A common product where lenders quote a periodic rate is credit cards. They regularly advertise it as a monthly rate, for example 2% per month. This seems temptingly low, but when annualized, the rate is a *mind-boggling* 24%.

Although quoting interest rates for periods less than one year was once a regular practice (a deceptive one in my view), it is no longer the case. It still never hurts to confirm that the rate is annual. Otherwise, it will be difficult to compare it to any other offer. A solution to this problem does exist, but first I want to describe one more potential complication: additional costs.

Fees, closing costs, etc.

When you borrow, the lender might charge you some type of fee. It might have different names, such as an application, origination, or administration fee. Strangely, most borrowers accept them without question. Regardless of the fee's name, it *increases* the cost of the loan. Another approach could have been to include these costs in the interest rate by quoting a slightly higher rate (and axe the fee). Cynically, one could argue that the purpose of these separate fees is to make the interest quotes appear lower to entice borrowers.

Let's use an example to illustrate:

A $10,000 loan for one year at 10% will cost you $1,000 in interest. But if the lender charges you a fee of $100, then the real loan cost is the interest cost plus the fee ($1000 + $100) $1,100. A simple calculation ($1,100 ÷ $10,000) shows the loan costs 11% and not the 10% quoted.

> All fees and charges increase the cost to borrow, and your real loan cost is your *total cash* outlay over the life of the loan. I ask that you read the previous sentence again. To make a wise financial decision, you must ensure you know all costs related to the loan.

The solution: APR

Thankfully, a solution exists to both complications, called "Annual Percentage Rate" or APR. A loan's APR is a rate that combines the base interest rate and certain fees the lender charges. It is quoted on an annual basis, and the even better news is you don't calculate it yourself! Lenders must quote the APR for *all* loans, and you use this rate to compare loans from different lenders.

Returning to the previous example, the 11% we calculated would be the loan's APR. While the lender may advertise a 10% base interest rate, it must also show an APR of 11%. If you were borrowing, which rate should you focus on? Correct. 11%, which is the APR. The 10% is sometimes called the "nominal" interest rate.

APR: Key points

While the requirement to quote an APR is excellent for borrowers because it is more transparent, pay attention to these points:

1. The APR may not include all fees. You must still inquire if any fees and charges are excluded from the APR.

2. Lenders could change a loan's APR for several reasons.

3. After you take the loan, the initial APR could increase if your lender charges additional fees or other costs later.

4. A loan's APR could also change depending on whether you have taken a fixed or variable rate loan. I'll describe this in more detail in the chapter *How much is Enough Debt (Part 2)*.

Compounding

So far, I have assumed interest is charged annually on the principal balance for the term of the loan. This method is referred to as "simple interest," which we met in the previous chapter. To illustrate, let's assume you borrowed a principal amount of $10,000 at a rate of 10% for 1 year. The interest cost would be:

$$\textbf{\$10,000 x 10\% x 1 = \$1,000}$$

If the loan term was 6 months instead of 1 year, the interest cost would be:

$$\textbf{\$10,000 x 10\% x 6/12 = \$500}$$

Returning to our example, let's instead assume interest is charged every three months and compounded. In this method, interest is calculated for the first three months and added to your loan balance. Interest for the next three-month period is then calculated using the *higher* amount. **Table 14** shows the calculations:

Table 14				
Period	**Principal**	**Rate**	**Months**	**Interest**
January to March	$10,000	10%	3	$250
April to June	$10,250	10%	3	$256
July to September	$10,506	10%	3	$263
October to December	$10,769	10%	3	$269
	Total interest for the year			**$1,038**

As you see, the effect of compounding means your interest cost is higher: $1,038 versus $1,000. Bear in mind the amounts in the example are small. Compounding could have a *significant* negative effect on your net worth with higher loan balances or interest rates, or longer loan terms.

Compounding is important, and it could be a particular problem with credit cards. We'll pick up this point in greater detail when we look at credit cards later.

Wrap up

You should now understand that interest rates, and how they are quoted, could be tricky. To protect your future financial self by making informed decisions, you must understand the loan you are about to take and its potential cost. Remember the cost is the **total cash** you pay over the life of the loan.

If you are planning to borrow, you should ask the following questions and ensure you receive a clear answer:

(a) What is the loan's APR?

(b) Is the loan's interest rate fixed or variable?

(c) What fees are excluded from the APR?

(d) What fees or charges can arise later?

(e) What could cause the APR to change?

(f) Is interest ever added to the loan's principal? (Remember, this is compounding.) If yes, how often?

Excellent! You should now have a good handle of the basics of borrowing and the potential effect on your net worth. Let's focus next on assessing what is a suitable level of debt.

The Debt Decision

Undoubtedly, being debt-free is liberating. You are not committed to a third party, no one has a first claim on your income, and you face no legal trouble from missed payments. While aiming to be debt-free is ideal, for most of us debt is inescapable, especially for large purchases like a home. Instead, the realistic approach is we should be *uncomfortable* with debt.

Being uncomfortable with debt means you do not take new loans willingly. Also, you do not calmly accept your current level of debt. Instead, you treat debt as an unwelcome visitor and do not allow it to overstay its welcome. You understand debt is a tool, but you remember that the correct tool is often cash. **You wait to use debt when only a loan can help you achieve a specific goal.**

Like you, I have occasionally taken loans. In this short chapter, I'll share the thought process I used, together with my actions, as part of my debt decision.

Question	Action
Will I consume my purchase at once? Or will the item have little value once I begin to use it?	If yes to either, I knew I should use cash instead. Not debt.

Question	Action
Is it realistic for me to save for a longer time to avoid borrowing?	I knew the major factor was whether I intended to buy a Need or a Want. I could defer Wants, which meant I should be patient; save, save, save; and buy with cash.
Is the purchase too large for me to use cash? Or am I buying an asset that could appreciate over time?	If yes, I knew using debt was fine. I also knew the interest cost could reduce my net worth. Therefore, to pay less interest, I tried to make the largest deposit possible or take the shortest loan term that I could afford.
Do I know what types of loans are available, the interest rate, and fees?	Because loans are expensive, I knew I should shop around and compare terms (especially APRs). I could not make a proper decision if I had only one choice.
While the interest rate is important, it is only one aspect of a loan. Do I understand the main terms of the loan agreement? Am I comfortable with the control I will give up to a lender?	Examples of questions I would pose are: Would I have to offer collateral? Could the interest rate change? Do I have the right to prepay? What fees could arise later?

Question	Action
Do I know what I can afford to pay?	Before speaking to a lender, I knew I had to estimate the payment I could afford and the loan term I would prefer. I also had to evaluate how much I could afford if my finances worsened in the future (I had to hope for the best but plan for the worst).
How much interest am I paying over the loan term? Am I okay with the total interest cost?	I knew I had to estimate the total loan amount (principal and interest).
Am I rushing this decision?	I knew some financial decisions made in haste, such as borrowing, could cause regret and stress for a long time.

Of the questions I asked above, we've already covered:

- Good debt versus bad debt. (You know that taking a loan to purchase Wants will always be bad debt.)
- The effect of interest on your net worth.
- The importance of a loan's APR.

In the upcoming chapters, I'll focus on these questions:

1. How to estimate the right loan size; and

2. How to prepare for a conversation with your lender.

When we've finished, you should have enough knowledge to make a wise financial decision about debt! Let's start with learning how to estimate an affordable loan amount.

Action 3

How Much is Enough Debt? (Part 1)

Let's now explore two questions:

1.   How to estimate the right loan size; and

2.   How to prepare for a conversation with a lender.

There isn't one correct answer for what is a suitable level of debt. Some of us are willing to accept a higher level of risk than others and will be comfortable with a higher level of debt. Also, at times, we may have no choice but to accept more debt than the guidelines I recommend in this and the next chapter. We aren't trying to arrive at one right number. Instead, we are trying to make the best decision after taking all factors into account. **Once you make an informed decision, you are in control of your money.**

The situation you want to avoid is relying on a lender to "tell" you how much to borrow. Yes, they have the final approval, but any discussion with them should be an informed one. You must have your own estimate of loan amount, installment, and tenor.

Let's start by looking at a valuable tool to help estimate the amount you can afford: loan calculators. You can find these free online or create them yourself with a spreadsheet. I use *Microsoft Excel*.

Whether you create them or use those online, they are incredibly useful. I'm sure after one or two tries to get familiar, you'll always use them. The alternative is to ask your lender for the information, but that quickly gets tiresome each time you want to change a variable. It's much easier to sit peacefully at home, adjust the inputs, and see the results at once.

There isn't anything complicated here. I encourage you to build the calculators yourself for the same reason we used a spreadsheet for budgeting. When you do it yourself, your understanding improves dramatically. I'll walk you through step by step.

Four components to a loan

A loan consists of four main variables, namely:

1. Installment (the amount paid, which is often monthly).

2. Principal (the amount borrowed).

3. Interest rate.

4. Tenor or term (the length of time to repay).

We've already covered interest rates and the importance of knowing a loan's APR. As a reminder, the APR is an annual rate; it includes certain fees and charges; and it could be higher than a loan's nominal interest rate. It is possible to calculate the APR yourself but unnecessary, as your lender must inform you (hooray!).

Returning to the four main variables, let's create calculators for each. By this I mean, once you enter three known variables, the fourth is calculated. You use the calculators to review the potential loan from various angles. Right now, let's create and understand them, and I'll show you how to use them in the next chapter.

A few points before we begin:

- The calculators are for installment loans, meaning those with a set repayment. Some loans do not have a precise repayment amount, for example credit cards or personal lines of credit. For those loans, you decide how much to repay above the minimum due.

- I'll assume all loans are repaid monthly (twelve payments for the year), although you can also change this variable.

- For three calculations, you'll need to enter an interest rate (this will be clearer when we start). You obtain a rate by either checking indicative rates on the lender's website or calling them to find out. Beware this may not be the final rate of your loan; we'll discuss why in the next chapter. But for now, a reasonable estimate works fine.

- For most loans, the bank will not lend you the full value of the item you wish to buy. Instead, you must make a deposit. For example, if the item costs $20,000, the bank might ask you to contribute $2,000, so they lend $18,000. For the calculations below, ensure you use the amount the bank will lend you, which means *after* deducting your deposit.

- Each loan type has a maximum tenor, and you choose a repayment period up to the maximum. Lenders usually show the possible term on their websites, or you can inquire.

Let's look at the first calculator.

How much do I pay?

When you think about borrowing, your first question is usually what will be your monthly installment. To calculate it, you need four inputs: loan amount, interest rate, loan term, and number of payments each year.

I show you how to create the calculator in **Table 15**, including the formulas to type. Open a new spreadsheet and type exactly what you see in **Table 15**. The columns and row references are there to help you.

Table 15: How Much Do I Pay?		
	A	B
1		
2	Loan amount	
3	Annual interest rate	
4	How many years?	
5	How many payments each year?	
6	**Installment**	**=PMT((B3/B5),(B4*B5),-B2)**
7	**Total interest over life of loan**	**=-CUMIPMT((B3/B5), (B4*B5),B2,1,(B4*B5),0)**
8	**Total principal + interest paid**	**=B6*(B4*B5)**

When you've finished typing the formulas, enter the bolded amounts below in the lighter shaded cells:

Cell B2 **100000** (Note 1)

Cell B3 **8** (Note 2)

Cell B4 **4.5** (Note 3)

Cell B5 **12** (Note 4)

Notes

1. The cell formatting could be *Number* or *Currency*. Right click your mouse when pointing at cell B2 and in the list that appears, you'll see an option for *Format cells*. Click it to see the formatting choices to the left ("*Category*").

    If you want a $ sign in front of the amount, choose *Currency*, but this isn't necessary. If you choose *Number*, click the box *Use 1000 Separator (,)* to place comma separators, which make the numbers easier to read. Click *OK*.

2. The cell formatting I used for the interest rate is *Percentage* (follow the approach in 1). If you choose the *Percentage* option, enter the number in cell B3 (**8** in our example). If you entered **8**, and then applied the *Percentage* format, the result will be 800%. Re-enter **8** to adjust. If you chose another option, for example *Number*, you must enter a decimal in B3 (for example, **.08**).

3. Format the number of years to two decimal places. After choosing the *Number* or *Currency* format, the option for *Decimal places* is to the right of the same window. Decimals are needed when your loan term includes a portion of a year. For example, if the loan tenor is three years and five months, the months will be 5/12 or 0.42, so you would enter **3.42** in cell B4.

    You could also use decimals in cells B3, B4, and B6 to B8. I used two decimal places.

4. If your installments are monthly, enter **12** in cell B5. If quarterly, then enter **4** or enter **2** if semi-annually. Use the *General* or *Number* format.

Once you enter the loan amount, interest rate, loan term, and number of payments, press *Enter* on your keyboard. Cell B6 will return an answer of **$2,211.24**. Your spreadsheet should look like **Table 16**.

Table 16: How Much Do I Pay?		
	A	B
1		
2	Loan amount	$100,000.00
3	Annual interest rate	8.00%
4	How many years?	4.50
5	How many payments each year?	12
6	**Installment**	**$2,211.24**
7	**Total interest over life of loan**	**$19,407.08**
8	**Total principal + interest paid**	**$119,407.08**

Congrats! You no longer need to rely on a lender for an estimate! Adjust any of the three inputs to arrive at a result that works best for you. For example, enter a higher or lower loan amount. Or change the interest rate if you saw a better offer from another lender. Or try to lower your installment by increasing the number of years.

Remember, this is your estimate, and your lender will make its own assessment.

Importantly, I calculated two other amounts:

- The total interest you will pay over the life of the loan (**$19,407.08**) and
- The total principal plus interest (**$119,407.08**)

As you now know, interest is the cost to borrow money. Like all costs, we must reduce it as much as possible. By doing the calculations yourself, you know the total interest you will pay and how expensive the loan could be.

Instinctively, you will focus on the $2,211 monthly installment to decide if you can afford it. What you may not think about is the interest cost included in the installment or the total cost of the loan. It is easy to overlook that you pay nearly $20,000 interest. When you realize your net worth will decline over time by this amount, you might feel more motivated to reduce the loan principal or repay it faster than you had intended.

What loan value can I take?

While your monthly repayment could be your first question, sometimes we already *know* how much we can afford (or prefer) to pay. Instead, we want to know what loan size we can get, using the installment we can afford. Looking at the example, let's assume you want to pay $2,211 each month. How can you estimate the loan size? Easy, once you have an estimate for the interest rate and the loan term.

Return to your spreadsheet and create **Table 17**, entering the formula as shown. Once again, I show the columns and row references to help you.

Table 17: What Loan Value Can I Take?		
	A	B
1		
2	Installment	
3	Annual interest rate	
4	How many years?	
5	How many payments each year?	
6	**Loan amount**	**=PV((B3/B5),(B4*B5),-B2)**

Follow the same cell formatting rules described in the first calculator. When finished, enter the bolded amounts below in the lighter shaded cells:

Cell B2 **2211.24**

Cell B3 **8**

Cell B4 **4.5**

Cell B5 **12**

Press *Enter* and cell B6 will return an answer of **$99,999.90**. Your spreadsheet should look like **Table 18**.

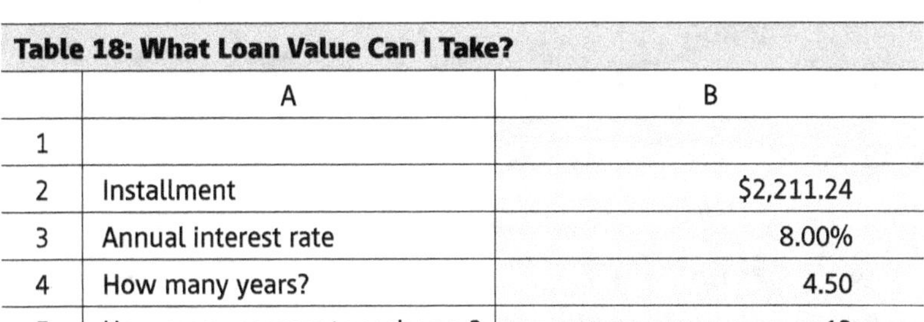

Table 18: What Loan Value Can I Take?

	A	B
1		
2	Installment	$2,211.24
3	Annual interest rate	8.00%
4	How many years?	4.50
5	How many payments each year?	12
6	**Loan amount**	**$99,999.90**

The result is close to, but not exactly, $100,000.00, because $2,211.24 is rounded, and we didn't enter the extra decimal values. These small differences have no effect on your decisions. We know $100,000 is correct because you used that number in the first calculator. Now you can estimate the potential loan size yourself by adjusting any of the three inputs!

How many years will I take to repay?

The third question you could have is: for how long will I be in debt? Let's return to the first example and assume you know you want to pay $2,211.24 each month, borrow $100,000, and you estimate the lender will charge 8%. How do you calculate the loan term? Easy.

Return to your spreadsheet, and by now, you should know the drill: create **Table 19** and enter the formula shown.

Table 19: How Many Years Will I Take to Repay?

	A	B
1	Loan amount	
2	Installment	
3	Annual interest rate	
4	How many payments each year?	
5	**Number of years**	=NPER((B3/B4),-B2,B1)/B4

Follow the same cell formatting rules we previously applied and when you've finished typing the formula, enter the bolded amounts below in the lighter shaded cells:

Cell B1 **100000**

Cell B2 **2211.24**

Cell B3 **8**

Cell B4 **12**

Press *Enter* and cell B5 will return an answer of **4.50**. Your spreadsheet should look like **Table 20**.

Table 20: How Many Years Will I Take to Repay?		
	A	B
1	Loan amount	$100,000.00
2	Installment	$2,211.24
3	Annual interest rate	8.00%
4	How many payments each year?	12
5	**Number of years**	**4.50**

You know 4.50 is correct from the first calculator. Now you have greater control to decide what loan term works best for you. Bear in mind the longer a loan exists, the higher the total interest cost.

This calculator is especially useful because it helps you estimate how quickly you can pay off a loan if you increase the monthly installment. Why would you want to do that? To reduce the cost of the loan and the future hit to your net worth.

What interest rate am I paying?

The last calculator provides the interest rate charged if you know the other variables. I imagine you would use this one less often because lenders must tell you the APR. But it still could be useful in certain circumstances.

Looking at the first example, let's assume you know you want to pay $2,211.24 each month; borrow $100,000; and the loan term will be four-and-a-half years. How do you estimate the rate the lender will charge? Again, easy.

In your spreadsheet create **Table 21**, typing the formula exactly as shown. Use the columns and row references as a guide.

Table 21: What Interest Rate Am I Paying?		
	A	B
1	Loan amount	
2	Installment	
3	How many years?	
4	How many payments each year?	
5	**Annual interest rate**	**=RATE((B3*B4),-B2,B1)*B4**

Follow the same cell formatting rules used previously. After typing the formula, enter the bolded amounts below in the lighter shaded cells:

Cell B1 **100000**

Cell B2 **2211.24**

Cell B3 **4.5**

Cell B4 **12**

Press *Enter* and cell B5 will return an answer of **8.00%**. Your spreadsheet should look like **Table 22**.

Table 22: What Interest Rate Am I Paying?		
	A	B
1	Loan amount	$100,000.00
2	Installment	$2,211.24
3	How many years?	4.50
4	How many payments each year?	12
5	**Annual interest rate**	**8.00%**

You know 8.00% is correct because we used it in the previous calculators.

Wrap up

Whenever I had to take a loan, I found these calculators incredibly helpful. They assisted me to zero in on what I could afford from different angles and understand the ultimate impact on my net worth.

As I mentioned at the start of the chapter, these are available online. But I believe creating them yourself builds confidence and helps motivate you to take control of your money by not relying on others. Of course, if you find it easier to use those online, feel free to do so. What really matters is how you use the results to make a wise borrowing decision.

How Much is Enough Debt? (Part 2)

In the last chapter I said there is no one correct answer to the question, "How much is enough debt?" While true, it is still important to be ready for a conversation with your lender. One aspect of being prepared is estimating in advance how much you want to borrow.

Lenders have made borrowing so hassle-free that you often do not need an in-person visit. **The easy access and approval can distract, and we ignore the importance of the commitment.** Loans are serious legal contracts. By accepting a loan, we pledge a part of our income to a third party—it is no longer ours. If we are unable to pay as agreed (called a "default"), your lender's approach changes from co-operative to almost combative, and they use all legal means to recover their funds.

You might struggle to repay in the future because:

- You overestimated what you could afford.

- Initially attractive loan terms could change into a burden later.

- You only viewed the future optimistically and did not consider the impact if your finances deteriorated.

- You allowed yourself to be influenced into accepting a higher level of debt.

You can avoid most future difficulties with a few simple calculations, and if you understood the previous chapters, you already have all the required tools and knowledge.

When borrowing, if you are not familiar with loan products, your first challenge is to choose the right loan. Lenders offer specific loans for different situations, and the terms offered vary by type. For example, you can't take a fifteen-year vehicle loan, but that tenor is possible if you buy a home.

For now, I'll assume you know which loan is appropriate, but I'll explain the main loan types in the following chapter *Speak and Think Like a Bank*.

When focusing on how much to afford, follow these steps:

1.   Gather information.

2.   Estimate a payment range.

3.   Confirm the payment fits in your budget.

4.   Decide the approach if you cannot afford the payment.

Once you try the approach, you'll see it is straightforward. I'll use an example to illustrate.

Gather information

To estimate the payment range, you'll need to:

a)   Estimate the loan size based on the purchase you wish to make.

b)   Decide what type of loan applies (for example auto loan).

c)   Research online for a typical interest rate on that loan type. Ideally, check a few websites, but they are likely to be similar due to competition.

d)   Choose a suitable loan term, but remember, there is a maximum tenor by loan type.

For this example, I'll use an unnamed loan until I discuss the major types. Let's assume these loan variables: principal $30,000

(after deducting the loan deposit); interest rate: 5% (variable rate); loan term 4 years; and monthly repayments.

Estimate a payment range

The loan details above should look familiar because we used that information when we explored loan calculators. Using the guidelines from the previous chapter, you have the inputs to estimate the monthly installment (the formulas are in **Table 15**). It should look like **Table 23**.

Table 23: How Much Do I Pay?		
	A	B
1		**Current**
2	Loan amount	$30,000.00
3	Annual interest rate	5.00%
4	How many years?	4.00
5	How many payments each year?	12
6	**Installment**	**$690.88**
7	**Total interest over life of loan**	**$3,162.18**
8	**Total principal + interest paid**	**$33,162.18**

The rounded monthly installment is $691, which when multiplied by twelve equals $8,292 (the total annual installment). Let's call this amount "**Current**," which is the start of the range.

Fixed vs variable rate loans

The next part of the range depends on whether your loan has a fixed or variable rate. Fixed rate loans are exactly what the name describes: the rate does not change during a specific period once you pay as scheduled. Variable rate loans, however, adjust based on the conditions the lender sets.

This is important because if the interest rate is adjusted, your loan installment will change. A rate decline is not an issue because you'll have a lower installment. The problem is if rates *increase*—your installment increases. You must therefore check if you can afford the higher loan payment.

Let's assume the rate increases by 3% (from 5% to 8%) over the four years. You have no control over the increase, so use a reasonably large change.

I've shown both calculators with the different rates side-by-side in **Table 24**.

Table 24		
A	B	C
	Current	**Simulated**
2 Loan amount	$30,000.00	$30,000.00
3 Annual interest rate	5.00%	8.00%
4 How many years?	4.00	4.00
5 How many payments each year?	12	12
6 **Installment**	**$690.88**	**$732.39**
7 **Total interest over life of loan**	**$3,162.18**	**$5,154.61**
8 **Total principal + interest paid**	**$33,162.18**	**$35,154.61**

At the higher rate, the monthly payment becomes $732. When multiplied by twelve, the annual payment is $8,784. Let's call this amount "**Simulated**."

Your annual repayment range is therefore $8,292 (**Current**) to $8,784 (**Simulated**). This means if interest rates are between 5% to 8%, your loan installment could be between $8,292 to $8,784.

Confirm the payment fits in your budget

Let's assume your budget looks like **Table 25** *before* the new loan.

I hid the outflow and monthly details to make the changes easier to follow. I hope you recall the percentages, which are calculated using total inflows.

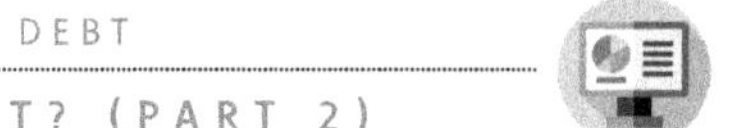

Table 25

	Jan-Dec (per month)	Total	
INFLOWS			
TOTAL INFLOWS	$3,000	$36,000	
OUTFLOWS			
Loan payments			
Total loan payments	$100	$1,200	3%
Needs			
Total Needs	$1,200	$14,400	40%
Wants			
Total Wants	$500	$6,000	17%
TOTAL OUTFLOWS	$1,800	$21,600	
Surplus/(Deficit)	**$1,200**	**$14,400**	40%

Next, amend your budget to include the new loan installment, beginning with the **Current** payment, as I show in **Table 26**.

Table 26

	Jan-Dec (per month)	Total	Current
INFLOWS			
TOTAL INFLOWS	$3,000	$36,000	
OUTFLOWS			
Loan payments			
Loan 1	$100	$1,200	
Loan 2	$691	$8,292	
Total loan payments	$791	$9,492	26%
Needs			
Total Needs	$1,200	$14,400	40%
Wants			
Total Wants	$500	$6,000	17%
TOTAL OUTFLOWS	$2,491	$29,892	
Surplus/(Deficit)	**$509**	**$6,108**	17%

To understand the impact of the new loan, use the budget profiles from *Step 9: Improve the Estimate of Your Target*

Surplus. The profiles are important because they remind you to always target a surplus, otherwise you will not achieve your financial goals.

The with-debt budget profile recommended the following percentages:

- 20% Surplus

- 30% Loan repayments

- 50% Needs and Wants

Remember, your total loan repayments should *not exceed* 30% of your inflows. Notice the percentage is 26% after you include the **Current** loan installment.

Next, repeat the approach using the **Simulated** loan repayment instead, as shown in **Table 27**.

Table 27			
	Jan-Dec (per month)	Total	Simulated
INFLOWS			
TOTAL INFLOWS	$3,000	$36,000	
OUTFLOWS			
Loan payments			
Loan 1	$100	$1,200	
Loan 2	$732	$8,784	
Total loan payments	$832	$9,984	28%
Needs			
Total Needs	$1,200	$14,400	40%
Wants			
Total Wants	$500	$6,000	17%
TOTAL OUTFLOWS	$2,532	$30,384	
Surplus/(Deficit)	$468	$5,616	15%

The result shows that both the **Current** and **Simulated** repayments fall within the suggested maximum 30% guideline.

Consequently, even if interest rates increased from 5% to 8%, you could still afford the loan. Of course, this assumes that your personal circumstances do not change. (Also, note the surplus is lower than the recommended 20%, which means you should re-assess Needs and Wants for possible reductions.)

Now you can relax a little, because having done the exercise, you are more prepared to handle the risk of higher loan payments in the future!

Discussion with your lender

The next step would be to meet your lender. In the conversation, you'll need to find out if your estimates are close to what your lender is using. Once close, your conversation will be productive. If their estimates are different, you'll need to understand why. In this instance, you should leave the appointment without committing. Return to your budget and repeat the previous steps using your lender's terms to ensure you can afford the loan. **Do not commit to any loan unless you are confident you understand how it will affect your budget.**

Let's say your budget can accommodate the **Current** but not the **Simulated** payment. In this case, you must recognize the higher risk. If borrowing is not urgent, think about saving for a larger deposit to reduce the loan principal. Aim to lower the **Current** and **Simulated** installments to a level where your total loan payments for both are less than 30% of your inflows.

Let's assume you must borrow at once. In this case, after borrowing, you should reduce expenses, save more, and pay extra towards the loan. Your goal is to reduce your loan principal to an affordable level (use the monthly repayment calculator). Once achieved, ask your lender to restructure the loan to reduce your monthly repayments to fit within the profile. This is not always easy to do. Therefore, before you borrow, you should discuss how loan restructuring works with your lender. This way, you avoid surprises later.

Estimate a revised loan principal

Do you remember you can use the loan calculators to estimate the loan principal (see **Tables 17** and **18**)? Let's assume when you include a **Simulated** payment, your loan repayment changes to 35%, as shown in **Table 28**.

Table 28

	Jan-Dec (per month)	Total	Simulated
INFLOWS			
TOTAL INFLOWS	$3,000	$36,000	
OUTFLOWS			
Loan payments			
Total loan payments	$1,057	$12,684	**35%**
Needs			
Total Needs	$1,200	$14,400	**40%**
Wants			
Total Wants	$500	$6,000	**17%**
TOTAL OUTFLOWS	$2,757	$33,084	
Surplus/(Deficit)	**$243**	**$2,916**	**8%**

To achieve 30%, your maximum total loan installments should be $36,000 x 30% = $10,800. You therefore need to reduce the annual payment by ($12,684 - $10,800) $1,884 or $157 monthly ($1,884 ÷ 12). Using your loan calculator, enter the lower installment of $575 ($732 - $157) as shown in **Table 29**.

Table 29

What Loan Value Can I Take?

	A	B
1		**Simulated**
2	Installment	$575.00
3	Annual interest rate	8.00%
4	How many years?	4.00
5	How many payments each year?	12
6	**Loan amount**	**$23,553.10**

It shows the required loan principal is $23,553 not $30,000.

Consequently, you must save the difference of $6,447 ($30,000 – $23,553) to increase your deposit before borrowing. Or if you cannot delay, this is the additional payment needed before asking to restructure the loan in the future. Unscheduled extra payments are commonly called "prepayments."

Approach if you cannot afford the payment

If the **Current** payment exceeds the 30% threshold, the best action is not to borrow at this time. Instead, save a larger deposit to reduce the loan principal. Use the calculator, as I showed above, to estimate a more suitable loan size.

If you borrow without reducing the loan amount, your annual surplus will be lower than the profile recommends. A smaller surplus means it will take you longer to achieve your medium and long-term goals. In addition, your "safety" buffer is reduced. Remember, even when you have debt, you must make annual surpluses. **Your surplus increases your net worth, which strengthens your financial security. A growing net worth provides you with a safety cushion to absorb the unforeseen.**

If you proceed, ensure that your surplus does not become negative or even close to negative. If debt could bring you to a financial state where you have no surplus, you must have a plan to exit this fragile situation. Your future financial self demands a properly thought-out strategy.

Key points

Before wrapping up, let me emphasize these points.

The 30% guideline

The with-debt budget profile is only a guideline. The real issue is should you borrow in the first place. If you must, it does not mean you should automatically aim to reach 30% of your inflows. You should *always* aim to take the *smallest* loan possible and repay it quickly to lower the interest cost.

You can repay it faster in two ways:

1. Save as much as you can while you have the loan and prepay occasionally. Or save the extra payments and pay off the loan in a lump sum at an earlier date.

2. Use a shorter loan tenor than what your lender is offering. This will make the monthly installments larger. For example, let's say your lender offers you a five-year loan. You can instead *deliberately* choose to repay the loan over two or three years. In this case it is fine if your total repayments are higher than 30% because you are making a conscious decision to repay the loan faster. If the installments become a burden later, you can ask your lender to increase the loan term back to five years to lower the payments.

> For both approaches to work, you must ensure your contract allows you to prepay and change your loan terms afterwards. Confirm what is possible *before* you commit to borrow. If you cannot prepay, it is wiser to borrow only what you can comfortably afford to avoid any chance of default.

Factor in unexpected events

We naturally decide what is affordable based on circumstances today. Instead, **we should pause and think about events that could restrict our ability to repay.** An example might be stability of employment. Uncertainty could exist in your own role, employer's situation, or industry. Ensure you factor the likelihood of any negative impact to you into your decision to borrow. If you must borrow, ensure you know how much you can realistically afford if those events happen. Use your budget to estimate the impact on your surplus if your income falls or expenses increase.

Emotion

While emotion should have no place in financial decisions, unfortunately, we can be swayed into taking a larger loan than we can comfortably afford. For example, buying a more expensive house because it has a dream feature or a fantastic location. In the moment, desire overtakes logic.

The only way to prevent emotion from influencing your decisions is to evaluate what you can afford first. In the example of buying a home, you should first estimate a specific high and low range. Then, when you begin scouting, you can quickly move on if the price is out of your range, even if it hurts a little to walk away.

Wrap up

This was a slightly long chapter because of the detailed explanations. In practice, once you have already created your budget and the calculators, the numerical changes only take seconds to do. The time is really spent exercising your mind to decide what works best for you.

Now you know how to objectively evaluate if you can afford a loan! The next step is to prepare for a conversation with a lender, which has its own pitfalls to avoid.

Speak and Think Like a Bank

Once you decide to borrow, you will eventually have to discuss the details with a lender, which could be a daunting conversation. The problem with financial institutions is they seem to speak a different language. In a way, this is true because they must follow several laws and these rules affect your conversation. Fear not! You can prepare for this discussion by learning about their world and becoming familiar with the concepts and questions that will arise.

Although this chapter refers to a bank, you can obtain loans elsewhere. Nonetheless, I'll use the terms "bank" and "lender" to capture all loan providers.

You can apply for many loans online. Although convenient, always remember you are making an important financial decision. It is better to meet in-person to have all your questions answered and to ensure you understand all loan options and conditions. I also believe a virtual approach could place the lender at an advantage.

Let's start by looking at the main loan features you'll meet; I emphasize that they could vary by loan product.

Credit score

Of all the terms and concepts you'll meet when taking a loan, this might be the most important to the lender. When you borrow, you are promising to repay the loan. This is a significant risk to a lender, especially since each borrower's situation is unique. Credit scores attempt to reflect these

infinite number of personal circumstances in a numerical way to help the lender assess the chance of non-payment. (Remember, when you do not repay according to your loan agreement, this is called a "default.")

Your credit score is a three-digit number. A lender interprets a high number to mean you are more likely to repay your loan. A low number implies you are less likely to repay. FICO[2] is a common credit scoring system, and its range and ranking of credit scores are shown below:

Score	Credit Assessment
Under 580	Poor
580–669	Fair
670–739	Good
740–799	Very Good
Above 800	Excellent

How does this affect you? If your credit score is low, either you may be unable to borrow, or lenders will charge a higher interest rate to compensate for your higher risk. If your credit score is high, lenders are more likely to approve your loan and they may charge a lower interest rate.

Credit scores are key to the business of lending to individuals. Anything that is important to your lender should be important to you. But credit scores are often used for reasons other than taking a loan. You must therefore review your credit reports and credit score regularly. You should also ensure you know what can affect the score. Credit reports often contain mistakes, and you will only know if you check them. Do not wait until you are ready to borrow!

---

2   If you want more information, you can research FICO and other scoring systems. A deeper understanding isn't needed for our discussion.

Fixed vs variable interest rates

Interest rates fluctuate, and these changes are an important risk for a bank. From the explanation in *How Much is Enough Debt (Part 2)*, you should remember loans have either a fixed or variable rate. Variable rate loans are linked to a benchmark, and if the benchmark changes, the loan's interest rate changes. Whatever the benchmark is, you certainly have no control over how it changes. In contrast, if the bank fixes the rate for a period, it means they commit not to change it once you follow the loan terms.

If you have a choice between a fixed or variable rate option, there is no right answer. If the same loan was offered at both fixed and variable rates, the variable rate option would tend to be lower. Although a benefit to you initially, you must accept the risk that if your interest rate increases, your loan installment will increase. Of course, you must be able to afford the higher payment. If you prefer certainty, you should seek fixed rate loans.

We have already covered the impact of interest on your net worth and the importance of reducing this cost.

Fees

The name of the fee is irrelevant: it is an additional cost.

Let me pull together the points related to fees that we previously met. You already know that you must pay attention to fees when borrowing. The name of the fee is irrelevant: it is an additional cost. Lenders are supposed to tell you the all-in cost of a loan, which you know is the APR. You also know that an APR might not include all fees. You must therefore confirm what fees are *omitted* from the APR as well as what *other* fees can arise before the loan is fully paid.

Banks charge fees for many services. Ensure you know *every* way you can incur a fee on each bank product you have. **Fees and charges add up unnoticed, and these outflows are often avoidable.**

Fixed vs variable payments

Loan repayments are either fixed or they vary. Fixed payments are set at the start of the loan and remain the same during the loan term. If the payments are variable, you decide how much to pay each month. Usually, these loans have a minimum amount you must pay. You choose the amount to pay above the minimum.

Obviously, loans with variable payments offer a lot of flexibility, but there are downsides. A fixed monthly installment ensures you diligently repay the loan. When you can choose the amount to pay, you must be disciplined. More importantly, loans with variable payments could have higher interest rates. Flexibility therefore comes at a cost.

Prepayment

I believe the most important feature to a borrower is the ability to make unscheduled payments. If you must borrow, a goal should always be to repay the loan faster than scheduled to reduce the impact on your net worth. Obviously, with a variable payment loan you can repay the entire balance whenever you wish. **If you have a loan with a fixed installment, you must ensure your loan agreement gives you the right to prepay.**

Lenders normally do not like prepayments. Consequently, they may discourage it by setting periods when you cannot prepay, or they may charge a penalty. Ensure you are familiar with the rules.

Secured vs unsecured

When you borrow, you promise to repay the loan according to the agreed terms. Banks reduce the risk of non-payment, by requiring collateral (also called "security") for certain loans. Remember, when you supply collateral, you give the lender temporary rights over an asset of value. This is sometimes described as the bank having a "lien" over the item. If you default, the bank will seize the asset and sell it to recover the amount owed.

If the bank has a lien over some forms of collateral, they will not allow you to access it. For example, if you secure a loan with cash, you can't use the cash until you repay the loan. Other times, you continue to use the item, such as your vehicle or home, but you cannot sell it without the bank's permission. Other loans are unsecured, which means the bank does not require collateral.

> The key point is unsecured loans are more expensive than secured loans. The difference in interest rates could be *substantial*.

Collateral value

Lenders will apply a *lower* value than what the collateral is worth. For example, let's say the asset you provide as collateral has an actual value of $100. The lender may only count 75% of the value, which means $75. The implication is you can only borrow up to $75.

Using a lower value provides the lender with a cushion in case the asset's value declines.

Refinancing

If you take a loan for several years, your personal circumstances will naturally change over that time. If your finances deteriorate, it may force you to adjust the loan terms, a process

called "refinancing." When you refinance, you effectively enter into a new loan to replace the old, although it may appear as one transaction.

Refinancing could take many forms. Examples include changing the monthly payment amount, switching between a fixed and variable rate loan, or taking advantage of lower interest rates. In addition, one may wish to increase the amount borrowed to obtain new funds.

This process is often not free and you should understand the cost to refinance. Remember, as you are ending the old loan and entering a new one, these costs could be significant.

Having reviewed the major loan features, let's summarize the types you'll meet. I again point out that these will vary by lender, so you'll need to ask about the specific options offered. These products are often governed by law or regulation, so please be aware I am not providing a legal explanation. I am focusing on practical understanding.

Loans for personal use

I think of these as three types:

1. Personal loan

2. Personal line of credit

3. Overdraft

All three tend to be unsecured, but you may have the option to offer security to lower the interest rate. Additionally, you use them for almost anything, but there is normally a maximum amount you can borrow, and the term is short (for example, up to five years).

The first, a personal loan, is a traditional one: you borrow a fixed amount and have regular monthly installments. It is best used when you already know the amount you wish to borrow.

The second and third type are similar. Lenders assign a limit, and you borrow up to that limit. You choose the amount to repay, and you can re-borrow up to the authorized limit. Because the loan balance fluctuates, they are sometimes called "revolving" loans. You only pay interest on the amount borrowed, not the authorized limit. A revolving loan is a good choice when you are looking for more flexibility or if you aren't sure in advance how much you need.

The difference between a personal line of credit and an overdraft is that an overdraft is linked to a checking account. The checking account can either have funds (your own money) or it can be in overdraft (you owe the bank). Let's say you have $500 in your checking account, and it has an overdraft facility with an authorized limit of $1,000. If you write a check for $700, the bank will cash your check, but it creates an overdraft of $200 (you owe the bank $200). The bank will charge you interest on the overdraft ($200) and not the limit ($1,000).

Vehicle loans

This loan is for the specific purpose of buying a new or used vehicle. The facility works like a regular loan with set monthly installments.

Home loans

Home loans are of two types:

1. Mortgage loans

2. Home equity loans

A mortgage is a loan to buy real estate. When you take a mortgage, you pledge the property you are buying as collateral. Importantly, lenders do not own the property—you do. But the mortgage gives them certain rights over the property. Specifically, if you default on your payments, the mortgage

allows your lender to seize your property (also known as a "foreclosure") and sell it to recover their funds.

A mortgage is the longest and largest loan many of us will take, so we'll consider this in more detail in Action 5: *Prepare for Major Life Events.*

A home equity loan is another form of secured borrowing. "Equity" refers to the value of your home less any mortgages outstanding. Let's say your home is worth $400,000 and it has a current outstanding mortgage of $300,000. The equity in your home is the difference of $100,000. The lender usually assigns a limit that is lower than the equity value, and you borrow up to this limit using the equity as collateral.

Credit cards

Credit cards require special attention, so I'll cover them in more detail in the next chapter.

The business of lending

Having explored loan products and features, let's focus on the actual discussion with a lender.

Always remember lenders are in the *business* of granting loans. This is the product they sell and how they make a profit. It is therefore in *their* interest to lend a qualified borrower as much as possible. But it may not be in *your* interest to accept what they offer.

Please let this point sink in. It is natural when you are in a comfortable office, facing charming professionals, to forget they are trying to *sell* you something. Often, lending personnel are partly compensated based on the number and size of loans they grant. I'm not suggesting they are trying to force you to do something. **If you enter a discussion where the other party is more informed, it is natural for you to be inclined to accept what they say.**

Think about visiting a doctor. Unless you have a medical background, you accept the doctor's advice. The same principle applies to lenders. If you are unfamiliar with what they sell, you have little choice but to accept what they offer. And if the person making the offer can personally benefit from the transaction, you could be in a tricky situation.

To repeat, lenders are in the business of making loans and they benefit from lending a qualified borrower as much as they can. Once you have enough knowledge, you will be better positioned to ask questions and ensure your loan is a smart financial decision.

Know what you can afford

One pitfall you must avoid is accepting a loan that is larger than you can afford. This could happen when you depend on a lender's recommendation. The only way to avoid this situation is to have your *own* estimate. **Effectively, you should tell *them* what you can afford.**

If you are a high-quality borrower, the lender may offer you a larger loan than you had planned. Remember, the higher monthly repayments lead to less financial flexibility and a larger total interest cost. The higher interest will reduce your future net worth.

If you follow the guidelines from the earlier chapters, you will have a good estimate of what works for your budget, and you can be in control of the conversation.

Debt-to-income ratio

Lenders often use a calculation referred to as "debt-to-income ratio." This compares your monthly "debt expenses" to your monthly gross income. Admittedly, debt expense is an odd term. It includes all loan payments, housing-related expenses (for example, property taxes), and often any other payment that is an obligation (for example, alimony or child support). What lenders include could vary, so it is best to inquire.

If your calculation is lower than the lender's benchmark, they interpret this as you can afford more debt. For example, let's assume your monthly gross income is $2,000. Remember, gross means before you deduct taxes. Let's also assume your total monthly loan payments and housing-related expenses are $500. Your debt-to-income ratio would therefore be 25% ($500 ÷ $2,000). If the lender's threshold was 35%, you are currently below. For the lender, it means you can borrow more because you can afford higher loan payments.

A lender's debt-to-income calculation will *never* be as accurate as your budget. I strongly recommend you only consider what your budget can afford.

Wrap up

I hope you feel that you are ready to go toe-to-toe with a lender! Remember, you do not have to know as much as they do. You should, however, be able to follow the discussion properly and ask the right questions. I'll also bet the person you deal with does not necessarily have more knowledge than what I provided you. Lenders may have more familiarity because they do these transactions every day. But you should not feel intimidated. At times, you might meet a career banker who has a broad range of experience, but these persons most likely focus on lending to businesses, not individuals.

Let's now turn our attention to an important lending product: credit cards. They are incredibly useful and convenient, but in the hands of the undisciplined or uninformed, they can be dangerous and destroy financial security.

Joys and Woes
of Credit Cards

A credit card is a small piece of plastic that everyone seems to have or obtains easily. It appears deceptively simple but is a powerful financial product. If improperly used, credit cards can decimate your finances.

Benefits

To begin, let's acknowledge their many benefits.

Transaction convenience

They undoubtedly make our life easier: take it out; swipe/insert/tap; sign/enter a PIN; and your transaction is done. Given most businesses no longer accept personal checks, without credit cards we would need to carry a personal vault to keep enough cash to buy anything. They are therefore especially useful for high-value transactions.

They helped the rise of internet commerce

It is unlikely online shopping and internet commerce could exist without credit cards. They have certainly contributed to the spectacular growth of online businesses.

Safety

Not having to walk with bundles of cash reduces our personal risk of robbery.

Rewards

If you avoid credit card debt, the rewards attached to the card could exceed its annual fee; therefore, you could actually "make" money from using the card.

Easy access to emergency credit/cash

The card's pre-authorized credit limit makes it an easy way to access either credit (remember, this means to take a loan) or cash in an emergency.

Itemized list of purchases

Credit card statements list your purchases, which you can use to monitor your spending. It also simplifies your financial record keeping, such as tracking your expenses, as we did in *Step 1: Track Your Inflows and Outflows.*

Dangers

While their benefits are abundant, there are accompanying dangers.

Addictive and easy to abuse

We agree they are easy to love because of their convenience. But a downside exists: they are dangerously addictive and easy to abuse.

Without a credit card, we'll have to use cash. With cash, we have a physical act of handing over several bills for our purchases. This action makes you pause because you *literally* see your money leaving you. It acts as a natural barrier to stop you from buying impulsively. But with a credit card, the psychological effect from depleting your cash is not present.

Fraud and identity theft

With ease of use comes two big challenges: credit cards are vulnerable to fraud, and you could become a victim of identity theft. Fraud and identity theft could lead to serious problems, especially if someone has been pretending to be you. Avoiding these traps requires a special level of vigilance, which could be difficult to maintain continuously.

Other dangers

There are several other dangers, such as:

- Most expensive form of credit
- Unclear interest calculations
- Fees
- The illusion of minimum payments

Given the importance of these other dangers, I'll discuss them in detail in the next chapter, *Understand Credit Card Debt.*

Credit card basics

To understand the other dangers better, let's briefly review how credit cards work. Even though it is a unique product, thankfully the basics are straightforward. The specifics vary by lender and card type, but the descriptions below should give you a good start.

Credit limit

As a credit card is a lending product, the bank will provide you with a credit limit based primarily on your credit score. They usually have an annual fee although no-fee cards are common. Credit cards are a type of revolving credit. You should remember this means you use it to borrow (up to the limit) and repay to create room to use it again.

The terms in the last paragraph should be familiar because we covered them in *Speak and Think Like a Bank*.

Let's assume you received a new card with a $10,000 limit and you used $7,000. You will have $3,000 remaining (your available balance). If you repay $5,000, you now owe ($7,000 – $5,000) $2,000. Your available room is then ($10,000 – $2,000) $8,000. You use and repay without needing your bank's permission, once the card is valid.

Dates and balances

It is important to understand not only what happens on different dates but also what the card balances on those dates represent. Let's figure them out.

Billing cycle

Credit cards are billed monthly (the "billing cycle") and these dates are important. The billing cycle varies, but let's assume you receive a new card on January 1, with its billing cycle from the first of each month.

Statement balance

At the end of the billing cycle, a statement is generated that lists your transactions during the billing period. It will show a "statement balance," which is the amount owed at the end of the billing cycle. For your new card this will be the transactions during January 1 to January 31. As you continue to read, let's assume your total purchases were $2,000.

Due date

The statement also has the payment due date, which could be two to four weeks *after* the billing cycle ends. Let's say in

our example the due date is February 21. Once you pay the statement balance of $2,000 by February 21, you will not incur an interest charge.

Let's think about this for a moment. If you bought an item on January 3, you pay for it nearly seven weeks later, yet incur no interest. This is a form of credit. Your bank effectively grants you an interest-free loan for several weeks. Once you keep paying your statement balance in full on the due date, you can take advantage of these interest-free loans.

The gap between the date you buy something and when you pay for it creates a challenge. You could easily forget the purchases you made weeks ago and be shocked when you see what is owed. If you weren't in control of your money, you may scramble to find the cash to make the payment in full.

Current balance

While your statement balance is what you owed at the end of the billing cycle (January 31 in our example), if you check your account online, you will also see an amount called "current balance."

The current balance is your up-to-date liability. It is the amount you owe at any given moment. Let's say you spent $500 between February 1 and February 21. On February 21, you could choose to pay either the statement balance ($2,000) or pay off the card completely—the current balance of $2,500 ($2,000 + $500). If you pay the statement balance, the transactions from February 1–21 will be reflected on your February statement.

Minimum payments

It is possible to pay *less* than the statement balance. The point to understand is once you pay less than the statement balance ($2,000 in our example), the unpaid amount is now an active loan that incurs interest.

Although credit cards allow you to pay any amount, your statement will show a "minimum payment." Let's say in our example the minimum payment is $55. It is easy to interpret this amount as what you are *supposed* to pay. But this is not the case. If you cannot pay the full statement balance of $2,000, you can pay *any* amount. **The bank is only informing you that the least you should pay is $55. If you pay less than the minimum, you could incur various penalties.**

I'd like to emphasize that in the example you owe $2,000 and should pay $2,000. If you had used cash for your purchases, you would not have an amount due. You should not passively decide to pay less than $2,000. Instead, if you knew you did not have sufficient funds to pay the statement balance in full, the wise decision would have been *not* to use the card.

Cash advances

Credit cards have one of the great conveniences of bank cards: accessing cash using an ATM. The giant difference between both types of cards is when you use your bank card, you withdraw cash from what you *already* have. I am of course assuming you do not create an overdraft in your checking account. When you use a credit card to obtain cash from an ATM, you *immediately* borrow from your lender. Your lender treats these withdrawals (called a "cash advance") differently from your purchase transactions and more harshly. I'll discuss this in greater detail in the next chapter.

Wrap up

This chapter was a pit stop, so-to-speak, to explain the basics about how the card works. I'll build on these points in the next chapter to illustrate the associated dangers.

Understand Credit Card Debt

Credit cards are like financial medication: when used as directed, they can be hugely beneficial; when we ignore directions, they can cause serious difficulties. Having covered the basics in the last chapter, let's take a deeper look into a few of these difficulties.

An *awfully* expensive form of credit

For most people, I expect credit card debt is their most expensive form of credit. Do you remember that APR is the best indicator of the cost of a loan? In the case of credit cards, they could range from 15% to 25%. Let that sink in for a moment…

In my wrap up to the chapter *Interest: The Not-So-Hidden Cost (Part 1)*, I suggested comparing what you earn on deposit accounts against the interest rate on loans. If you do, you will realize that your deposits earn a *tiny* amount compared to what you pay on a credit card loan. That's how expensive credit card debt is.

You already know that interest eats into your net worth, and one of your financial goals is to reduce your interest cost. So, pay attention! If you currently have credit card debt, you are paying a rate that's many times *higher* than even the next most expensive loan product. Read the previous sentence again.

Multiple APRs

Normally, when you take a loan, a lender quotes you a nominal interest rate. If there are no other fees, that rate is also the APR. You pay that rate over the loan term (once you follow the loan conditions). If you have a variable rate loan, the APR adjusts if the benchmark changes. It then remains constant unless the benchmark changes again.

Knowledge check: if you didn't fully understand the previous paragraph, please review the earlier chapters in this Action before moving forward.

Unfortunately, credit card interest rates are not that simple. **Credit cards have different APRs depending on the type of transaction, for example, purchases, balance transfers, and cash advances.** It gets worse. If you pay later than the due date or miss a payment, your rate could increase to a *penalty* APR. The penalty APR could be higher than the rate for the transaction types I listed.

In the example from the last chapter, the due date was February 21, and the minimum payment was $55. If you pay later than February 21, or less than $55, your regular APR (let's assume 15%) could jump to, let's say 25%, the penalty APR. Once increased, it remains until you restart regular, on-time payments.

Fees

Credit cards carry a range of fees, most of which are not part of the APR because they are not a condition of the loan. You should remember from our APR discussion that certain fees can be omitted from the calculation. For credit cards, examples include past-due payment fees, over limit fees, cash advance fees, balance transfer fees, and who knows what else! These fees are added to your loan balance, so your pain increases because you pay interest on the fee as well. Yikes!

Some fees are not a fixed amount. They are a *percentage* of the transaction, which could make them *significant*.

Complex interest calculations

If fees sound like a minefield, understanding interest calculations is even more challenging.

Do you remember how to calculate interest on a regular installment loan? Assuming you pay monthly, the month's interest is based on the loan balance multiplied by the interest rate. Revolving loans are similar, except that the calculation factors in changes in the loan balance during the month. Not so with credit cards—it is more complex.

Depending on regulations, calculation methods could vary, and lenders may have the flexibility to select an approach that could be quite expensive (if not punitive). It isn't possible to describe every way interest could be calculated, but let's pay attention to a particular problem: compounding.

Compounding

Let's return to the example from the last chapter to look at some of the difficulties. We were at the point when a statement was generated at the end of the billing cycle. The statement balance was $2,000 with a due date of February 21, and the minimum payment due was $55.

Let's assume you paid $500 on February 1 (earlier than the due date of February 21), so you owe $1,500. As you now have a loan, the lender will charge you the interest rate that applies to purchases (remember, credit cards have a range of APRs).

Let's assume the applicable rate is 15%, and you made no other purchases in February. You may think the interest charge for February would be $1,500 x 15% x 28/365 = $17.26. But you could be wrong.

Interest on credit cards could be compounded daily (you'll need to check your card agreement or statement to confirm). As a reminder, I explained compound interest in the chapter *Interest: The Not-So-Hidden Cost (Part 2)*. Daily compounding means interest is added to your loan balance *each* day. The interest calculation for the next day is then based on the slightly higher loan balance.

With a daily rate of (15%/365) 0.00411, that means on:

- February 1 you owe $1,500 x 0.00411 = $0.62
- February 2 you owe $1,500.62 x 0.00411 = $0.62
- February 3 you owe $1,501.23 x 0.00411 = $0.62
- Etc.

It is possible your credit card debt is the only loan that calculates interest in this way.

Subsequent purchases

Returning to our example. Let's say you resumed using your card in March and made a purchase on March 4. Remember, you have an existing loan because you did not pay the statement balance in full; therefore, each new purchase will be added to your existing loan. **This is important because you will incur interest on each new transaction from the date of purchase. You no longer have any interest-free periods.** Stop. Read this paragraph again.

In our example, the interest for March would be calculated and compounded daily on the unpaid balance from February 28. Then your new purchase on March 4 is added to your unpaid balance and interest is calculated and compounded daily until March 31. If you made several purchases during March, you will be charged interest on each from the transaction date.

Cash advances

Next, let's assume you use your credit card in March to withdraw funds (a cash advance). Lenders treat cash advances more punitively than a purchase transaction:

- They charge a fee *immediately* when you withdraw. This is not an interest charge. It is a fee to withdraw.

- The fee is not usually a fixed amount but a *percentage* (2% or 3%) of the amount withdrawn.

- You pay interest on the amount withdrawn *and* the fee from the date of withdrawal.

- The cash advance APR is usually much higher than a purchase APR. The purchase APR in our example was 15%. The cash advance APR could be 25%.

Do you feel poorer?

Remember I said credit card interest calculations were complex? With regular loans, it is possible to recalculate your interest charge if you apply the calculation described in the loan agreement. The calculations described in your credit card agreement are in a totally different league.

And don't forget, interest reduces your net worth—it makes you poorer. Credit card interest is especially expensive, which makes you even **poorer**.

The mirage of minimum payments

Let's quickly recap using our example. During January, you bought items totaling $2,000, which is your statement balance. I emphasize, this is the amount you owe. You should pay it *in full* to avoid creating a loan and incurring costly interest charges.

Secondly, if you cannot pay the full amount, you should pay the largest amount you can afford. Your aim is to make the loan as small as possible.

Thirdly, your statement would refer to a "minimum payment." This is not what your lender recommends you pay. **This is the lowest amount you must pay to keep from *defaulting*.** The minimum payment is normally a percentage of your card balance (around 2% to 4%).

Almost impossible to repay

You may not realize but it takes a long time (think *years*) to repay your balance if you pay only the minimum. This is because most of the payment is applied to interest owed and only a *small* part reduces the principal balance. If you have credit card debt, check this yourself by using an online calculator. The length of time to repay fully will shock you!

> The takeaway is, you will *never* get out of credit card debt if you pay only the minimum. You must pay much more than the minimum. Frankly, pay every dollar you can afford.

Enticements

Credit cards often have various enticements to influence you to use a particular card. Examples are introductory low rates, low rates on balance transfers, or various forms of rewards. We've already covered rewards, and I explained you could benefit if you use the card in a disciplined way.

While you could also benefit from a low-rate offer, review it carefully to ensure the offer truly works in your favor. Pay attention because low rates are normally temporary and escalate easily. Also, ensure that after the introductory period ends, the new card's regular APR is not even *higher* than your old card. I already mentioned balance transfers tend to have a

fee. It may take a long time for the benefit from the low rate to offset the cost of the fee.

Review all enticements carefully. You could be misled by what seems like a good deal if you don't understand the conditions.

Wrap up

Think about this for a moment. Once you continue to pay your card monthly but maintain a balance and incur the occasional fee, you are a bank's *dream* customer. They do not want you to repay your outstanding balance in full. They prefer if you pay just enough to keep your balance moving up and down.

I follow a simple rule in financial transactions: if you do not understand a transaction, you should avoid it. You cannot manage what you do not understand. Additionally, when something is unclear, you should ask yourself if it is confusing on purpose. Is it preventing you from making a wise financial decision?

Credit cards have several benefits and can be hassle-free when used and repaid fully on time. The problems begin when you do not pay your statement balance in full each month and create a loan. Many complications arise from this point, and they are difficult to understand.

It is, therefore, sensible not to use a credit card to obtain credit. **Put plainly, do not use a credit card to borrow.** If you must borrow, use another loan type that your lender offers. They are usually easier to understand and manage as well as much cheaper. This way, you could position yourself to obtain all the benefits of a credit card but none of the potential headaches.

233

Personally, after I understood credit cards (it is truly like quicksand), I adopted a different approach. I didn't wait until the due date to pay the statement balance. In our example, that would mean paying on February 21 for transactions between January 1–31. Instead, at each month-end, I obtain the card's *current* balance and pay that amount. That way, I always pay for purchases in the month I made them. No chance to incur interest or charges, miss a payment, or lose any sleep.

Debt Management Strategies

I hope I successfully convinced you that being debt-free is an important financial goal! Of course, it is perfectly fine to work towards achieving smaller goals on your path to becoming debt-free. For example:

1. The amount you owe is too high and you wish to reduce it to a more comfortable level.

2. You may be comfortable with your total loan balance but want to lower the overall interest cost.

3. You are struggling to cover all your outflows and wish to lower your total loan repayments to improve your cash flow.

Obviously, these objectives are interrelated, as an action to achieve one could also affect another. For example, reducing your total loans would also reduce your interest cost.

If you have one of these smaller goals as your short-term focus, let's explore strategies to achieve them. I'll start with two obvious actions.

Search for more surplus cash

Increasing your surplus could achieve all three goals. An increase will improve your cash flow, which you use to pay down your debt either by making a lump sum deposit or regular additional payments. And naturally, the loan reduction will lower the overall interest cost.

You can improve your surplus by:

☞ Reducing your Wants or making lifestyle adjustments to reduce Needs (your cost of living).

☞ Earning more income, usually by extra employment.

☞ Applying windfalls towards paying off your debt. By windfalls, I mean inflows that you did not expect. Examples could be performance bonuses, sales commissions, retroactive salary payments, tax refunds, or even cash gifts.

☞ Selling assets that you do not use.

Stop adding to your debt

Managing your debt is more difficult when you keep adding to it, which is easy to do with revolving loans such as lines of credit or credit cards. **You must make a deliberate effort to stop using them.**

Reduce the debt

Having described the two obvious approaches, let's look at other strategies.

To apply them, you'll need the current balance and interest rates on all your loans, so contact your lenders if necessary. You might already have your current loan balances if you recently did a net worth calculation.

Let's assume you have the loans outstanding in **Table 30.**

Table 30

	Balance	Current Repayment	Minimum Repayment	Excess	Interest Rate
Loans Outstanding					
Credit card A	$15,000	$600	$300	$300	25%
Credit card B	$8,000	$400	$150	$250	15%
Auto loan	$20,000	$350	$150	$200	5%
Line of credit	$3,000	$500	$150	$350	7%
Total loans	**$46,000**	**$1,850**	**$750**	**$1,100**	

Let me explain the headings:

- Balance is the amount to fully repay your loan now (not the original loan amount).

- Current Repayment is the monthly amount you pay now (it should agree to your budget).

- Minimum Repayment is the lowest payment allowed on the credit cards and line of credit (remember, you decide the payment for revolving loans). For the Auto loan, the amount is an interest-only payment.

- Excess is the difference between the Current and Minimum Repayments.

One approach is to focus on repaying the loan with the *smallest* balance first. When this loan is repaid, you focus on the loan with the next smallest balance. Repeat the process until you repay all debts.

Let me explain. One method to get cash to pay your smallest loan is to pay the minimum allowed on the other loans. For installment loans such as the Auto loan, you'll have to request an interest-only payment from your lender (they should grant it for a specific period). You then use the difference between your regular payment and the minimum payment to pay down the smallest loan. Once you fully repay it, you continue paying the *same* amount on the next smallest loan until you also fully repay it. And so on.

In **Table 30**, the Line of credit has the lowest balance of $3,000 and the total loan payments are currently $1,850. The approach is to keep paying $1,850 per month but only pay the minimum of $600 on the other three loans ($300 + $150 + $150). You use the difference of $1,250 to pay the Line of credit, by redirecting $750 from the other loans. If you continue doing this, you should repay the Line of credit in about three months.

Once you fully repay the Line of credit, you focus on the next smallest loan, Credit card B of $8,000 in our example. Again, you continue to pay $1,850 in total each month; this does not change. Your minimum payments on the two other loans are $450 ($300 + $150). Therefore, you pay $1,400 per month on Credit card B, instead of your regular payment of $400, until it is repaid.

You repeat the approach with the next smallest loan, Credit Card A of $15,000. Remember, you keep paying $1,850 per month because the total payment does not change. The objective is to pay as much as possible on one loan at a time. You continue until all loans are repaid.

As I mentioned, you'll need your lender's support to make interest-only payments on installment loans. While it should not be difficult to obtain approval, you'll only know when you ask.

This approach is useful because you feel accomplished and motivated from seeing your debts paid off sooner. You reduce not only the amounts owed but also the number of loans.

> But I hope you acknowledge that there is no magical approach to lower your debt. It requires discipline and commitment. And of course, you must not add new loans, otherwise you are trying to manage a moving target.

Reduce the interest cost

As you know, interest is an outflow that reduces our net worth. Given its impact, even if your current level of debt is affordable, you could still have a goal to reduce the overall cost. There are several approaches.

Highest interest rate

The first strategy uses the general idea previously described in *Reduce the debt,* but it is modified slightly. Instead of focusing your repayments on the loan with the lowest balance, focus on the loan with the highest interest rate. Repay that loan first. Then move to the loan with the next highest rate.

Returning to the example, the loan with the highest interest rate is Credit card A (25%). Follow the same approach as described, with your total monthly payment remaining at $1,850. You allocate it by paying the minimum on the other loans ($450 in total) and the remaining $1,400 ($1,850 – $450) on Credit card A.

Once you repay Credit card A, turn your attention to Credit card B, which has the next highest interest rate. You continue to pay $1,850 in total. Allocate the minimum of $300 to the other two loans and $1,550 to Credit card B until you fully repay it. Repeat until you repay all loans.

If you continue to pay the "Current Payment" on each loan shown in **Table 30**, you will eventually repay them. The two approaches just described are only more targeted efforts. With the first approach, the number of loans you have will reduce more quickly than using the second approach. With the second, you minimize your total outflows because you tackle the cost directly. The second will, therefore, lead to the highest cost saving but your loans do not end as quickly.

Ask your lender

The second strategy to reduce your interest cost is a surprisingly easy one: ask your lender. Once you have a recent history of meeting your commitments, contact your lenders and:

- Request a lower interest rate on your current loan.
- Inquire if there is a cheaper loan option to use.

It never hurts to ask. The response may work in your favor, especially if you try it together with the strategy described next.

Shop around

The third strategy is to shop around and search for better terms. Many individuals switch to autopilot after signing a loan agreement—they do not think about it much. Instead, they should scan the market every so often in case a competitor has a better deal. There might be a cost to switch, but if the "new" loan has much better terms, you could recoup those costs quickly after switching. Of course, you can also try to negotiate the costs down with the prospective lender. Rest assured though, your current lender will not want you to switch. I'll bet they may be more willing to work with you when they know you have another option.

Accelerate loan payments

The fourth strategy is to accelerate your loan payments, for example:

a) Pay before the installment's contractual due date. Let's assume your loan is due at the end of the month. Don't wait until month end; instead, pay at the start of the month. This action avoids the extra interest cost for the thirty

days, and if you do it regularly, it could result in substantial savings. This strategy is easy to apply to revolving loans. Once you are generating surpluses, it should also be easy to alter the timing of your payment.

b) Certain installment loans, like a mortgage, could offer more frequent repayment options, such as paying every two weeks instead of every month. Although the two-week payment is about half of the full monthly payment, the act of paying more often could lead to substantial savings in interest over the loan term. If you are skeptical, check with your lender. The result may astonish you.

Offer collateral

The final strategy is to offer collateral if your loans are currently unsecured. Collateral reduces the lender's risk of your defaulting. Consequently, lenders may be willing to offer a lower rate on a secured loan compared to an unsecured one.

Improve your cash flow

You could struggle to make ends meet if your loan payments are too high compared to your other outflows. In this case, your main strategy would be to ask your lender to extend the loan term, which is a form of refinancing. Lengthening the time to repay lowers your monthly loan payments and reduces your total monthly outflows.

You can also consider consolidating your loans, which means combining your existing debts into one loan. The aim is to make the monthly payments affordable. This approach could have the following benefits:

☛ You may be lucky to get an overall lower interest rate, especially if you combine high-interest debt into a lower-cost loan type (for example, credit card debt into a personal loan).

☛ You could obtain a fixed rate loan, which prevents your installment from increasing for a period.

☛ It could be more convenient to pay one loan instead of keeping track of many.

The major problem with extending repayment is you are not actively reducing the debt. You are only making the payments more affordable. **The significant downside is you usually pay more interest because of the longer term.** If, however, you were able to combine high-interest debt into a lower-cost loan, your total cost could be lower.

Because interest reduces your net worth, you should leave this strategy as a last resort. Instead, focus on actions that either reduce your debt directly or minimize the overall interest cost.

Credit card debt

After reading the two chapters on credit cards, I hope you understand that credit card debt is a minefield. Do your best to avoid it completely. If you already have an interest-bearing balance, repay it as quickly as possible.

If you have credit card debt, here are a few suggestions to help you reduce the balance. Again, there are no shortcuts.

1. The first step is to STOP using your card. Do not add new purchases because you cannot manage a moving target.

2. Never use your credit card to withdraw cash.

3. Never make only the minimum payment. You might never repay the debt with this approach. Instead, pay several times more than the minimum. Pay as much as you can.

4. Do not wait until the due date to make a payment. Pay early and as frequently as possible.

5. If you have any spare cash, use it to make a payment. It does not make sense to have spare cash and a credit card balance. Understandably, you may be uneasy about reducing your cash balance. The wisest financial move, however, is to pay down your card balance immediately. Rebuild your cash over time by saving what you would have paid on your card.

6. Ask your lender to transfer your credit card balance to a cheaper loan product. Lines of credit or other personal loans are cheaper than credit cards. Transferring to another credit card with a lower interest rate is an option, but after including fees, it may not be worth it. Your lender may encourage using a card with a lower rate, but you should focus on other options.

Wrap up

Now you have all the tools you need as a beginner to manage your debt! In the introduction to this Action, I described several types of financial know–how to help you manage your debt. I encourage you to look back at that list and ensure everything now makes sense.

To close, I would like to share a few thoughts about habits, specifically the habits of debt-free people. I hope it inspires you to be an awesome manager of your own debt!

Habits of Debt-free Individuals

At the risk of sounding like a broken record: I believe being debt-free is a core principle of financial independence. Of course, being debt-free may not always be possible. But once we have debt, we should find every viable way to repay it quickly. Being debt-free is more than a goal; it is a state of mind that creates lifelong habits. A habit is an action we do without thinking, and importantly, we can stop bad habits and learn good ones.

Let's complete this Action by looking at some habits of persons who are debt-free. Forming the right habits is critical if you wish to take control of your money. I am not suggesting that individuals with no debt are obsessed with money; they just recognize that money-related stress can be avoided. They are willing to invest time to secure their financial future, whether that means building knowledge or learning new habits.

They live within their means

Critically, they live within their means. Does this sound familiar? We met this idea in the chapter *Core Principles*. If they earn $100, they don't spend $105 because they know if they spend more than they earn the excess is usually funded by debt. In fact, persons who want to be debt-free live on much less than their income (for example, $75) often by "pretending" they earn less. Put another way, they pay themselves first. This means they immediately move their

monthly target surplus out of their operating bank account. Saving is the priority, and they ensure their surplus is available for their medium and long-term goals.

They also realize that most debt is consumption brought forward. We met this idea earlier. Consumption brought forward means buying something now with debt instead of saving and buying the item later with cash (the "buy now; pay later" behavior). They are acutely aware that debt is expensive, and they must minimize the cost to avoid a future decline in their net worth.

They make money from credit cards

Individuals focused on being debt-free understand that a credit card is an expensive form of debt. But that doesn't stop them from owning credit cards. Because they know how credit cards work, they "make money" from the rewards the card offers. They obtain all the benefits and the potential downsides do not affect them.

They have a budget

Debt-free persons live by a budget, which is not a straitjacket. They also do not spend much time actively budgeting. Once they begin to produce regular surpluses, they budget by autopilot because it is now part of their financial way of life.

They pay attention to details

Debt-free persons pay attention to their finances. They know their inflows and outflows in detail. They are unlikely to accidentally miss a bill payment or incur unnecessary fees. They check their credit card statements to ensure all purchases are valid, there are no recurring expenses to cancel, or fees that should be queried or reversed.

In summary, they make the effort to keep more of their money.

They plan and set goals

While debt-free persons enjoy living in the moment, they always have their gaze slightly ahead. It allows them to anticipate what is to come to plan appropriately.

They negotiate

They negotiate anything that could reduce outflows. This isn't the same as being frugal. They are just unafraid to ask for a waiver of fees, a discount on major purchases, or a reversal of a bank charge. Their philosophy is "it can't hurt to ask" and often, the answer is in their favor.

They say "no"

Debt-free persons know when to say no. For example, to the banker who offers unnecessary services or when to turn down invitations to events that they can't afford. They ignore peer pressure and other influences to stay focused on meeting their goals.

Wrap up

Fantastic! We've come to the end of Action 3, and I hope you feel empowered to make wise financial decisions about this critical area.

With your debt properly managed, it is time to focus on arguably the most important Action.

Action 4

Grow Your Income and Net Worth

A Continuous Focus

While the six Actions listed below are critical to achieve financial independence, if asked to choose the most important, I would select the fourth, our current topic.

1. **Control your inflows and outflows**
2. **Protect yourself and your dependents**
3. **Manage your debt**
4. **Grow your income and net worth**
5. **Prepare for major life events**
6. **Invest and plan for retirement**

I emphasize that a strong, full financial picture depends on completing all six Actions. Having said that, growing your income and net worth should always be at the top of your mind. **It should be a parallel activity to the others, meaning stay focused on this goal, even while you tackle the others.**

Although I believe it is the most important, ironically, this is a short section! Why? Because unfortunately, I can't *show* you how to increase your income. I can offer pointers, and I've already shared some ideas along the way. Beyond this, I can't show you how to achieve them because much depends on drive and ambition to succeed.

Let me explain why the Action of growing your income and net worth is critical.

Importance of net worth and income growth

In *Step 7: Calculate Your Net Worth*, I explained that net worth measures wealth. When we describe persons as "wealthy," we intuitively mean they have a high net worth and strong personal finances. Consequently, you want to increase your net worth over time.

Until you begin to invest for growth, your net worth will increase from your unused annual surplus or by reducing your debt. I'll explain the concept of investing for growth soon. I'll also return to this idea in Action 6: *Invest and Plan for Retirement*.

When we begin to take control of our money, controlling our outflows is the major way to increase our surplus. The reality is, however, tightening our belts by reducing outflows eventually reaches a limit. It is difficult to reduce outflows below a certain amount because we will always incur a minimum level of expenses. Besides, watching expenses closely eventually becomes frustrating.

Once reducing outflows is no longer possible, the only way to achieve a continuous surplus is to increase our income. In fact, producing long-term, sustainable surpluses is only possible when we earn enough income. Producing a consistently *increasing* surplus is only possible when our income grows over time.

For most of us, our best working years are between our thirties to fifties. During these years, we make the most income and, importantly, we have the most energy to work. It is critical, therefore, to maximize those years by earning as much as possible.

Approaches to grow your income

You can use various approaches to increase your income, but these aren't get-rich-quick schemes. Sustainable income growth requires you to invest time and be patient with the activity you intend to pursue. Let's look at a few options.

Manage your career upwards

I'll discuss this fully in the next chapter.

Higher education

In *Step 11: Invest in Yourself,* I explained that one of your best investments is to educate yourself. Higher education provides you with new skills, which should position you to earn more income.

Part-time employment

You could obtain more income from a part-time job or developing a second earning stream, such as a side business. As I said earlier, ideally, the second "job" should be something you are passionate about, a hobby you enjoy, or a cause you feel strongly about.

Become self-employed

An option that has the potential for outsized wealth creation is having your own business and growing its profitability. We met this idea in *Step 11: Invest in Yourself.*

The problem with income from regular employment is that it will always be "fixed" until your next promotion, or it stays within a known range if you include bonuses. When you own a business, however, the upsides are 100% yours, meaning your income grows as its profits increase. Naturally, the downsides are 100% yours as well, which is why it is risky.

But from a strictly earning perspective, the potential benefit from having your own business is theoretically unlimited.

Invest

Instead of owning and running a business, you can also consider investing in businesses through the stock market. This approach provides you with similar growth opportunities without having to actively manage a business. This action could improve your net worth because the amount you invest has the potential to appreciate. **Investing in businesses with long-term growth potential is, therefore, a key strategy to build wealth.** I'll return to the concept of investing in the final chapter *The End of Our Journey.*

It is worth recognizing that businesses do not grow indefinitely. They also face general headwinds such as economic slowdowns. During these times, for your net worth to keep growing, you will also need a steady (and ideally, growing) surplus. This leads us back to the importance of increasing your income over time.

Wrap up

Although various paths to earn higher income exist, I expect pursuing employment is the approach many individuals will take. It may even be the first step before exploring others.

When employed, the only realistic way to achieve increased income is to obtain positions of higher responsibility. Consequently, you must focus on long-term career growth. I'll expand on this idea in the next chapter.

Manage Your Career

For many persons, employment will be their major source of inflows. By "employment," I refer to a situation where you work for others, and your primary form of income is salary or wages. If this applies to you, the importance of career development to your future financial self cannot be overstated. **Realistically, to grow your net worth as an employee, your earnings must increase over time. To increase your pay, you must seek roles with greater responsibility.**

I know persons often feel stuck in their jobs and promotions or earning more income could seem unlikely. But it is not as challenging as it sounds. In summary, I believe once you create a track record of success, it opens doors to other opportunities.

Let me give you a few pointers.

Résumé as a career map

Regard it as a living document to be nurtured, continuously checked, and fed.

There is no better guide than your résumé to assess if your career is developing. It is not a document that you resurrect only when you apply for a new job. At that point, you face the daunting task to remember relevant job details since the last time you updated it. Instead, you should regard it as a living document to be nurtured, continuously checked, and fed. Use your résumé to ensure:

☛ You are not stagnating (you should be learning and developing even in your current role).

☛ Each successive role reflects career progression.

Update twice a year

If success is your objective, you should revisit your résumé every few months, or at least twice a year, even if you are not job hunting. The purpose is to add new contributions in your current role. If you're able to update it with meaningful achievements, you would have grown professionally over the past few months. **If you can't add new contributions, you are starting to stagnate in your current position.** It is time to motivate yourself to seek new ways to add value. Or if you believe you have outgrown your current role, you should seek a new one with either your current or a new employer.

Career ladder

When you review your résumé and the roles performed, you should be able to chart how your career progressed. To use an analogy, think of it as building a home. You first imagine the house and then draw the construction plans. Your career is similar. Ideally, you should envision where you wish to be when your career ends, and your résumé should reflect the deliberate steps you took to get there. Of course, your career may not end where you predicted, which is perfectly fine. **But your résumé should reflect the steps you took to advance your career, even if it is different from your original idea.** Each new position should be a higher rung in your career ladder, showing either depth or breadth of experience.

To focus on making proper career choices, consider the points below.

Twenties are the foundation for the thirties

While this sounds a little obvious, a successful career is normally in place by the time you are in your thirties. But to arrive at this success, you must work hard and invest to excel in your *twenties*. "Invest" here means spending time to learn and contribute, even if outside normal working hours.

We must all pay our dues and prove our worth. While you are toiling and frustrated, it's easy to lose sight of a crucial point: you will only reap the benefit of your hard work *later* in your career.

Think of your career like a tree. Think of your career like a tree. It grows into a towering structure of strength from a seed planted years ago. The seeds you plant today are the small tasks and actions that you find irritating or mundane early in your career. If you plant them poorly, you already know what you'll reap in the years to come.

What about if you are in your thirties or forties but have no meaningful career success? Don't dwell on missed opportunities in your earlier years. Start immediately to excel, doing whatever it takes to create a successful track record. Colleagues and bosses quickly notice. Even if your history was not stellar, I'm confident they will put your past aside once you convince them that your current drive to excel is genuine.

Decisions with a five-year horizon

The longer-term outlook helps avoid a rash decision today. Don't decide about new roles or opportunities by thinking only about what exists today. Instead, think about where you wish to be in five years (or a suitable future timeframe). Ask yourself, how would your current decision improve your career five years from now? It doesn't mean that in five years you'll be where you originally planned. Things change for many reasons, which is fine. But the longer-term outlook helps avoid a rash decision today. Additionally, focusing five years ahead will stop short-term distractions from influencing you.

Reach outside your comfort zone

Challenging yourself to move outside your comfort zone builds not only confidence but also breadth and depth of experience. **Taking risks, backing yourself to succeed, and then actually succeeding are critical steps to develop your career.** It is impossible to grow, develop, and achieve meaningful success if you're only doing what feels comfortable to you. Without a proven history of success, your employer is unlikely to offer you more senior roles.

When you are young, it is the perfect time to take risks. You have time either to pursue the risk successfully or to recover from an unsuccessful outcome. Eventually, your personal commitments will become important, for example, getting married or having children. When this happens, you will be less willing to take risks.

Do not job hop unless...

By job hopping I mean situations where persons stay in a role for a brief time before they switch to a new job. Do not job hop unless the new position shows clear and significant advancement. Employers view candidates who continuously change roles as lacking focus, commitment, or ambition.

> At some point, you must settle and commit to a role and an employer. This is the only way to build experience, contribute to an organization, and prove you are ready for more senior duties.

Also, it is worth noting that when you job hop, you will not meet the vesting rules for employer contributions to retirement plans. This statement will make sense when you read the chapter *Enter Corporate Life*.

Do not take a new job only for a higher salary

More income is always better, and a salary or wage increase is obviously a major factor for taking a new job. But it should not be your sole motive. If the job is essentially the same as your current role but pays more, ask yourself why. It could be a more stressful environment, and higher pay is needed to attract candidates. (This is only one reason.)

Sometimes earning a few extra dollars now is not worth it in the long term. Do not allow new positions with limited scope to learn or that have no career growth to tempt you.

In contrast, don't decline an offer solely because it pays less than what you currently earn. Jump at the chance if it offers a fantastic challenge or an opportunity to learn, especially if it builds on your other skills and experience. The future benefit may be multiples of what you currently earn.

Also remember salary is not the only form of compensation. Vacation, flexible working arrangements, a shorter commute, benefits, education support, bonuses, and retirement plans could be as important as base pay.

Be flexible and mobile

Early in your career you are unlikely to have dependents. During this time, adopt a flexible mindset and be open to travelling or working abroad. These are invaluable and eye-opening chances to obtain a wider perspective on life, work, and competition. Exposure to diverse cultures and experiences builds character and confidence.

Beware of social media

We are in an unprecedented time of openness and sharing because of the spectacular growth of social media. While

they provide many benefits, they also have drawbacks when your embarrassing moments, or words uttered emotionally, are available for all to see. An employer could believe these "innocent" posts reflect your character. As such, they may hesitate to offer you a position of greater responsibility. **Remember at more senior levels you are effectively an ambassador for your employer.**

Once something is online, recalling it is nearly impossible. Be careful what you make public and keep asking yourself how it could affect you in the future.

Associate with positive persons who wish to succeed

Daily, you must prove you can collaborate and achieve goals with your colleagues, regardless of their personality. Although you must accept this challenge, whenever possible, try to collaborate with people who view challenges and change positively. Negative persons will always find something to complain about and they drain you emotionally.

Positive people view obstacles as something to work around or overcome. They have an infectious passion to succeed, which attracts others like a magnet. **These similarly minded individuals collectively uplift each other and magnify strengths.** Ensure you are part of this group.

There is a cost to leaving an employer

When assessing the advantages of joining a new employer, it is easy to ignore the cost of leaving your current employer. I am not referring to a financial cost. I'm sure you will ensure you are no worse off financially. But hidden costs also exist:

☛ **Loss of your network.** You may already have an established network within the organization. You

257

know who to call to get something done, especially the informal channels. You also know how to maneuver the bureaucracy. At your new job, however, you start from zero. Sometimes the most difficult part of a job is not understanding your own duties but discovering and building relationships with the people you must rely on, directly or indirectly.

- **No "points" bank.** You earn "points" with your current employer by exceeding expectations and building trust. Having a stockpile of points is important. You "call" on them when you need your boss to be flexible or when you make an avoidable mistake. You'll know when you've run out of points—your boss gets "bossy." With a new employer, you start building points all over again, which takes time.

- **Becoming part of a team.** If you spend enough time in an organization, you're likely part of a team. If the team works well, it can be a rewarding experience. A new job means getting to know new people. This can also be enjoyable, but it takes time and patience to become an accepted member of an already-established team.

- **No safety net.** When you've been employed for a while, it tends to be a safe environment to take risks. Risks could be trying something new or leading a challenging assignment or project. Safety exists because you built trust and have proven accomplishments. Your leaders take chances with you and support you even if an outcome was less successful than planned. This safety would not exist immediately with a new employer.

- **No immediate promotions.** Companies tend to promote persons who have spent time with the organization and have a track record of success. When you move to a new job, you should mentally rule out promotions for two to three years, as it takes time to

contribute. It also takes time for decision-makers to get to know you.

Don't underestimate these intangibles.

Prepare yourself for the inevitable future corporate event

Most companies strive to treat their staff well; however, the reality is companies will not hesitate to take actions to benefit or protect the organization. Staff concerns over these actions will be heard but may not influence the decision. All employees should prepare themselves for the next event that affects staff, such as cost-cutting, reorganizations, or downsizing. **The best way to prepare is to stay as marketable as possible, especially by continuously adding value.**

You remain a valuable employee in several ways:

- **Keep your skills current.** Pursuing continuous professional development, such as formal qualifications or other forms of certification and training. Highly skilled staff will always be in demand.

- **Achieve broad success.** Look for opportunities to lead, manage staff, work with large teams, and obtain cross-functional exposure. Use them not only to build your profile and personal brand through name recognition, but also to grow professionally, add value to your employer, and succeed.

- **Focus on transferable skills.** University degrees and professional qualifications make us specialize, which narrows how others perceive our skills. Battle against this by learning transferable skills, whether learned on-the-job or through training. For example, being a good supervisor or manager is a skill learned by training and experience.

Regardless of your formal education, developing and leading successful teams is a transferable skill that adds value to any company. There are many examples of these skills.

☛ **Network and participate.** As you perform your duties, it is easy to interact with a specific and limited number of people every day. But this small circle does not build your personal brand or help you to learn about the organization and its decision-makers. Build courage and ask for networking meetings with people in other parts of the company, especially in areas where you may want to work. You'll be surprised how it could open doors for you.

Just know, having a series of short meetings is only a start. Follow up with an offer to contribute and participate. Building your name and connecting with others through successes is your ultimate goal.

Wrap up

If employment is your main path to earn income, ensure you invest time in your current role and aim for outsized success, while laying the groundwork for your next role. It is worth keeping in mind that new opportunities are sometimes only offered when you've *already* proved that you can succeed in the prospective role. Your bosses must be able to "see" you in the prospective role and believe you are capable. You demonstrate this ability by contributing *outside* your current role. Don't only do your job; show you can do more.

Financial Advising vs Selling

Until your income increases to a meaningful level, you need to manage your outflows carefully to produce a consistent surplus. This does not mean you should be miserly. You simply live by the philosophy that "it's not what you earn that matters; it's what you keep."

For most of us, our main or only inflow is our salary, while the sources of our outflows seem *infinite*. **Therefore, you need to be vigilant and ensure all outflows give you value for money.** The purchase of financial products is like any other outflow, but it has the added challenge that it sometimes requires long-term commitments. Consequently, you could have buyer's remorse for a long time if you regret your decision later.

Another problem with buying financial products and services is the industry is complex, with many rules that both institutions and individuals must follow. But it is difficult for most individuals to know or keep up with these rules. Consequently, advisers have stepped in to perform a critical role to help persons make wise financial decisions. The industry has many qualified professionals who work hard to help their clients succeed in several areas:

- Insurance
- Accounting, legal, and taxation
- Mortgages
- Banking products and services

- ☛ Stocks and other investments
- ☛ Financial or investment planning

Like most purchases, buying financial advice is a case of *caveat emptor*—buyer beware. The challenge for purchasers is knowing when they are being advised versus being sold a product or a solution. I am not suggesting that the product or solution is necessarily inappropriate. But a difference exists between advice that is genuinely in your best interest versus being offered the best product available.

Genuine advice

How can you tell if advice is in your best interest? One option should be that you take no action. Put another way, the adviser recommends you do nothing. In contrast, being offered the best *available* product means it may *not* be perfect for you, but it's the best *option* the adviser has. The distinction could be slightly hazy because there is a fine line between both.

Even when offered the best available product, it does not mean that the person "selling" is doing anything improper. They might be doing their best to match their employer's products to your specific situation. But if the adviser is genuinely focused on you, one possible recommendation must be for you to walk away. Unfortunately, this choice might not feature often with persons entrusted with selling.

Let's examine other signs that could indicate you are being sold something, instead of being advised:

- ☛ **Does the adviser earn a commission on what they offer?** Obviously, if someone earns a commission, they could try to maximize their income instead of providing you with the best solution.

☛ **Are you presented with less expensive options?** Expensive options may certainly have more features, flexibility, and other benefits. Often, however, the basic and inexpensive are suitable.

☛ **Are the terms of the transaction confusing?** Financial products could be complex, but those that individuals use and need the most are usually straightforward. If the option presented to you is confusing, complicated, or any calculations are unclear, these are signs that you should be careful before proceeding.

☛ **Are you informed of potential downsides?** If you are only aware of the positive aspects of a product or solution, it may be too good to be true. Downsides exist and you should know about both aspects.

☛ **How transparent are the costs or fees?** You should know all potential outflows throughout the life of the product or contract. If aspects are skimmed over, this is a bad sign.

☛ **Are you presented with slick marketing or an easy approval process?** A fancy presentation or a speedy approval does not reduce the importance of your decision. Think about a drive-through loan service where you get an approved loan in two minutes. Convenient? Absolutely. But it leaves you with the same financial strain as a less convenient option if you can't afford it. A fast process does not mean you need to make a fast decision.

No one point by itself automatically means you are being sold something rather than receiving advice. They are, however, certainly warning signs. You must pay attention and assess carefully before trusting that the offer is genuinely in your best interest.

Make a good decision

Faced with these uncertainties, how do you ensure you are making a good financial decision? Here are a few approaches:

- **Research.** If you try to negotiate with someone who has full knowledge and you have little-to-none, you can't blame anyone else if you make an unwise decision. Resources are abundant today and easily accessed, so you can prepare for any financial discussion.

- **Shop around.** The financial services industry is extremely competitive, and you have no reason to accept the first offer you receive. Be patient. It will help you feel more comfortable that you are getting a good deal.

- **Ask others about their experiences.** Seeking feedback is a terrific way to "get behind" the paperwork and understand how a product or transaction works in real life. Often, the way a contract is executed could be a little surprising.

- **Only enter transactions you understand.** This one is super simple but super important. If something is perplexing, don't assume you lack any knowledge or brainpower. It could be deliberately confusing. In which case, it is the perfect time to say, "no thanks."

- **Read the contracts for long-term transactions.** You will need to sign the contract, so make sure you read it. Ask about anything you don't understand. If you cannot get a proper answer, how can you be sure your adviser genuinely understands the transaction themselves?

- **Never agree immediately.** Because it's easy to be influenced by emotions and decide hastily, it is sensible to stop and reflect on the offer. It is especially important with large commitments or transactions that span several

years. During the "cooling-off period" your gut will often tell you if something doesn't feel right—don't ignore it.

When to seek advice

You may begin to wonder if there are situations when you *should* seek advice. The answer is: definitely. While you may feel reluctant to incur this cost, it is important to have a professional's opinion. It might uncover problems or identify benefits you missed. It may also confirm that you have done the major things correctly, creating peace of mind.

You should seek professional advice on technical matters, especially if you are unsure how the result could affect you. Obviously, that doesn't mean you should visit an adviser every time you have a question. Often some quick research can help when you only wish to understand a concept or rule. But at times, you need a better understanding about how it impacts your total financial picture. It may not be possible for you to connect these dots yourself.

Here are some areas where you can benefit from professional advice:

- **Taxation.** Tax laws change often. While basic research could help you understand individual rules, it is best if a reliable professional explains how it fits together in your personal situation.

- **Financial planning.** Once you are in control of your financial affairs, you should begin to think seriously about investing and retirement planning. At this stage, it is sensible to have an experienced adviser review your situation. This is because laws change, and new financial products and solutions are always coming to market. The relationship with your adviser does not have to be ongoing.

265

But a check-up every few years is smart, as professionals keep up to date. It's also smart to speak to an adviser at pivotal life events, for example when you get married. They can help with the family's finances, especially with matters such as tax filings, pre-marriage debt, and so on.

☞ **Legal matters.** It is best if legal professionals handle matters such as wills because of the potential complexities.

☞ **Investing.** If you are unfamiliar with investing, it is easy to confuse paying for advice versus dealing with someone who is trying to sell an investment. Ensure you treat designing your investment plan as a separate activity from executing the plan. Both aspects are independent: do not allow the discussion to overlap.

Wrap up

I am not suggesting that someone is trying to swindle you at every turn. My point is you need to be vigilant. Evaluate every reason someone is asking you to part with your money. Take responsibility for the decision and do not do something because someone else says it is best for you. In practice, this is not complicated, and you'll be surprised at how often you may hear yourself say, "no thanks."

In closing, let me emphasize: although completing all six Actions is important, the faster you earn higher income, the easier it will be to achieve financial peace of mind.

With your radar firmly set on continuously growing your income, let's consider a few major life events and help you plan for them.

Prepare for Major Life Events

Live Your Best Life

By now, I'm sure you remember the six Actions to achieve financial independence. But just in case, they are:

1. **Control your inflows and outflows**

2. **Protect yourself and your dependents**

3. **Manage your debt**

4. **Grow your income and net worth**

5. **Prepare for major life events**

6. **Invest and plan for retirement**

So far, you've controlled your inflows and outflows, protected yourself and your dependents, brought your debt under control, and are continuously searching for ways to earn more income. You are now ready to tackle another big challenge: life.

One of the core principles to avoid financial stress and remain in control is to keep your gaze slightly ahead. Looking ahead allows you to predict and prepare for your future needs. You already applied this idea when you estimated your twelve-month inflows and outflows. That activity required you to anticipate what was likely over the next twelve months. You do the same with events that arise during your life. We all progress through stages: we begin as dependents and grow to be young adults; become middle aged; and then have our golden years. During each stage we must navigate certain events.

The events vary based on our personal goals and ambitions. For most, life events include becoming employed, entering long-term relationships, having children, buying a car, buying a home, or preparing for retirement. Each has distinct financial challenges. While emotionally rewarding, they could have large, potentially multi-year financial effects. When they occur unplanned, they easily become a source of stress.

With a little preparation, however, you could navigate these milestones smoothly, even if they result in a temporary constraint, such as lower savings.

For context, you should recall the four ways to use your surplus:

1. Build an emergency fund.

2. Repay debt faster than scheduled.

3. Save for medium and long-term goals.

4. Invest and plan for retirement.

It often makes sense to approach these one at a time. Success is more likely when we focus on one thing, for example, building an emergency fund. Only when achieved, do you move to the next objective. Once your debt is under control, you have more freedom to focus on medium and long-term goals. Importantly, your debt does not have to be fully repaid, only responsibly managed. Ideally, you are aiming to have only housing-related loans outstanding. While it is better to be debt-free, if you only have good debt outstanding, you can more freely pay attention to upcoming life events.

Unfortunately, I cannot tell you the amount to target for medium and long-term goals. The scope will vary too widely due to personal circumstances, ambitions, and desired future lifestyles. Additionally, for this same reason, it is impossible to cover all events. What I can do is help you understand the financial aspects when setting certain goals.

Life events and your budget

Your companion along this journey will continue to be your budget. If you've worked through the *Steps*, you would have realized that with a little practice, you no longer spend much time actively budgeting. Once you know your inflows and outflows and create your budget, you just "live the budget." You only check in occasionally to ensure you are broadly on track. You are not counting pennies. You've learned a budget is not meant to paralyze you. **It is a picture of your future financial self—painted in dollars—that you are striving to achieve.**

Your budget is important when you think about life events because you must do three things:

1. **Allocate for major life goals.** We started with your target surplus as an amount to build your emergency fund or repay debt. Now, you'll allocate your surplus to the specific medium or long-term goal you wish to achieve, for example, a deposit on a home. You may even have more than one goal. If you jump back to *Step 2: Your Thirty-Day Financial Self*, I showed how to treat allocations from your surplus. Follow this approach to save for each medium-to-long-term goal.

2. **Update your budget when goals are achieved.** When the goal you were saving for becomes an outflow, update your budget to include the item. For example, if you were saving to buy a home, when you take a mortgage, update your budget with the loan installment and other costs of home ownership. You will stop allocating funds to this objective because it is now an outflow. You now begin a new allocation for your next goal.

3. **Reassess goals annually.** At least annually, reassess your medium and long-term goals and adjust your budget for the following year to pursue them. Use any twelve-month period suited to your situation.

As we move forward, I'll discuss the goals we normally pursue in earlier years and progress to those that arise later in life. Of course, your life doesn't have to follow this linear path; I am only using this approach to have a logical flow.

Because I only cover the common goals, if you have a different life event, follow the same general approach I describe:

- Ensure your gaze is slightly ahead to anticipate its arrival.
- Try to understand the financial impact.
- Adjust your budget by allocating funds to achieve the goal.

Let's begin!

Enter Corporate Life

The first major life event for many is entering the workforce. If you intend to stay employed until you retire, corporate life will be your major source of income. As we covered in *Manage Your Career*, your income must increase for your surplus to keep growing. The only realistic way to achieve this while employed is to obtain positions of higher responsibility. Consequently, you must focus on long-term career advancement.

In *Manage Your Career*, I described ways to advance. Although it may be daunting to think about navigating a career for thirty to forty years, many have successfully overcome the challenges you're about to face. Finding an experienced person to be a mentor could be an invaluable resource to provide general guidance and help you succeed.

Let's consider some financial matters you will have to navigate once you begin working.

General

As you begin to earn income, it is important to build good money habits early. Learning and applying the right habits from the start are significantly easier than trying to alter a bad one later. Read that sentence again and use the chapter *Core Principles* as a guide.

When you begin to work, if you are not ready to perform the Actions described earlier, you can begin by doing the following:

1. **Put aside 10–20% of your take-home pay.** Begin with your *first* paycheck, or as soon as possible, and transfer these funds to your savings account. Why? Our expenses easily inflate to reach our income because finding reasons to spend is easy. The earlier you begin this transfer, the easier it will be to adapt to living on the lower level of inflows. If the transfer is immediate and automatic, you effectively pretend it does not exist.

2. **Establish an emergency fund.** This is your first goal for the 10–20% allocation. As you are new to corporate life, you do not have job stability. To navigate this uncertainty comfortably, you need a strong buffer. It may be useful to review *Step 6: Build an Emergency Fund.*

3. **Avoid credit card debt.** Because credit cards are convenient, I'm sure you will get one. If you do, *always* pay the balance due on time, and never go into credit card debt. Always know how much you intend to spend by credit card. Let's say $500. Keep checking your card's current balance. When the balance reaches $500, stop using the card for the rest of the month. **Pay it off in full at month end, not the statement due date, which is later.** Then start using it again at the beginning of the following month.

   The two chapters on credit cards provide you with sufficient information to make wise decisions. If you must borrow, choose another lending product.

Welcome to the world of finance

Once you begin working, you get a rapid introduction to finance. Overnight, you are expected to be familiar with several aspects. Let's take a brief look at the key areas.

Banking

We've already covered an introduction to banking in the chapter *Basic Banking Products*, which should be enough to get you started. Additionally, we covered lending in detail in Action 3: *Manage Your Debt*.

Taxation

One of the largest outflows you will incur over your whole life is taxation. It affects income from almost all sources: your salary and other types of compensation and benefits; income from most investments; profits from sales of assets and investments; and so on. It also arises in other ways, for example, sales taxes, property taxes, and transfer taxes on various types of assets. Taxes can be due immediately or payment deferred until you retire or even on your death. Most people feel the impact of taxation directly, as our employer deducts the amount when we are paid.

Whether paid now or later, taxation reduces your income, and is the main form of revenue for most governments. They impose taxes by law; therefore, you have no choice but to pay. In addition, taxation has many rules and requirements that you must follow, which can often be complex. One usual requirement is that you must complete a return that lists all your income to prove you paid the right amount of tax. It is due by a specific date each year.

Although taxation affects us in many ways, it is strangely easy to ignore. Most likely we ignore it because we either accept we have little choice or because it is too difficult to understand. As one of our largest outflows, we should not surrender so easily. It is important to investigate the taxation impact of major transactions and seek proper advice. Help is important because reducing the amount of tax you pay is possible. Without professional advice, you may overpay.

Insurance

You will meet insurance in the workplace as group life and group health plans. We covered these topics and others relating to insurance in Action 2: *Protect Yourself and Your Dependents*.

Retirement planning

The one financial matter you should pay the most attention to is anything related to retirement. Understandably, when you begin to work, your primary focus is your salary. This is what you use to pay your bills and naturally you want to maximize this amount. But pause and **pay close attention to what your employer offers for retirement**. Your salary is payment for working today. Your retirement plan will pay you when you stop working in the *future*.

You have the advantage of time to let your money work for you.

You may wonder why the emphasis, especially if someone who recently began working has forty years until retirement. The answer is, it's the *perfect* time to put aside funds because you have the advantage of time to let your money work for you. The long timeframe benefits you in three main ways.

Compounding

We met compounding previously and I explained it in detail in the chapter *Interest: The Not-So-Hidden Cost (Part 2)*. It's especially important to your successful retirement, so let me remind you. Compounding refers to the process where interest is added to a starting balance and the new total is invested for another period. At the end of the period, the interest earned is added to the starting balance again, and the new total amount reinvested. And so on.

275

Let's look at an example. If you invest $5,000 for one year at 5%, it will return $250. When you compound, you add the $250 to the starting amount of $5,000 and you reinvest the new total of $5,250 at 5% (assuming the rate is unchanged) to earn $263. The calculations look like **Table 31**.

Table 31

Year	Starting Deposit	5% Interest	Ending Deposit
1	$5,000	$250	$5,250
2	$5,250	$263	$5,513
3	$5,513	$276	$5,788
4	$5,788	$289	$6,078
5	$6,078	$304	$6,381
6	$6,381	$319	$6,700
7	$6,700	$335	$7,036
8	$7,036	$352	$7,387
9	$7,387	$369	$7,757
10	$7,757	$388	$8,144
11	$8,144	$407	$8,552
12	$8,552	$428	$8,979
13	$8,979	$449	$9,428
14	$9,428	$471	$9,900
15	**$9,900**	**$495**	**$10,395**

When you invest your money for enough time, it can more than *double*. In the example above, $5,000 continuously invested at 5% can double in approximately fifteen years. Notice you haven't done anything other than make the initial investment. **If you increase the investment each month or year with an additional amount, you can supercharge your overall result.**

If you're interested, a shortcut exists to estimate the time it will take for the initial investment to double. It is called the "Rule of 72." Just divide seventy-two by the rate of return, which in our example is, $72 \div 5 = 14.4$ years. It's not perfectly accurate but it's close enough to be useful.

Tax deferrals

As explained earlier, you must pay taxes on your earnings; therefore, you receive the net amount. For example, if you earn a gross salary of $5,000 per month, you may receive a net pay of $3,500. "Gross" (or "pre-tax") means before deductions, and "net" means after deductions. Most of the difference between gross and net is a deduction for payroll taxes (there are other smaller deductions).

Let's then assume you fully invest the net amount at 5% per year. In fifteen years, your $3,500 investment would be worth $7,276. Not bad, as it effectively doubles in this timeframe. Now compare this result to the previous example when you invested $5,000 for the same fifteen years. Your investment would be worth $10,395, a difference of ($10,395 − $7,276) $3,119. It therefore makes a *substantial* difference if we invest gross instead of net.

> It makes a *substantial* difference if we invest gross instead of net.

The point to pay attention to is, certain retirement plans or products allow us to use gross earnings for investment instead of net. **If you take advantage of the long timeframe and use gross income, you can supercharge your result.**

Note, you don't escape the taxes due! You'll pay it when you use your savings each year during retirement. But by that time, you would have benefited from nearly forty years of compounding gross income.

Down cycles in the market

Financial markets are not static. They rise and fall regularly, sometimes many times in one day. When you have a long investment timeframe you can ignore these gyrations and focus on the long-term result. This creates considerable peace of mind.

Pensions

A pension is income you receive while you are retired. This is an important aspect of retirement planning and younger people easily overlook it. I did, and to this day, I regret not paying more attention in my first ten years of being employed. The basic operation is:

1. Either your employer or a private provider (for example, an insurance company) offers a plan.

2. You contribute money to the plan.

3. You contribute from either your gross or net income.

4. The funds are invested and grow tax free.

5. If you contribute gross income, you pay taxes as you draw income from the plan in retirement. If you contributed from after-tax income, you do not pay taxes again in the future.

Remember, this is important because when you contribute early, you benefit from compounding over a long time. Additionally, plans have various tax advantages. As the example showed, any opportunity to defer paying taxes could improve your overall return.

Here are some points to bear in mind:

1. **Many pension options.** There are several types of pension arrangements, both company-offered and private. The private options could enhance what your company offers. Or they can be your primary plan if your employer does not offer one.

2. **Eligibility rules.** Plans have different eligibility rules, so you'll have to understand which one is right for you. An example of an eligibility rule is an income cap. If you earn above a certain amount (the "cap"), you may not be allowed to contribute to that plan.

3. **Annual contribution limits.** A plan may have an annual limit for contributions, which means you cannot contribute more than this amount. You will need to know these restrictions.

4. **Free money.** Your employer may contribute to your plan. This is free money, so ensure you know the conditions for their contributions. Let's continue this in the next point.

5. **Employer contributions must vest.** Plans tend to have a "vesting period" for employer contributions. What you contribute is obviously yours, but what your employer contributes does not immediately belong to you. To be treated as yours, you must remain employed for a minimum number of years. This minimum time is called the "vesting period." Once the period passes, their contributions "vest," which means ownership has been transferred to you.

6. **Penalties.** There could be various penalties if you withdraw funds from the plan prior to retirement.

When you begin to work, there are several retirement-related matters to think about. The best way to start is to meet the persons responsible within your organization and ensure you understand what is offered. What I explained above will give you enough information to follow the explanations. It may be useful to have an initial meeting, do some private research, and have a follow-up meeting to discuss the details.

> Being unprepared for retirement is a regret you cannot afford from two perspectives. First, if you wait too long to start saving, you can never recover the lost time. Second, you want to ensure you live comfortably when you retire. The image of yourself living on limited income and forced to watch every dollar you spend should be a situation you want to avoid completely.

Share ownership plan

The last financial matter to mention is that your employer may offer some form of stock or share ownership plan. When you own shares in a company, you are a part-owner.

The basic idea of a stock or share ownership plan is that you get an opportunity to buy shares in the company once certain conditions are met. Certain benefits could also be offered, such as buying at a discounted price or tax breaks. Although these transactions will have limits (and vesting periods), ensure you understand what the offer is and how to take advantage of it.

Because I am only introducing the topic, you should be aware there are other rules.

Wrap up

In addition to the challenge of grasping your new job, you also face a myriad of financial matters to understand. And they are important. If you ignore them, you could put your future financial self at a big disadvantage.

Let's move to the next life challenge we tend to face once we begin to earn income: buying a vehicle.

Buy a Vehicle: The Basics

Owning a vehicle is a thrilling experience owing to the freedom it provides. Buying it, however, is a complicated transaction that has many aspects. For example, deciding used versus new; evaluating models and features; financing options; how much you can afford; insurance; warranties; and the sale and transfer of your current vehicle. The industry has simplified these steps to such an extent that it's as streamlined as buying groceries.

When we discussed loans, I pointed out that the ease of doing a transaction could make you forget it's a big financial decision. **If you did not fully think it through, you could have unexpected costs for several years and serious buyer's remorse.**

In this chapter, I'll explain the main points you should consider when buying a vehicle, so you can enjoy the wind through your hair for many years, regret free! Note, I'll use "vehicle" or "car" interchangeably.

Finance vs lease

Assuming you cannot purchase with cash, you'll have to decide whether to finance or lease.

☛ Financing means taking a loan to buy the vehicle. Either a bank or the dealer could offer the loan, although both are normally in partnership. When you repay the loan, you own the vehicle.

☛ Leasing is paying rent to use the car. At the end of the lease, you do not own the car.

Own vs rent

We arrived at the first major difference between financing and leasing. When you finance, you own the car when you complete the payments. It is your asset and has value. When you lease, you rent the car for a period, which is no different from renting an apartment. You own nothing at the end of the lease. I'll point out that you may have the *option* to buy the car at the end of the lease. To use the option, you pay an additional amount.

Installment size

The second major difference is the size of each payment. Monthly lease payments are normally lower than monthly loan installments for the same vehicle. Lease payments are smaller because you only pay for the vehicle's depreciation plus interest. (Depreciation is the decline in an asset's value from the passage of time and use. Leasing is a type of borrowing, so there is an interest cost.) On the other hand, when you buy, you pay the full selling price of the car plus interest, so you have a higher installment.

You may hear that leasing is "cheaper" than financing. But this is not an apples-to-apples comparison because what you get for each payment is different. But undeniably, leasing does require a lower outflow from you.

Restrictions

The third major difference is when you buy, you own the car and use it as you wish. With a lease, the car belongs to the

dealer; therefore, you must abide by several restrictions. For example, there is a mileage limit per year, and the vehicle's wear and tear must be from "normal" use. If you exceed the mileage limit, you pay an additional cost per mile. The dealer decides what is "normal" wear and tear, and you pay for anything considered excessive.

The related point to consider here is maintenance. With a lease, you pay for routine maintenance but not the more costly services when the car is older because the lease term would have ended. If you own the vehicle, however, you will bear these costs. But again, this may not be an apples-to-apples comparison. If you owned a vehicle for 10 years, you would have stopped paying installments well before the need for expensive maintenance. If instead you leased, you would have paid installments for 10 years continuously.

Complications

The last major difference is that a lease is a more complicated transaction than a loan. You should remember that complex transactions and confusing agreements are red flags. You need to decide if it makes the actual cost of the transaction less obvious. I suggest not to fixate on the lower installment— it is lower for a reason. Read that sentence again. Instead, ensure you understand all aspects of the lease. For example, the interest rate used in the lease (I suspect it may not be easy to find out), fees, as well as every way the potential cost could increase.

Bottom line, if you can live with the constraints of leasing, wish to drive a new vehicle every few years, and are okay with always paying a monthly installment, a lease should work for you. Instead, if you prefer to stop paying an installment eventually, are okay with the increased maintenance as the car gets older, and need the freedom to use the car as you want, then buying is a better choice for you.

A car is not an investment

Let's say I give you this proposal. I know a fantastic asset for sale, and I'll lend you $35,000 for five years to buy it. I also say there are costs for use and upkeep, so I'll lend you an extra $5,000. So, in total over the five years you must repay me $45,000 (including $5,000 interest). You say okay but ask what will the asset be worth in five years. I say $10,000.

What would your reaction be? You'd chase me away because it is a terrible deal!

Persons sometimes equate buying a car with making an investment or having an asset. But, if you agree my proposal is lousy, in essence, this is your car "investment." It's a different analysis if you use it to earn income, but for most, it's a means to an end, which is transport and convenience. Also, you get an emotional high from owning and using it, either as a status symbol or because of the independence it enables. Regardless, ensure you understand that you might be paying a lot of money for transport (and possibly ego).

A vehicle is a depreciating asset—it is worth less over time. I'm sure you've heard that a new car loses on average 20% of its value when it leaves the dealership. It gets worse. After five years, your car could have lost, on average, nearly 65% of its value. Of course, the depreciation varies by brand.

Financially, it is better to view a vehicle as a bundle of costs.

If a car were really an investment, you would earn income from it. But for most of us, the return is intangible: utility. And instead of earning income, you have new expenses from upkeep and other costs. Financially, it is better to view a vehicle as a bundle of costs that you incur over time. The balancing act is deciding whether having reliable transport and the other intangible benefits exceed the total cost of car ownership.

Remember, unless you use it to earn income, a car decreases your net worth.

The hit to your net worth could worsen from two potential costly mistakes:

1. Only thinking about affordability today and not over a longer-term.

2. Not considering the total cost of ownership.

I'll cover these more fully in the next chapter.

Trade-in vs sell it yourself

If you currently own a vehicle and decide to replace it, you'll face two choices. You either sell it yourself and use the proceeds as a deposit on your new car, or ask a dealer for a trade-in. A trade-in means the dealer assigns a value to your old car and reduces the price of the new vehicle by the trade-in value.

It is easy to get a bad deal on a trade-in, so you should treat the two transactions separately. The first is selling your old vehicle. The second is buying a new one. You should test the used-car market to know what your vehicle is worth and compare it to the trade-in value offered. The trade-in value may be lower, which is fine. The difference is effectively the dealer's profit. Consider it as the price of the convenience of doing both transactions with one party (the dealer) and decide if it is reasonable.

Bundling

Sometimes, the dealer may offer you a bundled deal, for example, the price includes insurance and/or maintenance. This sounds good in theory, but you should do a "sanity" check and investigate the cost of each aspect. By adding the cost of the separate parts, you can confirm if the bundled price is truly lower. Also ensure you know the conditions that could end the bundled deal or make it more expensive in the future.

Before wrapping up the basics of buying a car, let me make a few general points.

Marketing and salespersons on commissions

Try not to make a car purchase an emotional decision. Car manufacturers are expert marketers. They easily sway you into wanting something you either don't need or can't afford. Car commercials are especially tempting—they make you want to rush out and buy every new model! Be realistic and practical.

Also remember, vehicle salespersons work on commission, so always be a little skeptical about their "advice." Listen to what they say, ask a lot of questions, but shop around and investigate your options properly before deciding.

Additional features

Usually, cars are sold with a set of basic features and upgrades cost extra. Breaking down each upgrade makes it appear affordable. But the costs add up. Recognize this is an effective method of upselling. To combat the effect, enter the transaction knowing exactly how much you wish to spend and stick to it. This takes discipline when faced with so many "must-have" additional features.

Public transportation

If you are considering buying a car, it could mean public transportation is not available, safe, reliable, or convenient. While these are valid challenges, owning a vehicle comes with its own set of problems: much higher costs, traffic, and inevitable mechanical problems.

Frequency of change

Having an idea of how often you intend to change vehicles may influence aspects of your choice. For example, you may wish to change a car every few years (a financially unwise move). In this case, it makes sense to choose a brand that has a high resale value. Research a little because some vehicles lose value more rapidly, while others are in higher demand in the used market. Also, you should consider picking features and colors that appeal to a wider potential group of buyers.

Wrap up

You must keep several points in mind when deciding to buy a car, whether new or used. In the next chapter, we'll focus on certain financial aspects of your decision.

Buy a Vehicle: Your Budget

In the previous chapter, I explained several points to consider when buying a vehicle. In this chapter, let's explore the costs involved in more detail and the impact on your budget.

Creeping cost base

A car is a bundle of costs, with some value as an asset if you own it. Unfortunately, the costs generally exceed its value as an asset. Bearing this in mind, you have a critical matter to think about before committing to buy or lease a vehicle. You must assess how it affects achieving your other medium and long-term goals.

If you aren't confident about your financial security, you should be careful about adding new costs. Even if you earn a higher level of income, let's say, from a new higher-paying job, you should still be cautious. When we earn extra income, we instinctively wish to improve our lifestyle. A common way is to buy our first car or upgrade to a more expensive one. Both actions permanently increase your cost base because you are stuck with a new, higher level of costs for several years.

You should ensure actions of this nature do not compromise your future financial security.

Think total cost over five years (at least)

I mentioned in the last chapter that you could make two costly mistakes when buying a vehicle:

1. Only considering affordability now and not over the longer-term.

2. Not considering the total cost of ownership.

With any purchase that commits you to outflows for a lengthy period, you must think about your ability to afford it beyond today. Additionally, consider the total costs over this period; in the case of a car, I suggest at least five years. When you try to identify and estimate all costs, you could be surprised that they are much higher than you expected. Let's look at total costs first and then we'll consider affordability.

Create a total cost estimate

You can quickly and easily create a spreadsheet that analyzes total costs over five years, using **Table 32** as a guide. Notice I did the first year monthly, and you'll understand why soon. Use the first-year total to estimate years two to five. You don't have to be overly precise with timing or amounts. The aim is to get an idea of the overall costs to make an informed decision. Consult other car owners about their experiences to help with your estimates.

Let's briefly review the major items.

Installments

Include the lease or loan amount you'll pay.

Table 32

	Year 1												Total					60 mths
	Jan	Feb	Mar	Apr	May	Jun	Jul	Aug	Sep	Oct	Nov	Dec	Year 1	Year 2	Year 3	Year 4	Year 5	Years 1-5
Installments																		
Loan/Lease	300	300	300	300	300	300	300	300	300	300	300	300	3,600	3,600	3,600	3,600	3,600	18,000
Running costs																		
Gas	400	400	400	400	400	400	400	400	400	400	400	400	4,800	4,800	4,800	4,800	4,800	24,000
Insurance	350	350	350	350	350	350	350	350	350	350	350	350	4,200	4,200	4,200	4,200	4,200	21,000
Repairs & maintenance																		
Washing	50	50	50	50	50	50	50	50	50	50	50	50	600	600	600	600	600	3,000
Dealer maintenance			600			600			600			600	2,400	2,400	2,400	2,400	2,400	12,000
Small repairs									700				700	700	700	700	700	3,500
Major repairs													-	-	-	-	-	-
Miscellaneous parts						600							600	600	600	600	600	3,000
Tires															800		800	1,600
Enhancements																		
Music etc													-	-	-	-	-	-
Total Car Cost	1,100	1,100	1,700	1,100	1,100	2,300	1,100	1,100	2,400	1,100	1,100	1,700	16,900	16,900	17,700	16,900	17,700	86,100

Insurance

After the cost of the vehicle itself, insurance could be your next largest expense.

For this exercise, you should get an actual quote. It will only take a few minutes online. When doing so, you'll meet the options we covered in the basics of insurance and the cost of each type of coverage. Obviously, the more expensive the vehicle, the higher the premium. Premiums vary by insurer, so shop around to get a competitive quote.

Gasoline

This expense is easy to underestimate because the cost fluctuates, and your gas usage depends on how much you drive. Be realistic about usage and the price you might pay.

Repairs and maintenance

New vehicles should be serviced by the dealer to preserve your warranty, which could be an expense every three-to-six months depending on use. Your car's warranty will cover major repairs, but smaller repairs could add up. Used vehicles typically require repairs more often and need major part replacements compared to new cars. The costs could be significant when outside the warranty and depend on the vehicle's age and mileage. Manufacturers can guide when certain major parts will need either servicing or replacement. You should investigate these events and include the cost.

Do not restrict your estimate of periodic maintenance to only routine service visits. Also consider accidents that are not covered by insurance because the cost is below your deductible. Don't forget other mishaps, for example we all have hit our gates or walls at home, rubbed a curb when turning a corner, broken a taillight, repaired the air conditioner, and so on. If you lease, confirm how the dealer will treat these incidents.

The examples in **Table 32** are not complete. Include all the costs you realistically expect; don't be optimistic.

Your budget

Let's turn our attention to what you can afford, and yes, the only way to assess this is to refer to your budget. After completing your five-year cost estimate, insert the twelve-month details from year one into your budget and assess the impact on your target surplus. The techniques to apply are those from *How Much is Enough Debt? (Part 2)*.

You should also ensure that if your income declines or outflows increase unexpectedly, you can still afford the cost and achieve your target surplus.

Only after this review, and assuming your information is reasonably accurate, can you feel confident that you are making a wise financial decision.

Emergency fund

Given vehicle repairs can be both unpredictable and expensive (if out of warranty), having a proper emergency fund is an excellent way to deal with this uncertainty.

Wrap up

Whether you decide to buy a used or new vehicle, **keep in mind that the full cost of ownership is not only its price tag.** Consider all costs carefully and evaluate if they will leave you cash-strapped and prevent you from achieving your other goals.

A car is not an investment—it is a depreciating asset, with *additional* costs to use it. Plus, when you include interest on the loan or lease, it seems a bottomless pit of outflows. To be clear, I am not suggesting we should not own vehicles. I'm only underscoring it is an important financial decision.

Decide wisely.

Couples' Finances: Long-term Relationships

Being in a relationship is one of life's best experiences. As you get to know your partner, romance is the priority, and the time is emotionally charged. One reason why it's so great is "real life" does not interrupt for a while. But once you commit to a long-term relationship, life's important practical aspects become important. Money is one of the larger issues. Let's explore some financial aspects of entering a long-term relationship.

A long-term relationship is a commitment to share your life with someone, whether formally or informally. In this chapter, I'll refer to both these situations as "marriage."

A must-have conversation

A marriage has many aspects and changes, for example, living arrangements, sharing your life, and of course, your financial relationship. For many of us, talking about money early in a relationship is taboo. We aren't ready to ask our significant other about earnings, debt, or retirement plans. Although you may have discovered some of your partner's financial beliefs, such as their approach to spending and saving, or expensive hobbies and habits, realistically, these matters are less important early in the relationship.

Everything changes, however, once you commit to a life together. Money matters now affect you as well as your partner, and potentially your family, if you intend to have children. Consequently, before getting married, it is important to know

your partner financially, as ideally, you should plan your major financial goals together.

At some point, you both need to share details about your finances and discuss your philosophy and approach to different areas. Obviously, this should be an honest discussion to:

- **Learn about your partner.** Behaviors such as feeling entitled to unaffordable luxuries or extreme frugality may have root causes. Understanding why behaviors exist could help you relate better to your partner when discussing options.

- **Avoid future disagreements.** Arguments about money can derail an otherwise solid relationship.

- **Ensure your financial goals are compatible.** Goals could include buying a home, saving for your children's education, or plans for retirement. When you are ready to commit to a long-term relationship, you should know your partner's approach to the important matters, because philosophical differences could become big problems later.

- **Understand your partner's financial situation.** A pre-marriage financial conversation is necessary to learn about their financial health, just as you'd want to know about their physical health. Undisclosed large loans, outstanding bills, or credit card debt will eventually haunt the relationship.

Let's look at a few areas in more detail.

Pre-marriage assets

Either partner may have existing personal assets, such as property, land, cash, or investments. Together you'll need to understand how various questions will be answered. Will there be a prenuptial agreement, especially if a partner already has children? Will these assets be jointly owned eventually? Could they be used as collateral for new loans? And so on.

Pre-marriage debt

More important than assets is debt. Partners could have pre-existing debt from student loans, car loans, or credit cards. These could eventually strain a marriage, especially if one partner is in greater debt. You'll need to decide together how to handle this situation. Will the debt be serviced out of joint income or individually? Should the indebted partner try to repay quickly? Deciding on an approach is important, especially if you expect to incur debt together later.

Children

Key considerations will depend on whether either partner already has children, or if not, whether you have a common view on having children.

If one partner already has a child, does that partner bear the child's upkeep costs fully or only pay child support? These funds would not be available to pursue joint goals. In addition, the partners will need to decide how to distribute benefits from life insurance policies, retirement plans, or other assets when the partner with the child passes away.

If neither partner has children, then deciding to start a family ideally should be planned, with both partners on board. Children can be an irreplaceable source of joy and pride, but do not underestimate the costs.

Joint or separate bank accounts

Partners could choose to manage their finances differently; each approach has pros and cons. Key questions to be answered

would include whether to use joint or separate bank accounts and how to cover household expenses. The choice may depend on the level of financial independence each partner desires. Approaches could include:

- Separate bank accounts, with each partner responsible for specific expenses.

- Partners contribute agreed amounts to a joint account and pay household expenses from that account (see Income inequality below).

- Finances are fully integrated.

Income inequality

Another sensitive issue could be income inequality. When one partner earns more than the other, situations could arise where finding the right compromise is tricky. I touched on one example in the previous paragraph. For household expenses, do both partners contribute equal amounts or do they contribute in proportion to their income?

Communicate

Given the potential challenges, communication must be continuous. The financial conversation does not stop after the initial pre-marriage discussion. It should happen regularly, to ensure that you achieve your joint objectives and both partners take part in financial decisions.

Wrap up

After committing to a long-term relationship, the next step could be tying the knot with a ceremony. Let's briefly examine some financial points.

Couples' Finances: Newlyweds

Planning a ceremony to pledge lives to each other can be an emotional roller coaster. On one hand, you're euphoric, and on the other, you're stressed from the numerous decisions needed. In addition, planning a wedding can be a financial nightmare. One must balance one's dreams and ambitions with the reality of having to pay for them.

My focus in this chapter is to discuss the cost of these ceremonies, which could have different names. I'll refer to either "wedding" or "ceremony" to cover them all.

The cost of a ceremony could be shockingly high, or at least, potentially more than you intended. When creating your perfect day, here are a few financial points to consider.

Avoid debt

By now, I hope you understand you should avoid incurring debt easily. Either abandon the purchase entirely or wait until you have saved enough to pay with cash. "Buy now; pay later" is a recipe for future financial hardship. This principle especially applies to these ceremonies. **Do not borrow to pay for the event.** The last thing partners should do is start their married life by borrowing to pay for costs that have only enduring emotional value.

Alternative use of funds

Ceremonies could range from elaborate functions to intimate events, depending on which you prefer or can afford. While

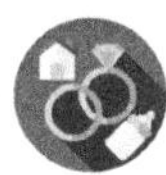

memories last a lifetime, what you spend is only for one day and one event in your lives. You should, therefore, not allow short-term decisions to affect you for years to come.

Think about life after your union. The ultimate question to answer is whether you could use those funds for future important outflows. For example, do you need a deposit to buy a home? The answer will shape the amount available to spend on the ceremony. There might be a better use of cash, which will advance your life together, as opposed to a one-day celebration.

You're trying to arrive at the right balance to have a more solid financial start as a couple. You're weighing the importance of a fantastic memory versus a less costly affair. Obviously, this is a personal judgment call. But do not decide based solely on your dreams for that day. Spend time thinking about what comes after.

Estimate the cost of your event

A wedding can be expensive; therefore, before you begin, it is sensible to estimate the total cost. This activity will also prepare you for conversations with various service providers, such as your wedding planner, caterer, or photographer. Eventually the question "how much are you willing to spend?" will arise and you should be ready to respond and negotiate.

Unless you were married previously, it is unlikely you can easily list all the costs of your choice of ceremony. Researching or hiring an experienced wedding planner could be helpful with this aspect.

To illustrate the types of costs, examples are shown in **Table 33**. The amounts used are only to illustrate how the scenarios work (explained next). It is not possible to estimate actual costs because ceremonies will differ due to cultures, personal tastes and so on.

Table 33: Wedding Budget

	1	2	3	4		1	2	3	4
Scenario	1	2	3	4		1	2	3	4
Guests Invited	100	150	200	250		100	150	200	250
Unidentified extra	20	20	20	20		20	20	20	20
Declined	-	-	-	-		-	-	-	-
Guests Accepted	120	170	220	270		120	170	220	270
	NUMBER				Price per	**ESTIMATED COST**			
Invitations	50	60	80	100	15	750	900	1,200	1,500
Wedding Planner						5,000	5,000	5,000	5,000
Venue/Décor									
Rental						7,500	7,500	7,500	7,500
Decorations						5,000	5,000	5,000	5,000
Tables	15	20	25	30	40	600	800	1,000	1,200
Chairs	120	170	220	270	10	1,200	1,700	2,200	2,700
Linen	15	20	25	30	20	300	400	500	600
Adornments	15	20	25	30	20	300	400	500	600
Food & Drink									
Food	120	170	220	270	50	6,000	8,500	11,000	13,500
Non-alcoholic drinks						1,000	2,000	3,000	4,000
Alcohol						3,000	5,000	7,000	9,000
Cake						750	750	750	750
Music						1,500	1,500	1,500	1,500
Photos/Video						3,500	3,500	3,500	3,500
Groom's Suit						1,500	1,500	1,500	1,500
Bride									
Dress						3,000	3,000	3,000	3,000
Shoes & Accessories						250	250	250	250
Hairstyling						500	500	500	500
Make-up						400	400	400	400
Bridal Party									
Groomsmen's suits	3	3	3	3	750	2,250	2,250	2,250	2,250
Bridesmaids' dresses	3	3	3	3	1,000	3,000	3,000	3,000	3,000
Flowers						500	500	500	500
Miscellaneous									
Bouquet/corsages						600	600	600	600
TOTAL						**48,400**	**54,950**	**61,650**	**68,350**

Scenarios

When planning your event, you can make a better financial decision by evaluating the potential costs under different scenarios. The example uses different guest levels for the scenarios because guest numbers drive many other costs, such as venue size, catering, and bar.

You could create a spreadsheet that looks like **Table 33**. The input cells will be those that are lightly shaded. When an amount entered is applied to the "Price per" item, a total cost is calculated. Let's assume wedding invitations cost $15 per invite. When you enter the number of guests in scenario 1 to 4, the spreadsheet should calculate the total cost of the invitations for each scenario. The total cost will be the price per invitation multiplied by the total number of invitations. For example, 50 invitations in Scenario 1 produces a result of $750 (50 x $15).

Other costs that do not depend on a cost per item are entered directly in the Estimated Cost columns in the scenario you are testing.

Of course, the activity could be simpler if you know the total amount you want to spend. But deciding on the final guest list and the total cost is normally a balancing act. In which case, seeing the cost under different scenarios could prove useful.

Scope creep

One of the bigger risks in planning a ceremony is scope creep. This means you start off planning for a particular wedding size or cost and then you begin to make changes. It could be to change the venue or menu, add guests, or several minor changes, with each change adding to the overall cost. Sometimes they snowball and affect other areas, for example, extra guests will increase catering, bar, seating, servers, and venue size. While you'll have to be flexible, your challenge will be to limit scope creep to an acceptable level.

Cost-effective decisions

The cost of nearly every wedding item can range from low to extravagant. Understandably, you might want the best in every area, but the total cost could easily get out of control.

At these times, you should remind yourself that the event is not about each piece of the wedding, but the result of the whole. More importantly, the most attention and memory will be about you. Making cost-effective decisions along the way usually does not detract from the whole event. Often only the most discerning persons can tell the difference between an inexpensive and expensive item. Once the event is about celebrating with friends and family, the majority are unlikely to realize (or even care) if you chose the more cost-effective option.

Before turning to life as newlyweds, the other likely major cost to mention would be the honeymoon. The principles discussed in this chapter continue to apply. Ensure you know what you can afford without going into debt and plan a honeymoon for this amount. Don't hesitate to leave the expensive dream destination for a vacation after your life together is more settled.

After the wedding

Let's summarize our discussion so far. **Your objective when considering the financial aspects of a wedding is not to regret the size of your bill later.** I previously mentioned that this could be a potentially stressful time. One way to gain control and reduce stress is by managing the overall cost.

Once the wedding and honeymoon are over, "regular" life will become more important. Money will feature again in many decisions to come. Let's look at a few important ones.

The family budget: spend vs save

Preparing a personal budget is straightforward but creating a family budget could be more complicated because another person is involved. But the same benefits from using a personal budget apply to a household budget. Once created together, it becomes a guide that removes guess work and emotion from major decisions, which should avoid unnecessary disputes.

The extent to which you combine your finances will guide what you include in the household budget. The aim should be to lay out a plan to achieve your top financial goals as a family, for example, buying a home, children's education, and retirement.

Debt

Debt has the potential to become complicated in a marriage. For example, if partners have pre-marriage debt, you'll need a plan to address this before adding new joint debt. Additionally, purchases such as buying a home may require both incomes to support the loan, which limits what each partner can do on their own. Again, the approach depends on the extent to which you combine your finances.

Major purchases

It may be a good strategy to set ground rules for major purchases. Let's say partners manage their finances separately and one partner wants to take a loan to buy an expensive vehicle. This would mean less overall cash available for *future* joint purchases and goals. An approach could be to set a limit and both partners agree to discuss purchases above this amount before committing. An expensive purchase could then possibly form part of the family's goals and be properly budgeted. Or it is dropped because other important goals require priority.

Emergency fund

Life has a way of throwing expensive curveballs. Having a household emergency fund will allow partners to be prepared for those events and avoid financial distress.

Insurance

Loss of income, sudden death, or serious illness are all events that arise unexpectedly. They might destabilize a household's finances because one partner must support the family single-handedly. This is a particular concern when the family depends on a partner who earns a much higher income. We covered these events in Action 2: *Protect Yourself and Your Dependents*. There, I explained the benefits of using insurance to protect against any resulting financial burden. Here's a quick reminder of the options.

Life

In the event one partner dies prematurely, the surviving partner could use the proceeds from life insurance in several ways. It could be a source of replacement income, a means to repay debt, or used to meet future obligations such as paying for children's education.

Disability

Disability insurance could be a source of financial relief if one partner becomes disabled and unable to work. Partners employed in jobs that pose a higher risk of injury should pay particular attention.

Health and critical illness

Medical care is expensive and is likely to increase over time. Critical illness and health coverage could help partially fund the cost of a serious medical problem.

Retirement planning

Even if partners had already individually begun retirement planning before marriage, revisiting the plan together is a good idea. Or if they did no active planning previously, it is certainly a smart idea to start when you get married.

Estate planning

"Estate" refers to whatever assets and liabilities you leave when you pass away. While estate planning is an advanced topic, two aspects are important and straightforward to understand.

Wills

A will is an important legal document that describes how you want your estate shared when you die. If you die without a will (referred to as "intestate"), a court decides what happens to your estate. Having a formally prepared will could protect your estate from excessive expense (for example, legal and probate fees) or lawsuits from unhappy heirs.

A will is especially important if the people you excluded could make a claim on your estate. This doesn't mean you are immune from lawsuits, but when your wishes are documented, your situation should be stronger.

Beneficiaries

After marriage, each partner should review existing investments, life insurance policies, retirement plans, bank accounts, and other financial contracts to update their named beneficiaries (or add a joint holder). If a partner dies, having up-to-date beneficiary details will simplify the legal process to access assets.

Wrap up

Family finances are a shared responsibility, requiring both persons to participate actively. If one partner bears the burden alone, it could eventually lead to strife. In addition, partners should avoid a situation where one has greater knowledge than the other about the family's finances. The less familiar partner could be in difficulty if the more knowledgeable partner becomes ill or unavailable, or worse, decides to separate.

Worrying about money does not bring partners closer together—it drives them apart. And there are several matters to consider. The challenges can be overcome but having shared goals would certainly make the situation easier. Obtaining advice from a qualified financial adviser also may be helpful with structuring the financial aspect of your life together.

Let's now turn our attention to the largest purchase most of us will make: buying a home.

Buy a Home

I already covered a lot of what you should know when buying a home in Action 3: *Manage Your Debt*. I'll pull it together for you here but refer you to the detailed explanations in the earlier chapters. I also explained several of the terms in the chapter *Speak and Think Like a Bank*. I recommend revisiting that chapter before reading this one.

Let me start by reminding you that lenders love granting loans to buy homes. To assist qualified buyers, they made the approval process ultra-simple. This convenience, however, creates a problem. You can be seduced by the painless process and forget the importance of the loan itself. Given the potentially large amount and lengthy period involved, it could be your biggest financial decision. You need to evaluate carefully before committing.

What is a mortgage?

We first met home loans in the chapter *Speak and Think Like a Bank*, and I explained a "mortgage" is a loan to buy a home. When you borrow to buy a home, you pledge the property as security for the loan. This pledge is called a "mortgage" or a "lien." If you do not pay as agreed, the mortgage gives lenders the right to "foreclose" on the property. Foreclosing means lenders take physical possession of it. Their ultimate purpose is to recover the funds lent. If necessary, they will sell the house and use the proceeds to repay the outstanding loan balance.

Action 5

The legal document you sign is commonly called a mortgage "deed." Another document you sign is the loan agreement (often called a "promissory note"). It describes the terms of the loan, such as the amount of the debt, length of the loan, the interest rate basis, and so on.

A mortgage is a secured loan (remember, you use the house as "security"). It reduces the lender's risk of your defaulting by giving them a way to recover their funds. It also benefits you because lenders offer a lower interest rate on mortgages compared to other types of personal debt.

Amortizing loans

Mortgages are amortizing loans, with a term potentially up to thirty years. An amortizing loan means each installment has two parts: an amount for interest and an amount for principal. The principal portion reduces the loan balance. The interest portion is the lender's income. Although you pay the same installment each month, over time, more of the payment reduces the principal.

An amortization schedule for a fifteen-year loan could look like **Table 34**. I presented it in years, but in practice it is monthly. To the right, I showed the installment split between principal and interest. Notice more of the payment is applied to principal as the loan declines.

Down payment

You will have to make a down payment on the property. Let's say the house costs $500,000 and the lender requires a 20% deposit. This means you pay $100,000 and borrow $400,000. A larger deposit will obviously reduce the loan and overall interest cost.

Table 34

Year	Starting Balance	5% Interest	Payment	Ending Balance	Interest	Principal	Total
1	500,000	25,000	(48,171)	476,829	25,000	23,171	48,171
2	476,829	23,841	(48,171)	452,499	23,841	24,330	48,171
3	452,499	22,625	(48,171)	426,953	22,625	25,546	48,171
4	426,953	21,348	(48,171)	400,129	21,348	26,823	48,171
5	400,129	20,006	(48,171)	371,965	20,006	28,165	48,171
6	371,965	18,598	(48,171)	342,392	18,598	29,573	48,171
7	342,392	17,120	(48,171)	311,340	17,120	31,052	48,171
8	311,340	15,567	(48,171)	278,736	15,567	32,604	48,171
9	278,736	13,937	(48,171)	244,502	13,937	34,234	48,171
10	244,502	12,225	(48,171)	208,556	12,225	35,946	48,171
11	208,556	10,428	(48,171)	170,812	10,428	37,743	48,171
12	170,812	8,541	(48,171)	131,182	8,541	39,631	48,171
13	131,182	6,559	(48,171)	89,570	6,559	41,612	48,171
14	89,570	4,478	(48,171)	45,877	4,478	43,693	48,171
15	45,877	2,294	(48,171)	(0)	2,294	45,877	48,171

Mortgage insurance

If you cannot make the minimum deposit (usually 20%), the lender will require you to get mortgage insurance. Its purpose is to protect the lender if you default. *You* pay the premium for the insurance, which is usually added to your monthly installment. **The premium consequently increases the cost of the loan.**

Mortgage insurance is *different from* homeowner's insurance. The premium you pay for homeowner's insurance protects *you* from various risks. Mortgage insurance protects the *lender*.

Loan-to-value

Usually when your loan-to-value (LTV) is at an acceptable level, you can request to cancel mortgage insurance. LTV is an easy calculation. It is your current loan balance divided by your home's current value. Returning to the example, if the lender requires a 20% deposit, it means the LTV requirement is $400,000 ÷ $500,000 = 80%.

Once your LTV is above 80%, you may have to buy mortgage insurance. A high LTV means you are a greater risk to the lender.

If your LTV is less than 80%, you should not need mortgage insurance; consequently, you should monitor when your LTV comes into line. For example, if your loan balance becomes $375,000 and your home value stays at $500,000, your LTV is 75%. You should no longer need mortgage insurance, and you should ask to stop the premium. Pay attention because it is a cost to you.

Credit score

As explained in *Speak and Think Like a Bank*, a credit score summarizes a person's credit report in a three-digit number. It is a major factor when the bank quotes an interest rate. A high credit score means you have a history of good credit behavior: you consistently pay what is due on time. It should help you obtain a lower interest rate. A low credit score means you pose a higher risk of default. Your lender may, therefore, assign a higher interest rate to your loan.

Fixed vs variable interest rates

Mortgages are either fixed or variable rate loans. Given its long life, understanding the implications of both is important. The first point to remember is interest rates are essential to the financial system and they continuously change.

In a fixed rate mortgage, your lender sets a period (for example, five years) during which the loan's interest rate and installment do not change. If general interest rates increase, a fixed rate loan would be in your favor. If, however, general interest rates fall during the set period, your installment will not decline.

In contrast, the interest rate on a variable rate mortgage could change when market interest rates adjust. If the rate changes, your installment is recalculated. This could be favorable if interest rates decline because your installment decreases. Of course, the reverse is also true. If interest rates rise, your installment and the cost of the loan will increase.

Prepayments

When you make a prepayment, the entire amount should reduce your principal balance, which lowers the total interest cost. Remember, lenders may not allow prepayments or they may charge a penalty if your loan has a fixed interest rate. Alternatively, your loan agreement may allow it without penalty once you give suitable notice. Having the flexibility to prepay is important, and **I consider it a *must-have* feature in a loan.**

Transferability / Switching

Borrowers are often encouraged to switch from their current lender to another. You could benefit by receiving better terms and a cheaper mortgage. To have as much flexibility as possible, ensure you confirm the rules for transferring before you commit to a loan.

Mortgage must do's

Here are a few suggestions for prospective buyers:

- Don't assume your regular bank is giving you the best deal. A mortgage commitment is too important and expensive. Shop around because minor differences in rates or fees can make a substantial difference over time. Use your loan calculators to help.

- Don't assume the terms offered are "take-it-or-leave-it." Negotiate everything, especially fees. Remember, lenders love residential mortgage loans—make them work for yours.

- Ensure you know the conditions for prepayments and how much is allowed.

- Understand the rules to switch to a different lender.

- Know how much you can afford *before* you enter a loan conversation. I'll discuss this in more detail below.

Homeowners insurance

Lenders will require you to insure the property. Of course, insurance is important because it protects your asset (for example, against fire), but it is an extra cost to factor in.

Tax deductions

Some governments offer incentives to homeowners (especially first-time homeowners) that can lower the amount of taxes you owe. It is important to understand which tax incentives apply to you. They could be valuable to help offset the costs of a mortgage and being a homeowner. Researching or consulting a qualified tax adviser could be crucial to learn about the options available and how to take advantage of them.

How much can you afford?

Your mortgage could span twenty to thirty years and could be your single largest loan. Consequently, it is important you

carefully consider how much you can afford. It's a delicate balance between choosing a location to live for many years and ensuring you can pay for it.

Only your budget matters

We've covered this in detail in the chapters *How Much is Enough Debt? (Part 1 & Part 2)*. The critical matter is knowing what fits in your budget, but still allows you to achieve your other medium and long-term goals. Only you can do this; do not rely on a lender's recommendation.

Part of the mortgage process is becoming "pre-qualified." In this step, lenders evaluate your application *before* you start your home search, and they inform you what loan size you qualify for. You use this amount to guide your price range.

Pre-qualification is useful because it simplifies the process and helps streamline your search. The problem to avoid is acting on a pre-qualified amount that is *higher* than what you can comfortably afford. For this reason, use your budget to make your own estimate. Apply the techniques from the chapters *How Much is Enough Debt? (Part 1 & Part 2)*.

Cynically, I could argue that pre-qualification is also a marketing technique to influence you to buy a more expensive home. Who wouldn't want to live in a better neighborhood or have a home with more space or amenities? I remember personally being pre-qualified for a mortgage. The amount I was approved for was twice what I had estimated for myself. I stuck to my estimate, comfortably afforded my mortgage, and had no regrets.

Payments under different scenarios

One of the more common mistakes is deciding on a loan based solely on your current situation. If you were taking a three-year personal loan, focusing on your ability to repay today could be suitable because the term is short. Mortgages, however, have three challenges:

1. They span most of your working life.

2. The interest rate for variable rate mortgages is adjustable at short notice.

3. When the set period for the fixed rate ends, a different rate could apply to the new period.

Owing to these challenges, you must simulate what your payment range could be, as explained in the chapters *How Much is Enough Debt? (Part 1 & Part 2)*. **It is especially important to assess the potential impact of interest rate increases for variable rate mortgages.**

Worst case

You should also think about the worst realistic event that can happen to you. Adjust your budget to reflect this event to assess how it changes what you can afford. You shouldn't automatically assume the worst event to be job loss. It may be more realistic to assume that you'll get another job at a lower income. The situations would obviously vary by personal circumstances. For example, you may have elderly parents and supporting them financially in the future could be a realistic possibility.

After this analysis, you may decide to take a slightly smaller loan to ensure your budget has enough cushion to withstand these events. You could achieve a smaller loan by:

☛ Saving longer to make a larger deposit.

☛ Purchasing a lower cost home.

☛ Accepting the risk of a larger loan but committing to prepay an amount by a specific date.

Costs of homeownership

You must also include in your budget the upfront and ongoing expenses that homeowners incur.

Upfront costs could include insurance, legal, and other fees. Ensure you have a full picture of these costs, and I strongly recommend not including these amounts in your loan. **Pay them at once, even if it means saving more initially.** Your mortgage will already be large. Do not inflate it, and worse, pay interest on these items for many years.

Examples of ongoing costs are property taxes, homeowner's insurance, repairs and maintenance, and utilities. Do not only think about the loan installment when you assess how much you can afford. Obtain a reasonable estimate of the new costs and include them in your budget to understand how it affects your other goals. When you factor in all costs, you might decide that a smaller loan is financially wiser for you. Or instead, you could feel confident that you can comfortably afford the commitment, creating invaluable peace of mind.

Wrap up

You should now have enough information to feel empowered to make a good mortgage decision! But a question that could arise in your mind is whether you should buy a home at all. Should you rent instead?

We explore this question next.

Buy vs Rent a Home

Finding a place to live usually means deciding between buying or renting a home. There are strong views about both approaches, such as buying is expensive or renting is paying the landlord's mortgage. Let's break down the various arguments to help you make a wise decision. What you'll discover is the "right" answer depends on personal preference and a mix of emotional and financial factors.

Permanence vs transience

A major factor is knowing what kind of person you are. Are you content staying in one location for a long time or prefer to be mobile? Buying a home incurs substantial upfront costs. If you are unsure about committing to one location, you would be better off renting to avoid these costs. Renting could, however, have its own downsides. For example, if your property owner does not renew your lease, you must deal with the uncertainty over where you will live.

Location

Some locations could be attractive because of a shorter commute, better schools, a nice neighborhood, or proximity to family. If you have a specific location where you want to live, buying or renting will depend on what is available.

Undesirable rental units

You may choose to buy because you are not satisfied with the options available for rent. They could be undesirable because they are unsafe, unsanitary, or rundown, or have unreasonable lease terms.

Desire to customize

Some persons want to alter their home to their preferences, for example, repainting, modernizing, changing interior designs, or adding outdoor structures. The benefit of owning is that renovations do not need a landlord's approval.

Responsibilities

Owning a home could be frustrating due to responsibilities for repairs and maintenance. Homeowners must take care of burst pipelines, leaking roofs, termite problems, and everything in between. And of course, homeowners bear the cost. Whereas with rentals, these are the landlord's burden. Your personality and capability might determine which approach is more appealing.

Retirement

If you prefer not to rent during retirement, then you must eventually buy a home. The wish to avoid renting is understandable. If your retirement finances are weak, it is sensible to avoid fixed payments when you stop working. Additionally, owning a home could give you options in retirement. For example, you could sell it and move to a less expensive house, providing you with cash in the process. Or you could leave your home as an inheritance.

Let's now look at some financial aspects.

Investment

Some view buying a home as either a form of "forced" savings or an investment. The idea has merit and arises because you "must" repay your mortgage. As you pay, the equity in your home increases. As a reminder, equity is the difference between the value of your home and the amount you currently owe on your mortgage. As the equity grows, you gradually own more of an asset that could appreciate.

Prices also decline

The point to recognize is housing markets also decline, although some locations may be more resilient than others. **Do not expect values only to increase.**

Although housing markets might be active, they are not liquid. A market is "liquid" when there are enough buyers and sellers to allow values to be easily realized. If there are not enough buyers when you are ready to sell, you may be forced to accept a lower price.

Down payment

Taking a mortgage to buy a home requires you to make a down payment. As explained in the previous chapter, the requirement could be 20% of the value of the house, which is a hefty sum.

Costs

You could view the cost of both options in three parts:

Upfront

A homeowner's upfront costs will obviously include the down payment, which isn't really a "cost," but you need funds

for it. But there will be costs such as legal fees. For renters, upfront costs should be limited to a security deposit, which the landlord returns if the property is undamaged.

Rent vs mortgage payment

A mortgage payment will be higher than renting a comparable home in the same location. It's worth bearing in mind this is not a direct comparison. When you rent, the payment is to use a space: you do not own anything. Whereas when you pay a mortgage, you are slowly buying an asset.

Ongoing

Homeowners have several ongoing costs to maintain and protect their home. The ongoing costs for a renter, however, would be comparatively smaller. They could include renter's insurance (which is cheaper compared to homeowner's insurance) and utilities (if not included in the rent).

Metrics

When trying to decide whether renting or buying is more beneficial, you can use two metrics to assess if rental rates or house prices are reasonable. If you're familiar with investment terms, you'll realize the metrics convey similar information as a stock's dividend yield and price earnings (PE) ratio.

Rent yield

This is also called rent-to-price ratio, and it is the property's annual rental divided by the property's current value. For example, if a property worth $1,000,000 can be rented for $70,000 per year, the rent yield is ($70,000 / $1,000,000 =) 7%.

How is this helpful? Think of it like this. If a property owner makes a low return, let's assume zero (to illustrate the point), then it is better to rent because renting is cheap. In this case, the renter pays $0 for the space. If the yield is high, it means the property owner earns a high return, which suggests it is a bad idea to rent because it is expensive.

Price-to-rent ratio

This ratio is the inverse of the rental yield. Using the example, you flip the calculation, which means the price-to-rent ratio is ($1,000,000 ÷ $70,000) 14.3.

If you know the historical ratio for properties in the location that you're scouting, this ratio could be useful. For example, if the average was ten, a ratio of fourteen suggests the properties could be expensive currently. Or at least future price appreciation may be at a slower rate than in the past.

The rule of thumb is, a lower ratio (than the historical average) means prices could be low, which favors buying a home. In contrast, a higher ratio suggests prices may be high, so renting may be a better choice.

Net worth

For many, a significant issue with renting is that they feel worse off because despite paying for years, they own nothing. But is this a reasonable conclusion? In summary, there is no easy answer. Paying a mortgage is more expensive than paying a rent because you are buying an asset. Rent is a payment purely to use a certain amount of space for a certain amount of time.

Let's think about this by first assuming you can afford to buy. You could instead *choose* to rent and invest the difference between the mortgage and rental payments. Let's assume you did this diligently over twenty-five years, the term of a typical mortgage. It is possible to have a larger net worth than a homeowner. This could happen if your investment

return exceeds the increase in house prices. Of course, the homeowner's net worth is in a physical asset, while the renter's net worth is in financial investments.

Several factors, however, complicate this analysis:

- The rate at which house prices increase can differ from the rate financial investments appreciate.

- Property is not a liquid asset, so there is no guarantee of a quick sale or even selling at the appraised value.

- Getting a house ready for sale may require a cost to update it to current trends.

- Future taxation policy and government initiatives could change the result for either approach.

- Demand and supply for housing in certain locations could significantly alter both house and rental prices.

- Changes in the economic environment and inflation could affect the outcome of each approach.

- Financial investments have different risks compared to physical assets.

- Persons may not consistently invest the difference between the mortgage payment and rent.

Three powerful factors may tilt a person's approach towards buying, despite the added expenses from owning.

1. While you can invest the difference between a mortgage and rental payment, realistically most people will not do so for twenty to thirty years. Entering a mortgage, therefore, is a forced savings plan with a clear result. You own an asset at the end of the loan.

2. We should not underestimate our pride in owning a home. A space you rent could never excite you in the same way, despite how fantastic it might be. Additionally,

most persons would prefer not to rent when retired. The peace of mind from knowing that you are in your own space with no monthly commitment is significant.

3. Home ownership is often supported by tax incentives, which help make it an attractive choice.

Wrap up

As I mentioned at the start, renting versus buying is not strictly a financial decision because the numerous variables and long timeframe make the outcome uncertain. This decision might require more judgment than other life events.

Let's now turn our attention to a few events that while important, (spoiler alert) ultimately have no financially correct answer.

No Financially Correct Answer

Certain life events are significant not only in the way they change our lives but also in their potential financial impact. Due to their importance, I can't exclude them from our discussion on life events. But the chapter's title gives away the conclusion: there is no financially correct answer. The variety of situations and range of approaches—from the inexpensive to the elaborate—make arriving at a financial conclusion difficult. Most likely, emotion will drive the decision and you'll manage the financial impact over time. Let's consider a few examples.

Higher education

In *Step 11: Invest in Yourself*, I said educating yourself could be one of your best investments. The return from investing in higher education should be to obtain better-paying employment because you have new skills. The more income you earn, the greater your opportunity to create wealth. You become wealthier because your surplus increases, and your net worth grows over time. **As there is a limit to controlling outflows, increasing your income is a critical focus for anyone hoping to achieve financial freedom.** I covered this in Action 4: *Grow Your Income and Net Worth*.

A good education is, unfortunately, expensive. For many, using debt is the only realistic way to pay for it. It is a form of good debt because it potentially leads to higher income, although the benefit is initially intangible (knowledge). Yes, the outcome is uncertain, but this is not consumption debt where you use the item quickly. Knowledge lasts forever, and it could benefit you for your whole life.

If you are stretching yourself to pay for higher education, a serious risk is not getting the value from your investment. Thankfully, you can follow several principles to give yourself a better chance to benefit:

- **Focus on in-demand professions and industries.** It does not make sense to pursue a field where a glut of qualified persons already exists. You are unlikely to receive a salary that compensates for your investment.

- **The institution's reputation matters.** The pedigree of the institution where you obtain your qualification is important. Consequently, the courses they offer may cost more than other schools. Often, the extra cost is worth it because employers respect the institution.

- **Experience counts.** Education is important but not everything. To receive higher compensation, you must have a blend of experience and education.

- **Be the best.** Top graduates in any program attract attention. It does not make sense to make a significant investment and then not distinguish yourself academically.

- **Obtain complementary skills.** If you have an existing qualification, build on it with complementary ones to show depth and breadth of technical ability. Unless you plan to switch careers, having two (or more) unrelated qualifications might not be beneficial.

Although there is no financially correct answer, you should invest as much as you can afford in your education. Do it as early as possible, to have a long horizon to reap the benefits.

Starting a business

We discussed the benefits of being self-employed in Action 4: *Grow Your Income and Net Worth*, but I want to raise it again, from a slightly different perspective.

One path to genuine wealth creation is to own your own business, but entrepreneurs face many risks and obstacles. It can be a frustrating journey to get your business started, convince lenders and investors of its viability, and attract your first customers to generate revenue. But many have faced these challenges and conquered them. To be a successful entrepreneur is often a case of "you'll never know unless you try." If or when to start are questions with no financially correct answer.

But similar to investing in your education, a few principles can guide you:

- **Most importantly: believe in yourself.** No one should be more passionate about your idea than you. You are always the Chief Marketing Officer. Passion is contagious and you'll need an infinite supply to overcome many sources of opposition. Your business will not succeed if you crumble when criticized by pessimistic stakeholders.

- **Don't compete in a crowded space; it's too difficult.** Instead, differentiate your business and prove that your idea/business/product is unique. Or show that you target an unfulfilled need. Or that it transforms something that already exists.

- **Expect to take risks.** Ideally, the best time to take risks is when you are young. You have enough time to recover if your idea is not as successful as you hoped. There are, however, many examples of successful entrepreneurs who began when they were older. A great idea does not depend on age.

- **Negotiating business finances requires a little financial savvy.** Some ideas from personal finance can help, but business finance is more complex and structured. It will be useful to take a few relevant courses if you don't have a suitable background. You'll speak to many stakeholders when starting or running a business. Even if they are interested in your concept or strategy, you must also convince them that you understand the financial side. You must expertly link how the activities drive the business's profitability and cash flow.

- **Expect to need capital.** Eventually you'll need capital to fund the business's growth, which may be more than you can afford alone. But the first investor in the business is you. It's not realistic to ask others to risk their funds if you aren't prepared to do so as well.

- **Learn how to lead and motivate.** When a business is small, the owner can do everything. Once it begins to grow, you must start hiring, which means working through and relying on others. This requires a distinct set of skills and experience. The faster you learn, the better chance you have to motivate employees to do more than the minimum to collect a paycheck.

- **Expect an initial loss.** Few start-up businesses are immediately profitable, which is why adequate capital is required. But you must judge when to cut your losses if you don't expect meaningful future success. Although you will be eager to succeed, if the business cannot sustain your livelihood, or worse, it needs continuous funding, it may be time to pull the plug. If you still believe in your idea, you should evaluate how to adjust your current approach before you commit new capital.

It is worth bearing in mind that you will have to separate your business and personal finances. Consider your business as separate from you, requiring its own financial management

and records. This will become clearer when you learn more about business finances.

Children

Of the events covered in this chapter, the fuzziest one for financial planning must be having children. While education and entrepreneurship are about you, having children requires you to support one or more dependents for about twenty years. Every parent has done it, but when it is your turn, it feels like an enormous responsibility with a significant financial commitment.

Trying to plan for them also creates headaches because a suitable time never seems to arise. When you're young, you have no money. When you're older, you must balance family with work demands, not to mention having less energy to keep up with them. Ultimately, you'll have to trust your judgment that your finances are adequate to handle the long-term commitment. Of course, many people have children without financial security—they figure it out as they go.

Having children is, therefore, the epitome of a major life event with no financially correct answer! But let's identify a few financial matters to plan for:

- **Stay-at-home parent.** During the critical early years, you'll need to decide if one partner will become a full-time homemaker and caregiver. If both partners work and both incomes support the household, it's easier to plan for the financial consequences of this decision *before* a child arrives.

- **Where to live.** You'll need to decide where you'd prefer to raise your children, especially if it involves relocating. If you are currently searching for a home and you eventually wish to have children, you should factor this intent into your choice.

- **Curb your enthusiasm.** It is easy to be surprised by the costs that arise following your child's birth. Try to obtain an estimate of what to expect if you prefer to save for these upfront/additional costs. But thankfully, many needs have inexpensive solutions. It is easy to go overboard with equipment (crib/stroller/car seat/and so on) and other preparations. Retailers tug at your emotions and influence you into costly purchases. When your child quickly outgrows them, you'll probably look back and regret spending so much.

- **Incremental costs.** Realistically, you'll absorb and manage the costs for clothing and food within the overall family budget. But other costs will be additional, for example, extracurricular activities or orthodontics. These occur at various stages as your child grows, so factoring them into the family budget in a reasonably organized way is possible.

- **Future financial support.** Eventually, you'll need to decide whether to provide financial support for university education and beyond. If you would like to assist with your children's higher education, it will become one of your medium and long-term goals.

Wrap up

These three events that have no financially correct answers bring us to the end of this Action. While the events covered could never be complete because personal goals vary widely, I hope I've tackled the more popular ones.

Five Actions for building strong personal finances are now complete! The last Action to discuss is investing and retirement planning.

Action 6

Invest and Plan for Retirement

The End of Our Journey

Congratulations! You made it to the end! Let's recap our journey, to show how much progress you've made.

1. I started by explaining that the foundation step to taking control of your money is knowing your inflows and outflows. This is critical because it is impossible to manage what you do not know.

2. With a precise idea of what you earn and spend, you created an annual budget to achieve a target surplus.

3. You learned that your net worth is important, and you build wealth by growing your net worth. Your net worth grows when you produce an annual surplus consistently.

4. You learned to allocate your surplus to achieve goals.

5. You created an emergency fund. It is your personal insurance plan for unforeseen events.

6. You learned the valuable role of insurance in managing certain key risks.

7. You created a plan to repay your debt faster than scheduled, focusing initially on all consumption debt. You learned to pay attention to loan interest because it reduces your net worth.

8. With your debt under control, you began to plan and save for medium and long-term goals.

Your progress will also be evident if you compare when you were financially stressed versus now being in control.

Signs of Financial Stress	Signs of Control
Living paycheck-to-paycheck	You are in control of your expenses and live well within your means
Having too much debt	Your debt is under control, or you are debt-free
Having unpaid credit card balances	You make money from credit cards, enjoy all their conveniences, but pay no interest
Every unexpected expenditure is a crisis	You have a pool of emergency funds
Having no savings	You have annual surpluses
Fearing tomorrow	Your gaze is always slightly ahead, and you plan for life's major events
Depending on others for advice or making the easiest choice from lack of knowledge	You invest in yourself and make wise decisions confidently
Forced to rely on government support in retirement	Government programs will be your cushion because you have your own investment and retirement plan

The Six Actions

You should now be able to recite the six Actions from memory and realize that the previous recap is an expanded description of the first five Actions:

1. **Control your inflows and outflows**

2. **Protect yourself and your dependents**

3. **Manage your debt**

4. **Grow your income and net worth**
5. **Prepare for major life events**
6. **Invest and plan for retirement**

After successfully completing the first five, you should be generating surpluses consistently. Even better, your surplus should be increasing as your income grows because you are not increasing your expenses at the same rate. At this point, you are ready to focus seriously on investing and direct part of that surplus to your financial future: retirement.

Are you wealthy?

In the chapter *Start at the End*, I raised the question if financial security is the same as being wealthy. Having now read the various Actions, it's worth considering this question again. As a reminder, I believe the answer is "no" because wealthy persons have three main characteristics:

1. Their income easily exceeds their expenses, which means they continuously produce surplus cash that they use to invest.

2. They own assets that earn income.

3. They can afford a higher cost lifestyle, which means spending on Wants easily exceeds Needs.

Instead, you are certainly on the path to becoming wealthy. The critical milestone to creating wealth is producing a steadily increasing surplus.

Retirement

Retirement is the only certain life event for everyone. What is also certain is you cannot predict your capacity to work in your sixties and beyond. Because retirement is a known event with a critical uncertainty, the advice you will always hear is to start planning for retirement as soon as possible. This

advice is perfectly sound. **If you can set aside any funds before you begin to generate steady or increasing annual surpluses, you should do so.**

Many of us, however, face a problem acting on this advice. For investing and retirement planning to be effective, you must use funds that you will not need for decades.

Do not think about using your retirement funds to pay for other outflows. Also, you should not use your retirement funds for any other goal. If you want to use these funds before you retire, think about it as stealing from your future self.

Unfortunately, this principle sometimes conflicts with the way certain financial products are structured and sold. For example, you will hear of retirement plans that allow you to withdraw if you need to make a deposit to buy a home. Withdrawing for this reason only makes sense to me if you consider a house an investment. Put another way, you exchange a financial investment for a real estate investment, and you intend to convert the property to cash when you retire by downsizing to a smaller home.

It's easy, however, to understand why people might continue to live in their home instead of downsizing. It is fully paid, and they are comfortable with their community. In this situation, you can't say in one breath that you are saving for retirement but in another you are saving for a house deposit. These statements conflict with each other.

You invest your retirement savings to achieve a long-term objective. When you disrupt the pool of investments by withdrawing money, you lose the benefits they were designed to achieve.

Notice the idea of investing is beginning to arise.

Investing

Investing is an action taken to make your money work for you, either to generate income or growth or both. The money invested is your "capital" or your "principal." When you invest to earn income, the value of the capital itself does not change. In contrast, when you invest for growth, you hope your capital increases in value over time.

Risk and return

Once you are trying to generate income or growth, you must start taking risks. The alternative is to take no risk. For example, by leaving your surplus funds in a bank savings account and earning a tiny amount of interest. Because you take no risk, you earn practically no return. Leaving surplus funds in a bank account is, therefore, not investing.

Risks arise in many ways, but common sources for individual investors are:

- **Capital is unavailable.** To earn higher returns, you must invest your capital for longer periods. Often, when your funds are committed, you cannot get them back until the investment term ends. If you must break the investment, you may face expensive penalties or even receive less than what you originally invested.

- **Losses.** The longer someone else has your money, the greater the chance they might not repay. Of course, it does *not* mean they *will* default; the risk is just higher. Let's say you have an option to invest your funds for either one or ten years. If you choose ten, you clearly place a higher level of trust that your capital will be returned compared to a one-year investment.

- **Capital value can fluctuate.** Financial markets behave like living organisms. They always move and experience

steep rises and falls. When you invest for growth, you must accept your investment will fluctuate in value, which could be unnerving.

The common thread in the points above is a long period. **To earn a proper income or achieve growth, you must commit funds for an extended period.** Long periods make the cycles of ups and downs in financial markets easier to stomach.

Compounding

Another benefit of an extended period is you take advantage of compounding, a concept we met in earlier chapters. Let's use an example to help with recall. Would you rather have $10,000 per day for thirty days or one cent that doubled in value every day for thirty days?

While getting $10,000 every day may sound like the right answer, it is not. $10,000 per day for thirty days will give you $300,000. In the second option, the effect of compounding will get you over $5 million dollars, as shown below.

Day 1	$0.01
Day 5	$0.16
Day 10	$5.12
Day 15	$164
Day 20	$5,243
Day 25	$167,772
Day 26	$335,544
Day 27	$671,089
Day 28	$1,342,177
Day 29	$2,684,355
Day 30	$5,368,709

Of course, this is an extreme example, which assumes a 100% return compounded daily. **The point is, over the long term, continuously reinvesting your returns is a fantastic strategy. You cannot obtain this benefit over a short period.**
Critically, for most of us, investing and retirement planning go together. Investing means putting your excess funds to work for you. You will only have enough excess funds when you produce surpluses continuously. Your investments need enough time to earn income and capital growth. When most of us have enough surplus funds, our time horizon tends to coincide with our need to plan for a successful retirement.

Cash management vs investing

A question that arises is, what to do with the funds that you set aside for goals other than retirement? Can these be invested? The answer depends on the nature of the goal and the period involved. Let's look at a few examples to illustrate and introduce the concept of cash management.

1. **Planning a wedding**

   Assuming you expect the ceremony within one or two years, you would not want to commit these funds for a long period. Neither should you risk a decline in your capital. Your primary aim is to ensure the funds are available when you need them. While you would be happy to earn a small amount of interest in the meantime, accepting risk to maximize return is not your priority. Keeping these funds safe and accessible is therefore cash management, not investing.

2. **Saving for a house deposit**

   The same principle from the previous point applies here, even if you plan to save over a longer period, let's say five years. As these funds are earmarked for a specific purpose

in a specific timeframe, you should not risk any capital loss. Consequently, growth-oriented investments are not an option. You could deposit the funds for one to two years to earn a slightly better return, but protecting your principal is the priority. Put another way, you'll be happy to get a return that's better than a bank savings account, but only if your capital is safe. Again, this is cash management, not investing.

3. Creating a college fund

If you intend to save for your children's university tuition, and you start when they are young, you could have a time horizon of 10–15 years. This should be enough time to take advantage of the benefits explained earlier. In this situation, speaking to a qualified adviser about an investment plan is a smart move.

To summarize, nothing is wrong with wanting a better return than interest from bank accounts. It is, however, worth remembering that bank accounts are protected by deposit insurance, up to certain limits. For individuals, they are as safe as you can get, which is one reason why the returns are low. Trying to get a slightly better return, while having access to your funds, plus protecting your capital, are understandable aims. **But this is not investing.** It is better to think of this activity as cash management. The objective is to use your cash as efficiently as possible.

Wrap up

Wow, it's been an incredible, and I trust, rewarding journey! Let's revisit the goals I set at the start. I wanted to:

1. Educate and empower you to make real-life wise financial decisions.

2. Teach you the fundamentals of personal finance and show you how to take control of your money.

3. Show you how to achieve a steadily increasing surplus and grow your net worth.

I did my best to accomplish these objectives and truly hope I succeeded.

So where do you go from here? Once you are ready to invest and plan for retirement, I recommend you meet a financial planner. Let them review your situation and work with you to prepare an investment plan. Can you do this yourself? Of course. If you do not have complex investment goals, it is easy to learn how. But that may be a topic for another book!

Until then, enjoy the tremendous peace of mind from your newly found financial independence!